"*Learning by Heart* is an important series of stories that could and should spark many discussions. Highly recommended—and hard to put down."

—Ulrik Juul Christensen, MD, CEO of Area9 Group

"I admire Tony's gumption, his refusal to follow conventional wisdom, his unflinching honesty about his own failures, and his unshakable belief that there's a better world out there—and that he was destined to improve the work of teachers everywhere."

—John Merrow, founding president of Learning Matters

"*Learning by Heart* transforms the young Tony Wagner's pain into a journey of compassion, imagination, wit, and, finally, triumphant success. Fast paced, original, and beautifully written, it is one of the most honest and useful memoirs I've read in recent years."

—Rebecca Pepper Sinkler, former editor of
The New York Times Book Review

"*Learning by Heart* revels in rich storytelling to reveal why classrooms—or conversations—demand deep listening for anyone ready to learn the compelling lessons of the heart. His life quest and this book delivers."   —Hal Gregersen, executive director of
the MIT Leadership Center

"Part memoir, part manifesto, *Learning by Heart* is a powerful counterblast: a full-blooded testament to the inescapably personal nature of teaching and learning."

—Sir Ken Robinson, *New York Times* bestselling
author of *The Element*

D0170118

Tony Wagner is a Senior Research Fellow at the Learning Policy Institute. Previously, he held a variety of positions at Harvard University over the course of more than twenty years, including four years as an Expert-in-Residence at the Harvard Innovation Lab and the founder and codirector, for a decade, of the Change Leadership Group at the Harvard Graduate School of Education. He also spent time as a high school teacher, K–8 principal, and university professor in teacher education; was the founding executive director of Educators for Social Responsibility; and is the author of *Creating Innovators* and *The Global Achievement Gap* and coauthor of *Most Likely to Succeed*.

Learning
by Heart

AN UNCONVENTIONAL EDUCATION

Tony Wagner

PENGUIN BOOKS

PENGUIN BOOKS
An imprint of Penguin Random House LLC
First published in the United States of America by Viking,
an imprint of Penguin Random House LLC, 2020
Published in Penguin Books 2021

ISBN 9780525561897 (paperback)

THE LIBRARY OF CONGRESS HAS CATALOGED THE HARDCOVER EDITION AS FOLLOWS:
Names: Wagner, Tony, author.
Title: Learning by heart: an unconventional education / Tony Wagner.
Description: New York: Viking, 2020. | Includes bibliographical references.
Identifiers: LCCN 2019027347 (print) | LCCN 2019027348 (ebook) |
ISBN 9780525561873 (hardcover) | ISBN 9780525561880 (ebook)
Subjects: LCSH: Wagner, Tony. | Educators—United States—Biography. |
Student-centered learning—United States. |
Motivation in education—United States.
Classification: LCC LA2317.W32 A3 2020 (print) |
LCC LA2317.W32 (ebook) | DDC 370.92 [B]—dc23
LC record available at https://lccn.loc.gov/2019027347
LC ebook record available at https://lccn.loc.gov/2019027348

Printed in the United States of America

1st Printing

DESIGNED BY MEIGHAN CAVANAUGH

For my grandchildren: Sasha, Sydney, Kiran, and River

May they always remain curious, creative,

and courageous in their own learning

And for Robin, who taught me how to write a memoir

CONTENTS

INTRODUCTION

WHAT DOES IT MEAN TO LEARN SOMETHING "BY HEART"? For most people, the phrase connotes committing something to memory—like a passage from a book, a poem, lines from a play, or perhaps an equation. But what about the phrase "getting to the heart of the matter"? It suggests something very different, doesn't it? Something you can't arrive at by rote.

This is the story of a boy—and later a young man—who rebelled against memorizing most of the things he was required to learn in school. Indeed, he refused to "take to heart" many of the things most adults told him. The lessons he was assigned and the world he was handed made little sense to him. And so he was driven to try to get to the heart of things, to explore what was truly important about a book, a moment in nature, a concept, an experience of another person, a time in history.

He wanted to understand what was really vital, after all, in order to make a meaning for his life and to work with passion and purpose.

It is my story, and the questions of what's most important to learn and how things are best learned continue to haunt and inspire me.

ONE

The Dropout

WHEN I TALK TO PEOPLE WHO HAVE PLEASANT MEMORIES of their school years, they rarely mention the classes they took. Those who remember school fondly are far more likely to recall it as a time in their life when they had fun with friends. Or they excelled at a sport or joined in an extracurricular activity that excited them. Almost invariably, they say classes were easy for them, and so they got along with their teachers and brought home good grades that pleased their parents.

For many students—those for whom school is hard for whatever reason, or who are not popular or good athletes—school is tedious at best, torturous at worst. I was such a student. School for me was a giant jigsaw puzzle with many hundreds of tiny pieces—a puzzle that came with no picture to guide me or tell me how it was all supposed to turn out. I was lost.

From first through sixth grade, I went to a small, coeducational private day school half an hour's drive from where my family lived. I have only hazy memories of my classes and teachers there—things scrawled on the blackboard that we were told were important for us to know; heavy, dull textbooks that had to be lugged to and from school every day. What I remember most vividly was being an outlier. Most of the other kids were from the suburbs, and they saw each other frequently, after school and on weekends. But not me. We lived too far away. And so during recess, I wasn't invited to join in their play. I mostly just watched from the sidelines.

I was also slow to learn to read. Some kids naturally learn much later than others, and then, all too often, parent anxiety and teacher pressure fester and turn a late reader into an insecure learner. For several years, my mother dragged me to a tutor once a week. Mrs. Gray was patient and warm, unlike my teachers at school, and by fourth grade I was proficient. But the beginner reading books, organized by level of difficulty, and the assigned textbooks bored me, and I took no pleasure in reading them. I liked the smell of the blue ditto sheets, fresh off the mimeograph machine, that were sent home with us every night, but I hated doing the same math problems over and over. They were even worse than the reading assignments. I didn't do the homework most of the time.

About a year or so after I'd really gotten the knack of reading, I fell in love with it just for pleasure. At first it was a series of books called *We Were There*. Each book was a fictional retelling of a real historical event featuring one or more kids as the main characters. I don't remember where I got the first one, but it took me awhile to get into it. By the age of eleven or so, I was reading most every night—for myself, not for school.

I trekked the Oregon Trail, fought at the Battle of Gettysburg, dumped tea at the Boston Tea Party, nearly froze to death with Admiral Byrd at the South Pole. But it was the books about World War II that most captivated me: I'd watched, horrified and helpless, as the Japanese Zeros screamed out of the sky and bombed our fleet at Pearl Harbor; I ate bugs to survive in the jungle during the Battle of Bataan; I charged ferociously at the German pillboxes above the beaches of Normandy.

I went on to read about the different ground campaigns of the war. The German general Erwin Rommel, known as the Desert Fox, fascinated me by the way he kept sneaking around the desert, attacking the British, then slipping away. Then I got interested in battles between big ships. I begged my parents to let me watch *Victory at Sea*, a TV documentary that each week depicted a different naval engagement of the war, using original film footage. The program always closed with the first verse of "The Navy Hymn":

> Eternal Father, strong to save,
> Whose arm hath bound the restless wave,
> Who bidd'st the mighty ocean deep

Its own appointed limits keep;
Oh, hear us when we cry to Thee,
For those in peril on the sea!

The music gave me shivers and made me feel sad. All I felt when they sang the hymns at our little Episcopal church each Sunday was impatience for the service to be over. I tried to imagine what it must have been like to be on a destroyer, manning a gun under fire from a Japanese battleship, terrified that a kamikaze would fly into us.

I knew what I would have done if I'd been in the war. I'd have been a fighter pilot, like my dad. In *We Were There at the Battle of Britain*, I flew a Spitfire and blew the German Messerschmitt Bf 109s and the Focke-Wulf Fw 190s out of the sky as we battled for air supremacy to save Britain from invasion. After finishing that story, I sought out others about aerial combat during World War II. I learned the names, armament, and performance characteristics of every fighter plane that fought in the war. I wondered which was best: the American P51 Mustang or the British Spitfire. The P51 was faster and had more guns, but the Spitfire was much more maneuverable, like a sports car.

On my father's bureau, I had seen a small silver-framed photograph of him wearing his officer's uniform and standing next to the nose of his Spitfire. There was so much that I wanted to ask him—not just about his plane, but what it had really been like to be in the war. Like so many World War II vets, though, he rarely talked about his experiences.

I did get some answers many years later when, at the age of seventy, Dad sat down to write a short account of his war experiences, "for his children and grandchildren," he said.

The outbreak of the war in Europe in 1939 found my father selling insurance, taking a few courses at Johns Hopkins University, and playing golf. "My school and college record was spotty at best," he wrote. "My life was golf and good times."

His other passion was flying.

While he had only three hours' experience in a friend's small private plane and had never soloed, he wanted to join the Army Air Corps. But he didn't have the required college degree, and there was a year's wait. At a Labor Day party in 1941, my father met a former Royal Air Force pilot and asked for help. It turned out that the RAF was desperate for pilots—having lost so many in the Battle of Britain the previous year—and so in November 1941, at the age of twenty-one, my father found himself as the only American cadet in a British Flying Training School. Of the sixty pilots in his cohort who graduated and received their wings, only half survived the war.

My father graduated at the top of his class, although he'd cheated on his Morse code exam, he confessed. Because all plane communications were by radio then, he never saw the point of learning it.

After serving as a flight instructor for several months and surviving a midair collision that required him to bail out over the Bristol Channel, Dad was offered his choice of assignments. He asked to be posted to the Forty-first Squadron because they were flying one of the hottest fighter planes of the war—the legendary Spitfire MkXII. For the next several years, he flew numerous offensive and defensive "sorties"— "scrambling" to chase after German fighter planes, escorting bombers on runs over France, strafing ships and locomotives, getting shot up by antiaircraft guns and limping back to base. His pilot's log reads like a script for a classic World War II movie:

"Cover for bombers at Abbeville; Hugh Parry hit."

"Rear cover for 300 B17s returning from Paris area; about 50 FW190's about; saw one of our own Spits shot down in flames."

"Typhoons [a British single-seat fighter-bomber] at Le Havre bounced by six FW 190's; mixed with them; we got two."

"Met nine ME109's and FW190's head-on with 20 more above over Abbeville; Tom Spack and Dick Hogarth missing; Sargent Fisher shot up, claimed one 190 destroyed."

Despite the daily horror and constant danger, it was the happiest time of his life, my father once admitted to me. He was doing something that he loved—and doing it very well.

Four days before D-Day, he was shot down off the coast of German-occupied Guernsey in the English Channel.

"I sat in my dinghy all day long . . . two airborne life boats were dropped by a special air-sea rescue squadron, only to blow away beyond my reach," he wrote in his memoir. "Finally, at dusk, the Germans sent a French fishing boat out to get me. As I stepped ashore in Guernsey harbor, a German officer saluted me and said, in broken English, 'For you, the war is over.'"

He spent the last year of the war in Germany at an infamous POW camp called Stalag Luft 1. Something that kept him going there, he told me in one of the rare moments when he talked about his war experiences, was his dream of owning a farm.

After Dad returned home in June 1945, he persuaded the girl who had spurned him before the war to marry him. I was born the following July and spent the first year of my life at Spook Hill Farm, my parents' new home in rural Maryland. One of my favorite pictures in the family album is of me dressed in a snowsuit, being held close by my beaming dad.

I rarely saw him smile beyond the borders of that photograph. Farming was hard work and there was no money in it, as my father was soon to discover, and he and his new bride had been raised in privilege. The daughter of a mining engineer turned successful stockbroker, my mother had grown up on a large estate in Middleburg, Virginia—fox hunting country. She had gone to Sarah Lawrence, then one of the most elite and progressive women's colleges, for three years. They were both unaccustomed to doing with less. So he sold the farm and took a string of jobs as a professional fund-raiser, and we moved from place to place: Baltimore to Buffalo to Indianapolis to Princeton to Baltimore again. My mother had to manage the moves while taking care of me and my younger sister and brother.

Country life was in my father's blood, though, and so when I was six, he bought another farm in Maryland. This time, he had a full-time tenant farmer run the place while he commuted daily to Baltimore, where he had formed an investment group to buy underperforming companies, turn them around through better management, and then sell them at what he hoped would be a profit.

Noon's Delight, as the new farm was called, encompassed rolling grassy hills dotted with patches of green woodland, all sweeping down to an intimate, emerald valley. A stream called Piney Run snaked along the valley floor, sometimes fast, sometimes slow. Glints of sunlight sparkled on the spots of swift water, while in the slow pools, beneath the shade of an ancient oak, wary fish lurked. And throughout all the fenced hillside pastures and in the valley, our herd of Black Angus mooed and munched their way through the day. For the next six years, the farm was my work, my play, my solitary sanctuary from school.

My father left early and came home late, and weekends were for golf. I think he might have been more enamored of the pastoral fantasy of living as landed gentry on an "estate" rather than the reality of running a farm. My mother wasn't involved with the farmwork. She spent much of her day carpooling kids to school and managing the household, though she always found time to read, dabble in photography and watercolor, and occasionally play the piano or listen to her favorite opera. Earle, the resident farmer who lived with his family in a small house in one corner of our valley, did all of the work, with a little help from occasional hired guys, his kids, and me.

Besides our herd of cattle, we had a few of most every kind of critter, and my job was to trudge down to the big white clapboard barn every night to feed the hungry hordes. Pigs, horses, our two Great Danes, the chickens, of course, and those damned geese, which my father had named after his least favorite sister-in-law and her husband. Get too close to them, and they'd nip you with their sharp beaks.

After feeding time, I'd flick off the light switch and linger as inky darkness crept across the valley, watching the animal shadows root and chew, listening to their snorts and grunts, feeling the heat rise from their bodies on cold nights. Walking slowly back to the house, to face that night's homework, I craned my neck to see the endless sky sparkling with stars. The Milky Way, solar systems, galaxies, the universe—what were they, how did they get there? I had so many questions.

Haying was the hardest chore. The bales were huge and heavy—too much for me to lift—but I could roll them into piles of three or four, making it quicker work for the guys coming along in the wagon. It was always hot and humid in haying season. After only an hour out in the fresh-cut pasture, I'd be soaking wet, with itchy, loose strands of straw sticking to my skin. There was often no stopping, as thunderstorms frequently sneaked up over the hills in the late afternoon, and all the hay had to be picked up and brought to the barn before the rain came on. I'd ride on top of the bales on the last wagon back, wrung out and parched, half delirious with exhaustion, but proud.

When I wasn't needed to help with the haying, my time was my own, and the farm was my cosmos to discover.

I hiked the hills with my dog, Smutty, to see what was

beyond, only to find more hills, more woods, and more pastures on distant farms. I ventured into the hardwood forests and clambered up a rocky outcropping so I could look down through the ash and maple canopies beneath me and wonder what lived there in the spooky shadows.

Then, sweaty from my explorations, I scrambled down the hillside to the valley where the stream meandered, splashing in the waist-deep pools of icy, blue-green water. I dammed the flow in the shallows, watching it forge new rivulets around my sticks and rocks. Finally, worn out from my adventuring, I lay back on the grassy bank and watched islands of white clouds drift slowly across a lazy sky.

WE HAD A VISITOR to the farm the summer I turned eleven. I don't remember his name, but he was a business associate of my dad's from out of town, and so he spent the night with us. At dinner that evening, he asked me if I liked to fish and if there were any fish in the stream. I'd seen some in Piney Run, I told him, but I had never tried to catch one.

"I brought my rod and reel," he told me. "So let's give it a shot tomorrow if you're game."

Shortly after dawn, I led the visitor down the hill from our house to the part of the stream where there was a still pool. He handed me the rod, showed me how the reel worked and where to throw the hook, baited with a worm I'd dug up in the garden. Pretty soon, I felt a fish tug, pulled to hook it, then let the fish thrash a bit in the water to wear it out, as he'd told me, before finally winding it into my net. It was just a catfish, so we threw it back, and I tried again.

While we were sitting on the bank waiting for the next nibble, the visitor asked me how I liked school. No one had ever asked me that before, and I wasn't sure whether or not I could be honest. But he'd taken me fishing. No one had ever done that before, either.

"I don't like school," I admitted. "But I read a lot outside of school—stuff that really interests me."

He nodded as though he understood.

We didn't get any more bites, and soon he looked at his watch and said it was time to go. He had to drive back to the city.

Trying to get to sleep that night, I wondered why the visitor had asked me about school. That made me think about why I didn't do my homework. Why couldn't we just read about things that interested us for class?

A package arrived in the mail for me a few weeks after his visit. Inside, there was a brown box and a note. "Thanks for taking me fishing" was all it said.

I opened the box carefully and peered inside to find a spider web of tiny wires, with different colored pieces stuck on the ends, a black plastic knob, a coil of wire, and bolts and screws of different sizes. It looked like a little pile of junk. At the bottom of the box, I found a booklet of printed instructions: "How to Build Your Own Transistor Radio."

Wow. Building my very own radio. I was fascinated—and totally overwhelmed. So many wires and pages of instructions in small print. I couldn't imagine turning this mess into an actual radio. I read the first page of the manual:

What You Will Find Inside:

Page #1: From Transmitting Station to Receiver, the Whole Picture.

Page #2: A little information about the parts you will be using in this project, schematic-symbols diagram.

Page #3: Assembly procedure.

Page #4: Operating and experimenting procedure.

Page #5: Assembly figures.

Page #6: Antenna and ground ideas.

Page #7: Parts list & glue on templates.

It went on to list the tools and parts that I would need for the project: scissors, needle-nose pliers, wire cutter, #2 Phillips screwdriver, small straight-blade screwdriver, sharp knife and/or wire stripper, awl or ice pick, paper paste, medium sandpaper, wire for antenna. I didn't know what half those things were.

I took the list to Earle, our tenant farmer, who often ended his day working on equipment in the shop next to the shed that housed the tractor and other farm vehicles. He was a big, gruff man with a thin mustache and an enormous tattoo on his right forearm of a cobra wound around a pole, its fangs bared. He looked at my list, then at me, and shook his head.

"It's for a project," I explained. "I'm going to build a radio."

Clenching a Camel between his tobacco-stained teeth, Earle gave half a grunt and began taking down tools from the peg board above his work bench. Then he put them into a cardboard box.

When he was finished, he handed me the box and said, "Now, you bring all of these back as soon as you're done, y'hear?"

Back in my bedroom, I began by carefully laying out the contents of my box and reading the parts list, trying to figure out what was which in the tangle. The first thing I had to do was cut out two paper templates and glue them to the two small boards that came with the kit. One board was the bottom of the radio and would hold the electronics: the capacitors, diode, coil, and resistor. The other was to be the front of the radio, which would have the tuning knob, the antenna and ground wire connectors, and the two connectors for the earphone.

I used the awl to make two pilot holes for the machine screws needed to fix the front panel to the base panel. Then I attached the variable capacitor to the front. That was for tuning into stations. So far, so good.

After installing the four machine screws up through holes marked on the template on the base, the instructions got more complicated. "Locate: 3 Coils, Diode, and Sea Hex-Nuts. It is highly important that the 3 Coils be placed in the proper places. L-1 has three dots that are Red, Red, and Black; L-2's dots are Yellow, Violet, and Black; and L-3's dots are Brown, Gray, and Brown." I tried to keep it all straight in my head. "Using the above procedure, 'fish-hooking' the wires, attach the Coils, Diode, and 2 Wires from the Variable Capacitor, 1–4 inches from 'Phones' & 5 inches from 'Ground' Wires from Front-Panel as shown, under the Sea Hex-Nuts."

What the hell? This was too hard. I couldn't follow a word and decided I'd never finish the radio. And if I did, it probably wouldn't work anyway. I got up and abandoned the jumble on the floor.

A couple of days later, I screwed up my confidence and tackled the radio again. I made absolutely sure that I had correctly identified the different coils and took each step slowly, rechecking my work before moving on to the next. Once I'd completed these steps, all I had to do was attach the supplied earphone to its two wires on the front. Finally, the instructions said: "Proceed to Testing, Operating, and Experimenting on the next page."

But there was a catch. "A substantial antenna is an absolute must, for the ultimate pleasure of crystal radio experimentation . . . Antenna Wire, 50–100'; 14 gauge," the next page of instructions informed me. "Stranded wire is the most practical here. The wire can be insulated or uninsulated and if 14ga. isn't handy or practical, then use what you have that would be a close substitute."

It was time for another visit to Earle. I returned his tools and showed him the page about the antenna. "Humpf" was all he said as he uncoiled wire from a reel and cut it to the right length.

I spent the afternoon rigging the wiring. I had a little porch off my second-story bedroom and strung the antenna around its railing. By the time I was done, my mom had already called me to dinner twice, the second time with a menacing *Tohhh-nnny!* So I left the wire hanging there and went down, reluc-tantly.

Would it really work? I kept thinking as I pushed the food around my plate, pretending to eat, hiding peas under my knife. *No, how could it?*

It was dark by the time I got back upstairs. I attached the antenna and ground leads and earphone wires to the front panel, then turned to the instruction book. "Put the Earphone into your ear and slowly rotate the Tuning Control, listening for stations. If stations are heard, then proceed." *What would I hear?* I wondered. "If not then: 1) Check all your wiring, step-by-step, making certain all assembly and connections are correct. Make certain you have a proper Antenna/Ground, as per instructions on Page #6." Now I worried that Earle might have given me the wrong kind of wire. "To check your Earphone, brush the Antenna Wire on the lower Earphone Terminal, and if a 'clicking' is heard, Earphone is OK. To check the Diode (D-1), brush the Antenna Wire on the #4

Terminal, and if 'clicking' is heard, then Diode is OK. Make certain that L-1, L-2 & L-3 Coils are in their proper places, as per Step #4 in Assembly Procedure."

My hands shaking, I put the earphone in my ear and slowly turned the tuning knob. Nothing. Not a sound. I knew it. I knew I wouldn't be able to make it work. I couldn't get anything right.

But then I checked everything again. Earphones clicked. Diode was okay. Coils were in the right places. I reconnected the antenna wire, put the earphone to my ear, and turned the knob again. Static! Real static. I must not have attached the antenna wire securely the first time.

I kept turning. There was music, and then, on another station, a radio announcer. "Philadelphia," he said. I was listening to *Philadelphia*. On a radio that *I* had built. I listened through the evening, finding more stations, with lots of interference in between. That night at bedtime, I was so excited that I couldn't even read. I'd done it. I'd done it all by myself. I wished the visitor would come back so that I could show him.

The last page of the pamphlet described some experiments you could do with your radio, like changing the size and location of the antenna or moving the antenna jumper to different terminals. The one that most intrigued me involved comparing how many stations I could receive at daytime versus nighttime. There were so many more at night, and I wondered why.

My parents had bought a *World Book Encyclopedia*, and so I started reading about radio frequencies and the atmosphere.

I discovered that the ionosphere is a layer of the atmosphere, fifty to six hundred miles up, and the radio signals were bouncing off it, and when the sun goes down, the ionosphere's composition changes. The fewer charged ions at night enabled the radio signals to travel to a higher level of the atmosphere, where the ions sometimes vibrated at the frequency of the radio wave, taking some of its energy, and bouncing it back to earth. It was hard reading, and there was a lot I didn't understand, but I was learning. Learning a ton. Why couldn't school be like this?

SOON AFTER I TURNED TWELVE, my world unraveled. My parents sold Noon's Delight and built a house on the edge of the sixth fairway of the golf course where my father played. They said it was so that we could be closer to the school I was going to for seventh grade—an all-boys day school in the city of Baltimore called Gilman, where my father had gone.

Playtime was over, the teachers—who were all men—told us at the beginning of the year, though it felt like summer outside. It was hot and I wanted to be splashing in Piney Run. Instead, every fifty minutes I had to shuffle to a different class, where they assigned piles of homework. And I had to wear a coat and tie to classes because it was the uniform. What was the point of a tie? It only got in the way, and I hated the feeling of it around my neck, like a noose. I dreaded being dropped off at Gilman each morning.

To make the time pass faster in classes, I played out a fantasy with my collection of Scripto mechanical pencils. They were spaceships, taking off and landing from the pencil slot at the top of my scarred wood desk. They went to faraway places to explore. The crew lived in the clip, and the rest of the pencil housed a giant atomic engine in the shape of a coiled spring. Sometimes the ships had battles, and they'd be damaged and the crew would have to evacuate. The red eraser that popped off the end was their escape pod. I wished I could do that— escape, bail out, get away from there. Go back to the farm.

Eighth grade was even worse than seventh. The teachers said they had to "whip us into shape" for high school, so there was even more homework. Plus, they started giving quizzes and tests practically every day. I never studied for them. I didn't know why, but I couldn't make myself memorize boring facts just to pass a stupid test.

I figured out a new way to pass the time in study hall, though: listening to baseball on a tiny Sony transistor radio. The kids were all talking about the World Series, but I didn't care; I just wanted to see if I could get away with it. I slipped off to the bathroom and threaded the wire from the earplug up the front of my shirt and then down my shirtsleeve. I cupped the earpiece in my hand and put the radio in my pocket. At my desk, I'd put my hand up to my ear, slip in the earpiece, and whisper the score to the other kids when the teacher had his back to us.

Everybody at Gilman was sports crazy. Behind the imposing brick buildings, the athletic fields for all the different sports seemed to stretch forever. We were required to play a sport every day after school. If you weren't standing in the hot sun or shivering in a nasty wind all day waiting for something to happen, then you were sprinting around a cinder track, trying not to fall, or running over somebody, or somebody running over you, chasing a ball and hoping not to get hurt. My father had played varsity football here. I couldn't imagine it. I didn't really like any sports.

There was one class I looked forward to—religion. The teacher, Mr. Finney, didn't assign a lot of homework, and we didn't have to memorize a bunch of facts for tests. We studied stories from the Old Testament and talked about them. When we read about Cain and Abel, he asked: "Was God right to let Cain off easy after he killed his brother?"

This was my first experience of a class discussion where the teacher asked us for our honest opinions. There were no right or wrong answers, only how well we explained our points of view. Most of all, we were talking about important questions—about how to live our lives. It was learning through dialogue and engagement with ideas, and the class made a deep and lasting impression on my young mind.

Not long after the end of the semester, my parents hosted a New Year's Eve party at the house for a bunch of their country club friends. I hung out on the stairs, eavesdropping. One of the men wandered out of the living room, drink in hand, and spotted me.

"So, how'z sschul going?" he slurred, as he leaned heavily on the newel of the banister.

"Fine," I said, looking off to the wallpaper.

"What do you want to be when you grow up?"

"I think I want to be a religious philosopher," I announced. "Except that I'm an agnostic, and I don't know if you can be a religious philosopher if you don't completely believe in God."

He stared at me for a moment and then walked back to the party.

Early in the new semester, my parents and I were asked to come into the school for a conference with the principal. I had done well in Mr. Finney's religion class, but it wasn't enough to save me; I had lousy grades in everything else. We were told that I would not be "invited" back to Gilman for high school.

I'd hated the place and was glad I wouldn't have to go back, but I was afraid now, too. Was it possible I'd end up at a school where I'd be even more miserable?

It was raining and chilly on the September day when my parents drove me up to Avon Old Farms, a boarding school in Connecticut. Walking into the quadrangle, I shuddered: the only way in or out was through one of four archways tunneled into the center of the four buildings, each constructed out of huge blocks of red clay–colored stone. In the walls there were small windows like the slits for self-defense built into medieval castles. The roofs were steeply slanted slate with little turrets and tall chimneys knifing into the gray sky. A series of thick, dark wooden doors fitted with enormous wrought-iron hinges enclosed the classrooms on the ground floor. The dorm rooms were on the second and third floors.

As my parents and I walked down a flagstone path toward my dormitory at the far end of the quad, a senior told us about Avon's history. "Theodate Pope Riddle, one of the state's first licensed female architects and the school's founder, wanted to create the feeling of a Cotswold village," he explained. "So in 1927 she spent millions bringing all these craftsmen over from England, and they made everything by hand—the wooden beams, the iron door latches, the hand-blown glass. The brownstone came from a quarry nearby."

Why did she go to all that trouble to build a place that felt more like a fortress than a school? I imagined that there might be moats and drawbridges beyond the quad, guarded by tinmen dressed in chain mail, and jousting was probably a varsity sport.

My parents helped me carry my suitcases and stuff to my room, and then we headed back to the car. Mom gave me a cool hug. Dad shook my hand and said, "Work hard, son. I don't care what you do so long as you are the best." Then they were gone.

Back at the dorm, I looked around my room. Bare wooden walls, built-in bunk bed, and a cramped closet with a couple of drawers. A small flip-top desk and wood chair, with one tiny window for light. God, it was noisy. Guys running up and down the hall, yelling and jabbering. I could hear everything. The door from my room to the hallway was open at the top and the bottom, like a bathroom stall. So they could spy on you, I thought.

Avon took kids who didn't have good grades or test scores, and it had a reputation as a place for jocks. We had to play a sport every season. I did football, wrestling, and lacrosse because my father wanted me to, and I hated them. It was Gilman all over again, only now the kids were bigger and tougher. That bastard Art Drury once floored me with a sucker punch to the jaw because he said I was too loud. The jerk was a trained boxer, looking for an excuse to show off. If you weren't a jock—and I wasn't—you might as well go crawl into a closet for four years and hope they'd leave you alone. But they didn't leave me alone.

Classes at Avon were also no different from those at Gilman, and so I was no different as a student. "The Battle of Hastings was fought in 1066 between the Norman-French army of Duke William II of Normandy and an English army led by King Harold Godwinson. . . ." Suddenly, the litany stopped. "You should be taking notes. You never know what will be on the semester exam." Did I have to copy down *everything* he said? No way. I couldn't keep up.

The Pythagorean theorem was something about triangles. I didn't get it. And what the hell was pi? For some crazy reason, I memorized it to more decimal places than I was supposed to: 3.14159265.

Domain, class, order, and phylum—I couldn't keep them straight. The textbook had colored illustrations of men's and women's anatomy, but what I really wanted to know was what girls looked like with no clothes on.

Conjugating verbs? *Veni, vidi, vici* was the only phrase I could remember, but it sure wasn't going to help me conquer Latin. I came, I saw, I flunked.

I began to detest all of my classes—except for English. The teacher, Mr. Ramsey, was a little weird—the way he held his cigarette between his long, thin fingers as if it were something delicate, and shot streams of smoke straight up into the air every time he took a puff. But I really liked what we were reading.

The Old Man and the Sea was about an old fisherman, Santiago, who'd gone eighty-four days without catching a fish. So he decided to go way out to sea, all by himself in his small boat, searching for a big catch. He caught a humongous marlin and spent two days reeling it in before finally killing it. But the fish was too big to bring into his skiff, so he had to lash it to the side. Then sharks came and started eating his beautiful catch. "My brother," he called the marlin. He tried fighting the sharks off with a rudimentary weapon—a penknife lashed to an oar. He killed some, but he couldn't kill all of them.

"So why does Santiago seem obsessed with the baseball player Joe DiMaggio?" Ramsey asked us.

I shot up my hand, squirming in my seat.

"Wagner?"

"I think it's because he admires the way DiMaggio continues to play and to try his best, even though the bone spur in his heel is hurting all the time. The old man is hurting, too, but he knows he can't give up—that he has to keep trying to catch fish."

Ramsey smiled, then took a puff of his cigarette. "So do you think the outcome of the story would have been different if the boy, Manolin, had gone out with the old man?"

That's what I liked about this class. Sometimes he asked us questions that would never have occurred to me. Just like Mr. Finney had.

Our next assignment was to write a short story. I decided to write my own "Old Man" tale. I wrote about a guy who's been a guide in New Hampshire's White Mountains his whole life. I wrote about the way he took people up some of my favorite mountains—like Mount Lafayette on the Franconia Ridge. I described the view from the top, how you could see across the densely wooded Pemigewasset Wilderness to the jagged peaks of the Presidential Range and Mount Washington. But the man is getting old, like Santiago. He isn't going to be able to guide people, or even hike much, anymore. His knees and back hurt a lot. So he decides to take one last hike to Mount Lafayette, by himself.

He takes my favorite trail, the Falling Waters Trail, up to the ridge. The sun is setting as he crosses the ridge and heads for the summit. When he finally gets to the bare rocky top at dusk, the sky rumbles with thunder and he sees lightning zigzagging in the distance.

I'd put that in because I was trying out this thing Mr. Ramsey called foreshadowing—trying to give the reader a hint of something that's about to happen, without giving it away.

He can tell it's going to rain, so he finds a rocky outcropping just below the summit to crawl under. He's tired, really tired.

Here's how I ended the story: "Slowly, he surrenders to the soul-satisfying silence of slumber."

It took me forever to write that sentence. I kept rewriting it until I was finally happy with it. I wanted to use this thing called alliteration that Ramsey had taught us about. I wanted the sentence to make long *ess* sounds—sounds that might soothe you to sleep. I left the ending uncertain on purpose. Maybe he just fell asleep, or maybe he died. The reader had to decide.

It was such a challenge to get the story right—to use all the senses, and to bring together some of my best memories of the New Hampshire mountain trails—while making up this character. He wasn't like anyone I'd ever met.

Ramsey went ape over it. Read it to the class and gave me an A. The first A I'd ever gotten in school.

At the start of tenth grade, I couldn't wait for English class. But right away I knew it was going to be different. Mr. Stanley, a bald-headed hulk of a man who smoked stogies, had this tight, little half smile that wasn't a smile at all. It was more of a pit bull's snarl.

The first book we had to read was *The Return of the Native* by Thomas Hardy. *Booooring*. And then we had to write an essay on it: "Analyze the evidence that suggests that Eustacia had supernatural qualities. What impact do these suggestions have on her as a character?" I didn't know what he was looking for, so I just made up some BS. Got a C minus.

Finally, Stanley gave us a creative-writing assignment. We were supposed to write a physical description of one of the other kids in class. I wrote about this tall, blond athletic kid, and the way he moved, like a leopard on the prowl.

After we handed in our papers, he chose a couple to read out loud. I was hoping that he might choose mine. But instead the worst happened. He started reading a description of a boy who had braces, glasses that slipped down his nose, and greasy black hair. The paper went on to describe the way the boy picked and squeezed the pimples that dotted his face, and everyone started looking at me and laughing.

Stanley looked at me, too, with that little half smile—as if he were really enjoying it, making me squirm. My cheeks burned. I'd never felt such shame.

For the rest of tenth grade, I did the minimum, just enough to pass. Often, trying to doze off at night, I fantasized about leading a group of rebels in a takeover of the campus, freeing the convicts. But I could never figure out where the prisoners—we students—would go or what we'd do. Besides, no one was going to follow me. I was more alone than ever.

In the fall of 1962, at the beginning of my eleventh-grade year, a teacher came into the dorm partway through evening study hall and told us to assemble in the refectory immediately. They'd never done this before. Walking out into the icy night, everybody was trying to guess what was going on. No one had a clue.

As we sat down at the long dining tables, the headmaster stood up at the platform at the front of the room. He cleared his throat and talked into a mike so that everyone could hear: "The Russians have deployed intercontinental ballistic missiles in Cuba. The president has just announced a naval blockade of Cuba. It will be sustained until the Russians remove the missiles." Kids shook their heads in stunned disbelief.

"Gentlemen, this is a perilous time for our country. There has never been a confrontation like this between two superpowers since the dawn of the nuclear age. No one knows what the outcome—" His voice caught in his throat. "So let us pray tonight—each in our own way—for the president and for our country. You may return to your rooms."

Squeezing through the exit, everyone was quiet. But then, outside, one kid shouted, "Just let those communist bastards try something! We'll blow them back to the Stone Age."

A couple of kids cheered and some laughed nervously. I shook my head and walked away from the crowd to where the lawn met the woods.

Jesus. This was for real. Back at Gilman, when they set off the air raid sirens and had us crawl under our desks, I'd figured it probably wouldn't help us much. I'd seen the films of the bomb going off. But now there were so many more, and they were much more powerful. There was no place that was safe.

Why? Why was this happening? I looked up. The sky was clear, the stars shimmering. If there really was a God, He wouldn't let this happen, wouldn't destroy the whole world in seconds. I wished I had a God that I could believe in—that I could pray to: *Please, God, don't let this happen.*

Classes, tests, grades, getting into college—it all seemed even more trivial now.

I took up smoking and often sneaked out of the dorm after study hall for a quick one in a dark classroom. I'd wear a glove so they couldn't smell it on my fingers, and always chewed a breath mint afterward, but I knew I'd get caught—and I was, several times. As punishment I was given hours of physical labor around the campus on Saturday work details.

We were allowed to go into town on Saturday nights, as long as we were back before the 11:30 p.m. curfew. Midweek, kids would start talking about who was giving what kind of party in town and whether there'd be booze. I'd go, but then stand in a corner, drinking beer. I knew that if I went back to school with the smell of alcohol on my breath, I'd be expelled.

I finished junior year in my usual fashion, with another collection of C's and D's on my report card. Most of the kids studied—at least some of the time—and didn't seem to care about having to memorize and regurgitate boatloads of dull crap. Why did I always question everything? Why hadn't I just been able to fit in and do what I was supposed to do, like everybody else?

There was the usual confrontation with my parents when I came home from school. They'd grill me with their questions: *Why wasn't I trying, didn't I realize how important it was to do well, to get into a good college?* Blah, blah. I promised to do better. It was practically a ritual now.

On the train back to school for the beginning of my senior year, I felt nauseous. The pressure would be intense. All the kids talked about how tough the twelfth-grade English teacher was. His name was Sid Clark, but everybody called him the Mole because he was short and round with a long nose, and when he was on duty, it was almost as though he were tunneling around, looking for trouble, with that huge, black four-cell Maglite of his.

English was even worse than I thought it would be. The Mole lectured the entire senior class of fifty at once, and he made it a habit to call on kids to answer some obscure question on *The Canterbury Tales*, or some other antique book, with no warning. He glowered at you until you whispered a reply, and when you didn't give him what he was looking for, he'd ridicule you. "Did your dog eat your textbook again, Wagner?" If you were stupid enough to doze off, as I did a couple of times, he threw his eraser at you. Kids would hoot and howl when he did that. I lived for the Saturday nights when I could get off campus.

My coping strategy worked for about a month. I'd been to another party in town, but for the first time, I was late getting back. It was only twenty minutes after curfew, though, not the end of the world. Then the flashlight hit me straight in the eyes, blinding me. I'd been caught.

"Wagner, you're late!" the Mole barked.

Not *him*. Anybody but him. Of all the teachers, why did it have to be the Mole on duty?

"I had trouble getting a cab," I mumbled, trying not to slur my speech. I'd probably be grounded for a couple of weekends if he didn't smell the beer on my breath. I'd chewed a couple of mints in the cab, just in case. I needed to keep it together.

"Wagner, you're a fuckup!" he growled, stepping closer and sneering in my face. "You've always been a fuckup, and you're always gonna be a fuckup. Get to your room."

God, where did that come from? His words rattled around my brain as I stumbled through the darkness back to the dorm. Judge and jury ruling on my seventeen years. My future, too. I'd been sentenced to a life of fuckupedness. And I was sure that he was right—that was the worst part. Salty tears streaked my cheeks as I staggered up the steps to my room.

Pulling the covers tight around me, I struggled to fall asleep. I couldn't stop thinking about the dreariness of the last three years. I knew I was never going to get into a decent college with C's and D's in just about everything. Maybe I wouldn't get into college at all.

First thing the next morning, I called for a cab to take me to the train station, where I bought a ticket to New York City. I didn't have permission, and I knew I would be expelled for it. But it didn't matter. In my mind, I was already a dropout.

I walked the streets of New York for three days, replaying the Mole's vicious attack in my head. I'd never heard an adult say "fuck." What a shit he was to say that to me. And I was furious with myself for having run away. Maybe he didn't smell the beer, and I would have been punished only for being late if I hadn't run away. Now what the hell was I going to do? I had no idea.

Stanley and the Mole were not the only abusive school authorities I was to encounter in my school years. Nor was Avon the worst school I attended, or the last from which I dropped out. But it was the first time I had actively rebelled. I had taken a huge leap into the unknown. It was liberating, but only for a brief moment as exhilaration quickly gave way to naked fear. I didn't know it then, but I was running from the smoke straight into several fiery, tumultuous years of education. Like steel, I was eventually tempered and strengthened by them—though only after more painful experiences.

I EVENTUALLY CALLED MY PARENTS to say I was coming home. The headmaster had already told them that I was not to return to school. My mother met me at the train station. We drove in silence to the house. "The talk" came that night after a tense, wordless dinner.

"You've got a couple of choices," my dad said in a quiet but hard voice. "You could enlist." What, and get ready to go to war with the Russians? That wasn't happening. "Or get a job pumping gas," he continued. I couldn't think of a job I wanted less. "Or go to public high school." Public school was where the greasers went. "Or maybe you can find another boarding school that will take you. It's your decision." He looked disgusted with me.

I couldn't choose "none of the above," so I took the last option. My parents hired a consultant to find a boarding school that would take me. There was one school that would admit me, he said, Searing, in Somers, New York, about an hour north of Manhattan. I took the train up by myself and then hailed a taxi to the address on the admission letter.

It was a gun-smoke gray November day. The school's "campus" consisted of two Victorian houses situated on a wooded hillside overlooking a small field full of weeds with a soccer goal at each end. Paint was peeling off the dilapidated buildings, and there were no nets in the goals. Ruth and Otto Swan, the owners of this for-profit school, lived in the smaller of the two houses. The other had been chopped up into classrooms and dorm rooms. As I approached the front porch, I spied a loose knot of boys lounging around in beat-up, straightback wooden chairs, playing cards.

A tall guy with slick black hair looked me over coolly. "What school you get kicked out of?"

Searing, it turned out, was a "last chance" school for fuckups like me. Every one of the twenty or so boys there had either been tossed out of or flunked out of another school. There were only three or four boys in each class, and although we were theoretically supposed to be in different grades, we all listened to the same dull lectures and did the same mindnumbing assignments.

A few weeks after I arrived, kids and teachers gathered

together in the common room, staring in shared silence at the only TV the school had. The president had been shot. Chaos. No one knew anything. But then Cronkite came on and gravely announced that the president had died.

I rushed out to the porch. I didn't want them to see me crying. I just wanted to be alone. It felt like a replay of the Cuban missile crisis the year before—adults doing crazy things in a senseless world. But I couldn't think about that now. I had a school year to survive.

They didn't assign very much homework at Searing—probably because they knew none of the kids would do it—but the threat of the New York State Regents Exams the following spring loomed over me. I had to pass the tests in all the major subjects in order to graduate. Trouble was, I had no idea how to study.

And so with plenty of time on my hands and little to do but play cards after class, I read a great deal. Hemingway, Fitzgerald, Steinbeck—none of the books that were actually assigned. Or if they were, I'd be sure to finish them ahead of time. Teachers ruined good books by lecturing about their structure, while asking us nothing about what we thought or how the books *felt* to read.

That winter I discovered Thomas Wolfe. I read all four of his sprawling novels in three weeks. Hemingway's guys—just like the jocks at school, and like my father, too—prized toughness over everything. Wolfe's characters were different; Eugene Gant and George Webber were sensitive and thoughtful, seeking to understand the world and their place in it.

They were the first men I'd encountered in literature or in real life who didn't seem embarrassed by their emotions and try to hide them. Feelings were part of how they knew things. They *felt* the world as much as they thought about it, as I did. Reading those books, I began to realize that maybe I wasn't some freak of nature.

Later that winter, I stumbled across a book of aphorisms by a Polish author, Stanisław Lec, in a corner of the room that passed for a library at the school. I was amazed at how he could capture a little bit of wisdom or a life dilemma in just a few words, and I wrote down some of them:

"When smashing monuments, save the pedestals—they always come in handy."

"Optimists and pessimists differ only on the date of the end of the world."

"Is it progress if a cannibal uses a knife and fork?"

"If a man who cannot count finds a four-leaf clover, is he lucky?"

Then I tried writing some of my own. Most were kind of crappy, I knew, but I crafted one that I liked because it pretty much summed up my views on adults and life:

Is life nothing more than a question-and-answer period, where the questions go unanswered, and the answers go unquestioned?

Working on my aphorisms, I became excited about writing again, for the first time since sneering Stanley had humiliated me. I decided to see if I could find a creative-writing teacher. I knew that it couldn't be my English teacher at Searing. With pipe smoke swirling around his head, he always seemed to be in a bit of a fog. But the other English teacher at school was very courteous and friendly toward me and the other kids—maybe because he was British, I thought. He wasn't trying to be liked, as my young biology teacher was. He just seemed to respect us. I finally mustered the courage to ask him if he'd teach me creative writing. "I'd be delighted" was his reply. It would be an extracurricular activity, he said, with no grades or academic credit.

Each week Mr. Edwards gave me a new writing assignment, and then we'd meet and talk about it. One week, it was a childhood reminiscence. The next week, a description of nature. Then a monologue. Then a humorous story. He encouraged me to write about things that I knew or had experienced rather than try to invent things entirely in my head. I spent more time on these "assignments" than I did on all of my real classes combined.

One week, he suggested I try a dialogue, and so I wrote one based on some stuff I'd overheard in the dining room.

"Tony, you've really captured the male adolescent voice with this," Mr. Edwards said. "Simply marvelous how you've shown the hurt in the teasing without any description. But the part where the teacher intervenes seems a bit artificial. Next time, you might try reading the lines out loud to yourself to see if they ring true."

I'd made up the part about the teacher stepping in. That was why it didn't work. But what I really liked about Mr. Edwards was that he always commented on at least one thing that I'd done well in a piece. And he'd point me to something to work on, too. He was constantly encouraging me, making me want to work harder, like a good coach.

For everything else, I was doing only what I had to in order to get by. Despite my shitty grades and low SATs, I'd been accepted at Randolph-Macon, a small men's college in Virginia. A guy I was friendly with from Avon had gone there the previous year and said he liked it. That was good enough for me.

Spring came early that year, and everybody was obsessed with the Beatles. We'd open the windows after class and flood the campus with music, "Can't Buy Me Love" and "I Want to Hold Your Hand" blaring out, hour after hour. A teacher would switch off one radio and another would take up the chorus. With the end of high school so near, I was beginning to feel hopeful for the first time. But then Mrs. Swan, Searing's owner, called me into her office.

Mrs. Swan rarely came over to the school building, and when she did, it was usually because some kid was in serious trouble. She was a big battle-axe of a woman, with a clipped German accent and a huge set of gray braids wrapped around her head like a crown.

Frowning, she sat me down in front of her desk.

"We found your stash."

Stash? What the eff . . . And then I remembered. I'd put a couple of Coke cans in the reservoir of the toilet in my dorm to keep them cool. The toilet still worked, so what was the problem?

"I am suspending you. Your parents will be notified, and you will be sent home for the next three days, and won't return until after spring break next week. I hope you will use this time to think about being more responsible and setting a better example for the younger students."

It was a long train ride home. I didn't know what kind of reception I'd get from my parents. My mom met me and asked me to tell her what had happened—even though I knew Mrs. Swan had already phoned her.

"Let me understand this," she said, suppressing a smile. "Your punishment for cooling your Cokes in the back of the toilet is three extra days of vacation?" We both roared. These days, my mom and I were kind of buddies, and sometimes she talked with me about the books she was reading and shared her favorite operas.

After spring break, I was counting the weeks until my release. Then Von Hilda called me into her office again in late May. Now what had I done?

"The Regents scores came back." *Oh, shit, here it comes.* "You got a forty-nine in biology."

I stormed out the door, crying. I *knew* it. The bio teacher was just back from the peace corps. Class was mostly bull sessions, and I hadn't learned much. Now I wasn't going to graduate. I banged my hand against the wall, over and over.

"Just kidding," she shouted down the corridor a few moments later. "It was a ninety-four."

I couldn't believe it. Why did she do that to me?

After that, I didn't want to bother going to graduation, but

I had to because my parents had driven up from Baltimore. I sat squirrelly on my folding metal chair as Mrs. Swan gave her prepared spiel. A couple of faculty came up to hand out awards to students. I wasn't paying attention. I couldn't wait for the whole thing to be over.

Then Mr. Edwards stepped up to the lectern. "Searing has inaugurated a creative-writing award this year," he said, "and it goes to Tony Wagner."

Stupefied, I was slow to stand up. Finally, I stumbled to the dais and took the small wrapped package he offered. His warm hand enveloped mine in a gentle handshake. "Congratulations. You've earned this. Good luck."

THE SUMMER AFTER I finished high school, I read two books that were, in retrospect, vital to my intellectual awakening. The first was John Steinbeck's *The Grapes of Wrath*. It seemed as though we'd studied American history every couple of years since elementary school, and teachers always talked about the Great Depression, yet I had no sense of the suffering of the people who had lived through it. Most stunning to me was Steinbeck's portrayal of how greedy banks and corporate farmers had taken advantage of the Okies and used the police against them. When people tried to organize, the cops murdered them. Why hadn't they taught us how it felt to live in different times, instead of just barraging us with the dates and facts? Too much of learning then, as now, was rote memorization. The kinds of assignments we were given and the homework we were made to do were incredibly boring and pointless. To me, it was not work worth doing.

The second book was even more influential as I tried to make sense of my years of schooling. Called *Summerhill*, it was an account of an experimental boarding school founded in Suffolk, England, by a journalist-turned-teacher named A. S. Neill. In *Summerhill* Neill outlined his educational philosophy. He believed that children were innately wise and that school should not get in the way of their natural development: "We set out to make a school in which we should allow children freedom to be themselves. In order to do this, we had to renounce all discipline, all direction, all suggestion, all moral training, all religious instruction."

Teachers and students decided the school's rules together in weekly meetings, with each person having one vote. Kids were free to go do music or art or woodcraft or play outside whenever they chose. Classes were optional, and there were no tests or grades. Occasionally, Neill would "set an exam for fun," for instance, asking students, "Where are the following: Madrid, Thursday Island, yesterday, love, democracy, hate, my pocket screwdriver." Schoolwork was playful.

Neill summed up his approach in a line that I found especially striking: "When my first wife and I began the school, we had one main idea: *to make the school fit the child*—instead of making the child fit the school." I thought about the ways in which adults had pressured me to "fit" a school and berated me when I didn't, from my teachers' negative comments on my report cards to the never-ending lectures from my parents. Like most children, I had blamed myself for my failings: I was lazy, or just not very smart. I was a "fuckup," after all. The Mole had said it, but I knew that other teachers, and even my parents, believed it, too.

But what if it had been the other way around? What if instead my parents had found a school that fit me? Did such schools exist beyond the shores of England? What would it have been like to go to one? How would my life and my learning have been different if I had?

One answer was clear to me: my learning would have been organized more around my interests and questions, as they were for the children at Summerhill. Neill believed real learning occurred only when a child's motivation was intrinsic—not the need to perform well on a test and please a teacher or parent, but the desire to understand something the child took a natural interest in.

Despite being labeled a "reluctant reader," I had devoured books about the Second World War while trying to learn about my father, who had volunteered to be a fighter pilot. I wanted to know what it felt like to live with danger and to fight for something I believed in. I had read up on radio waves, frequencies, and the ionosphere as an eleven-year-old, all the while refusing to do homework. I had taken the time to ponder complex concepts such as agnosticism after I'd been encouraged to formulate my own interpretations of biblical stories. I had played with different literary forms after being challenged to write a short story. Neill was right. When I was interested in something, and given freedom and encouragement to follow that interest wherever it led, I was an eager learner. Even a good one.

Another compelling aspect of Summerhill was the easy and informal relationships between students and teachers. When I looked back on my school days, I realized that while Mr. Ramsey had taught English in an engaging way, he had not made the sort of profound impression on me that Mr. Finney, who taught religion at Gilman, and Mr. Edwards, my chosen writing coach at Searing, had. It wasn't just that I was interested in what they were teaching, it was also that these teachers conveyed a sense of caring about me as a person. "Nobody cares how much you know," the saying goes, "until they know how much you care."

Finally, Neill's ideas of play intrigued me. He felt many essential things were learned in children's play, things that were more important than what could be learned in books. Unstructured play provided opportunities for kids to learn how to get along with other kids and be creative, he wrote. Years later, reading the works of many education theorists, I came to see how children use forms of play, not only to gain social skills or as an outlet for imagination, but also to make sense of the world around them. Infants are scientists, argues Alison Gopnik, a philosophy professor at the University of California, Berkeley, and they experiment through play to "construct" an understanding of the nature of things.

At the time, I knew how much I missed my unencumbered

play in the hills and woods of Noon's Delight. But I'd never before thought about play as a way to learn. Now I began to see my five years at summer camp in New Hampshire in a new light. I didn't think of them as having anything to do with my education, but my days there were all about learning through play. It wasn't the free play of Summerhill or the farm, though. It was different—somehow more serious, more purposeful.

TWO

School of the Open

MY PARENTS DIDN'T LET ME WATCH MUCH TV, BUT I'D BEG
for the Lone Ranger with his silver bullets, white hat, and a
horse named Silver. He went around helping the good guys
and fighting the bad ones. Tonto was his Indian sidekick, but
he didn't talk very much, except when he called the Masked
Man *kimosabe* ("ke-mo sah-bee").

Even though my cowboy hat was black, my six-gun shot
only caps, and my Tonto was a Great Dane named Smutty, I
was *the* Lone Ranger on the farm, ranging the hills, looking
for adventure, protecting our heard of Black Angus from cattle rustlers. I'd count the weeks until summer when I'd be
free to roam the land, get sweaty, and then go strip and splash
in Piney Run.

But then, the summer I turned ten, my parents announced

that I was going to a camp up in New Hampshire called Mowglis. My father had gone there, but he'd never told me anything about the camp—only that it was near the mountains on a lake called Newfound. I was to be loaded onto a train from Baltimore to Boston, then a bus from Boston to the camp.

And suddenly it was happening. With a deafening horn and urgent clanging of a bell, the huge diesel lumbered down the track and pulled up to the station platform where my mother and I were waiting. I was already dressed in the Mowglis gray wool shirt and shorts my mom had ordered so that the camp counselor could recognize me. A grown man in a uniform like mine skipped down the steps, told me his name, and shook my hand. I gave my mom a short tight hug and followed him on board. As the train pulled slowly from the station, I took a seat and pressed my nose to the window, wanting to wave to my mother, but she had disappeared.

At each stop of the journey, more kids boarded, some in Mowglis uniforms, others in different uniforms, going to different camps. Once we got to Boston, those of us with gray uniforms were herded onto buses for the slow drive north. I remember nothing of the trip, only that my stomach was in knots. It was my first time away from home, and eight weeks felt like a very long time.

The bus eventually pulled down a dirt road to a flat, dusty outdoor area, which I would soon learn was the hub of the camp. We came here for announcements and to check our duty assignments for the week. Every evening, we'd line up here, stand at attention, and salute while the flag was taken down and a bugler played "To the Colors"—it was from a record—over the PA system.

On one side of the assembly area, there was a large building called Grey Brothers Hall, stained a dark chocolate brown like all the other buildings in the camp. A porch wrapped around the front, and inside there was a stage at one end of the plain, pine-sided hall, with a stone fireplace, big enough to stand in, at the opposite end. A large canvas curtain hung across the front of the stage. It was decorated with a life-sized painting of forest animals and a boy. He was naked and playing on the ground, surrounded by wolves. Two cubs were playing with him, while some adults watched. An enormous black bear stood over the boy, like a guard. A black panther was poised on a rock, looking at the boy. In the distance, there was a tiger that seemed to be sneaking up on them.

Two more scenes were painted on the wall on either side of the stage. In one, a teenager with rippling muscles, wearing just a blue cloth around his middle, stood between two slender tree trunks, each with a few pale-blue leaves. The trees bent toward him in the shape of cupped hands. The young man was smiling at a giant snake that was completely wrapped around him. They seemed to be friends. In the other mural, the man had a long, curved knife in a sheath hanging from his neck and stood with his hands resting on two animals—the panther and the bear. A gray wolf stood just behind them. The paintings were simple, with a cream-colored background— almost like drawings you'd color in a coloring book. All were signed in the lower right-hand corner: Wah-Pah-Nah-Yah. I wondered if the artist was an Indian, like Tonto, and what stories the vibrant paintings were telling. I stood for the longest time, gazing at them.

I wasn't familiar with Rudyard Kipling's *The Jungle Books*, so I didn't immediately recognize the characters. The boy and the young man was, of course, Mowgli, who had been found in the forest when he was little and was raised by a pack of wolves as though he were one of them. The pack's cubs were his "grey brothers." Kaa, the snake, was indeed a friend. Baloo, the bear, was his teacher, and so was Bagheera, the black panther. Many of the names of places in the camp came from *The Jungle Books* as well. The sleeping cabins were Baloo, where the youngest kids, like me, slept; Toomai (the elephant handler), Akela (the wolf pack leader), and Panther were for older boys; and Den was for the most senior campers, who were fifteen and sixteen years old. The cabins were each a short walk away from the main path, which led gently down the hill from Grey Brothers Hall through a grove of tall pines for perhaps a quarter of a mile before ending at the lakeside.

The cabins were simple. Dark brown planks ended halfway up the building, with the remaining space to the low roofs open to the air. Inside, the pine walls and roof were unfinished, their two-by-four supports exposed like the ribs of a skeleton. Twelve to fifteen pinewood beds were lined up in two rows the length of the building, with a low, open-shelved bureau standing sentinel beside each one. Two counselors had their beds at the ends of the cabin—close enough so that they could hear and shush the whispering that sometimes erupted after taps.

The porch at one end of the dorm had just enough room for a couple of plain wood tables and benches, where we would play board or card games on rainy days. All were covered with crudely carved initials, some deeply etched into the weathered wood. Many of the cabins were ancient—more than fifty years old—and I wondered if I might find my father's initials somewhere.

In front of every dorm, there was a tetherball court, which consisted of a ten-foot metal post that had a hard rubber ball suspended on a line from the top. In our free time, pairs of boys faced off. The first person to wind the line completely around the pole won. Knots of boys would stand and watch, yelling encouragement for a friend, while waiting their turn. The game, like so many other competitive sports, held no appeal for me, perhaps because I was slow and chubby as a kid. When it came to picking players for the softball team, I was always one of the last kids to be chosen by a team's captain.

Continuing down the main path, past the pine-needled paths to the sleeping cabins, there were trails snaking off to the right and left that led to activity areas. One ended at the archery field, another at the rifle range; still another led to the soccer field and softball diamond. Before you arrived at the waterfront, one of the last side paths ran off to the right, uphill toward a thick stand of trees—white pine, maple, ash, birch. You'd walk for a couple of minutes before you could see the dozen stone steps leading up to a simple stone archway, a bell suspended just beneath its peak, that defined the entrance to an open-air chapel. This would become a very special place for me—a place where I went, alone, when I needed to get away from the cabin noise and incessant teasing and figure things out.

That first Sunday afternoon, summoned by the slow ring of a bell, I lined up with my Baloo cabinmates and counselors to go to the chapel. We walked in silence along the path, then up the steps and through the archway, which was just tall and wide enough for us to pass through, two by two. Defined on all four sides by a neat, knee-high stone wall, the space held twenty long, straight-backed wood benches, stained the same brown as the camp buildings, ten to each side of a center aisle leading to an altar. As we made our way to these makeshift pews, an organ, almost completely hidden from view in a little shack behind the altar, played slow, solemn, churchy music. Sunlight filtered through the thick canopy of trees arching above us.

We stood and sang a hymn from the printed sheet left on the benches and were then told to sit down. As the dull drone of the organ died away, I heard strange new birdcalls—musical notes I'd never heard on our farm in Maryland. I looked closely at the altar for the first time. It was made of moss- and lichen-flecked fieldstones of varying shape and size, held in place by some invisible mortar. There were no cloths, no polished brass candlesticks. There was only a pale-white birch bark cross on the altar, a few delicate ferns waving in the wind on either side of it.

Mr. Kingsley, the camp director, got up from the front bench and faced us, standing in front of the altar. Like the rest of us, he was dressed in Mowglis's matching shirt and shorts—only his shirt had a blue pocket with a white *M*, signifying that he was one of the senior counselors. Junior counselors got a gray pocket with an *M*, I was later to learn, while we campers had no pockets.

Smoothing back his slick black hair with one hand, he welcomed us. In a somber voice he told us how Mrs. Elizabeth Ford Holt had created what she called a "school of the open" back in 1903. This was a place where boys like us, who grew up in crowded cities and suburbs, could be in nature and learn outdoor skills. She had written to a famous author named Rudyard Kipling for permission to name the camp after Mowgli. Mr. Kingsley explained how Mowgli had to learn to be clever and tough to survive in the jungle, and how his animal friends had helped him. The animals also taught him to love and respect all who lived in the forest.

Then Mr. Kingsley read from a page written by a colonel named Alcott Farrar Elwell who had taken over from Mrs. Holt as director of Mowglis in 1925 and run the camp for twenty-seven years. It was something about developing the good in every boy's character. I found it hard to follow, and I fidgeted as Mr. Kingsley talked. The rough-hewn bench scratched the back of my bare thighs, and I had to brush away the mosquitos that were swarming around us.

I didn't know what I was doing there. I lived on a farm and wasn't some kid who'd never been to the country. Yet I was captivated by the stuff our counselors had told us we'd be doing. Most every day, we'd go to "industries" and work for ribbons—in activities like archery, woodworking, arts and crafts, drama, camping, tennis, riflery, canoeing, and sailing. And swimming, of course, but in a cool, clear lake, not a swimming pool. We'd take day hikes every week, and overnight hikes, too. It all started the next day. I couldn't decide what I was most excited to try first.

Mr. Kingsley finished his talk with a short reading from the Bible. Like all of the other Bible readings I'd heard in our church back home, it made no sense to me. I was relieved to finally be able to stand up and take my turn filing down the aisle, through the chapel archway, and back to my cabin.

That night, after a noisy supper in the cramped dining hall, we walked to our first evening campfire. These campfires were held in a grove off the main dirt road. Eighty or so primitive wood seats were arranged in semicircles around the blackened stones of the fire pit, where a tepee of wood stood, waiting to be lit. Our chairs consisted of four-foot-long planks of pine with slanted backrests at one end and footrests at the other. A long board was nailed down the length of one side, holding the pieces of wood together. With our short legs, we younger kids could stretch out, but the older kids had to sit with their knees bowed in front of their faces.

Once we'd all squirmed into our seats, Mr. Kingsley stepped down from his perch on what was known as Council Rock and lit the fire. As the flames leaped up into the twilight, he told us how you had to earn four ribbons in order to be inducted into the inner circle, close to the fire. The older boys who sat there seemed so confident in the way they strutted around camp, as if it belonged to them.

After campfire, we returned to our cabins, brushed our teeth in the dancing light of kerosene lamps, and did our business at the latrine. Yawning, I crawled onto my hard bunk with its thin mattress covered with cotton ticking and snuggled under the scratchy wool blankets, piled high against the cool night air. A counselor turned down all the lamps but one, which he placed on a bench in the center of the cabin. Then he sat down and began to read.

He had chosen one of the Hardy Boys mysteries, perhaps *The House on the Cliff*, one of the early books in the series. Joe and Frank Hardy and a couple of their high school buddies are out riding motorcycles in the countryside when they decide to visit an abandoned house high on a hill, where an old miser had lived until he was robbed and murdered. The sky is growing dark as they enter the house. They hear a shriek and take off. Then Frank persuades the others to go back. They go inside the house again, there's thunder and lightning outside, and they hear another scream. Part of the ceiling caves in as they rush out the door. In the end, Joe and Frank find a secret cave in a cove, with stairs leading up to the old house. They're captured, but get free and rescue their father, a famous detective, who had been tied up in the house for days.

Hunting for Hidden Gold, *The Shore Road Mystery*, *The Secret of the Caves*—during my years at Mowglis we heard dozens. Camp was the only place where I had stories read aloud to me. Suspense, excitement, and adventure filled the darkness beyond the thin halo of kerosene light every night. Tired as I was, I never wanted the reading to end.

. . . .

WHEN I RETURNED TO CAMP the next summer, on the first day in Toomai, I noticed there was a new kid, different from the other guys. He had oily jet-black hair, combed straight back, deep brown eyes, and dark reddish-brown skin. He wore thick black-framed glasses and spoke with an accent. It wasn't southern, but it had a kind of drawl. He wasn't shy, he didn't hang back, though while the rest of the kids were fooling around, he just watched with alert eyes and half a smile.

His name was Jimmy West. We began to talk after the first few days, and I learned that he was from Oklahoma and that he was a full-blooded Cheyenne Indian. He had come to Mowglis with his dad, a counselor.

Jimmy could be with the other guys and laugh at their jokes, without trying to be like them or be liked by them. He didn't tease me about my protruding front teeth or call me "Buck Fang," the way all the kids in my cabin did. I'm not sure why he wanted to be friends with me, but maybe it was because he saw me as kind of different, too; and I didn't join in with all the aping of the way he talked. After the first week or so, he asked if I wanted to join a couple of kids who were going to learn Indian lore from his dad.

Mr. Kingsley had introduced Mr. West at one of our first campfires that summer. When Jimmy's father stood up for his introduction, I had been awed. He was enormous—much taller than any other counselor, with wide shoulders and bulging biceps.

Mr. Kingsley told us that Mr. West's Indian name was Wah-Pah-Nah-Yah, which meant "Light-footed Runner" in Cheyenne. He had been born in a tepee in 1912 in Oklahoma and had first come to Mowglis as a counselor in 1939. He was a famous artist and teacher, Mr. Kingsley said, and he had painted the stage curtains in Grey Brothers Hall in 1940.

So he had done the paintings that had entranced me the previous summer. I had never met an artist before. And he was a real Indian, too, not like Tonto. I couldn't wait to have him as my teacher.

We met every afternoon in the camp's dusty library, a cramped room tucked into a corner of Grey Brothers Hall. It was quiet. Very few kids came for books. Mr. West set the four of us—Jimmy, two other boys, and me—to work making costumes we'd wear for a performance of traditional dances at the end of the summer.

We began with the small headdress, called a roach, which was cut from a strip of leather. The decorated roach would stretch the length of the top of my head, from my forehead to my neck, like a Mohawk haircut. We learned how to pull a row of U-shaped metal wires through the leather with pliers, and then carefully push through the quill ends of the white feathers, which we'd wrapped in fine, multicolored threads, one onto each wire. We glued a wisp of dark plume to the end of every feather. Then we attached a leather thong to each of the four corners of the roach, which we'd tie under our chin when we wore it.

Mr. West explained that the feathers we were using were

taken from turkeys and dyed to look like eagle feathers. Eagle feathers were awarded to warriors for bravery, he said, but because eagles were now endangered, only Indians were allowed to have eagle feathers, and they had to be used only in religious ceremonies.

Mr. West worked alongside us, decorating four feathers that were much larger than ours. They looked as though they might be real eagle feathers. He wasn't making a roach, and I couldn't figure out what he planned to do with them. With fine thread, he secured a horsehair bundle to the end of each feather. Next, he beaded over the thread and down the quill, using different combinations of turquoise, silver, red, and black beads to make a distinct design for the base of each feather.

I watched, mesmerized. How could such large hands create patterns so small and intricate and beautiful, while my child's hands struggled just to push the feathers down onto the wires protruding from the roach without stabbing myself? Mr. West could see I was struggling. He patiently put his enormous paws over mine and gently guided them, without words. My hands grew more sure with his teaching.

Having finished our headdresses, we worked on the other parts of our costume: two round, feathered bustles. A smaller bustle would be knotted around our neck and hang down our back across our shoulders, while a larger one would be tied around our waist and cover our back breechcloth. Again, we wrapped the quill end of each feather with fine thread. I chose a deep red thread to match the red plumes I'd glued to my feathers' tips. Finally, we sewed a simple beadwork design onto the round leather patches that held the bustle feathers.

While we labored, Mr. West told us about the Cheyenne. Long ago they had been farmers, but they were moved off their land and became hunters. They had to adapt to survive. And he told us about the Cheyenne religion.

He explained that the Cheyenne are animists. They believed that all creatures and places possess souls. Ma'heo'o, the Cheyenne's Divine Creator, had made the animals to help him create the earth, even before he had finished making man and woman. The very last thing he created, after he'd put humans on earth, had been the buffalo, which would provide the Cheyenne with food, shelter, and clothing.

Like the Christians, the Cheyenne had a prophet, called Motse'eove, or Sweet Medicine. He predicted the coming of the white man, and the horse and the cow, and the challenges they would bring. He said that it was better not to have a single all-powerful leader to face these tests. Following Sweet Medicine's teachings, the Cheyenne created a system where forty-four chiefs came together to make any important decision. Four chiefs were chosen from each of the ten bands of Cheyenne, along with four wise elders for the whole people.

Sweet Medicine also taught that if someone did something wrong, they should have another chance. Even after the white man attacked the Cheyenne for no reason, the Cheyenne forgave and continued to try to make peace because of his teaching. Similar to what I'd learned in church, the Cheyenne believed that everyone should strive to be a better person. But they had no churches, no dull sermons or droning hymns, no praying to a man in heaven. They worshipped nature, pure and simple. By then, I didn't think I believed in God or the Bible stories; I no longer said my prayers at bedtime, as I'd been taught. Yet being in the stillness of the woods by myself felt kind of like praying, praying to nature.

Mr. West's stories of the Cheyenne fascinated me. His voice was deep and rich and resonant, nothing like Tonto's stumbling English. The pictures he painted with his words were so different from the images of whooping warriors attacking settlers on TV.

As Mr. West told us these stories, we continued to work on our costumes. We made felt breechcloths that would hang down from our waists to our knees, in both the front and the back. Mine had an eagle, the color of the sun, and snow-white lightning bolts on a blood-red background. We also made matching plumed armlets to be tied above our biceps, a leather band of bells to secure below each knee, and sheepskin anklets. I was glad that we were given moccasins to wear but didn't have to make them, too.

Midway through the summer we began to practice our dances and chants—but dressed in our camp uniforms, as our costumes were not yet ready. Mr. West would put a record player on the window ledge of the library, with an album of Indian music, and turn up the volume, and we'd trudge out to the hot, dusty assembly field. Sometimes boys would stop and watch us practice. When they did, I would lose my concentration. I'd think about how ridiculous we must look to them, prancing around and chanting—especially me. I couldn't move to the music the way the others did. My legs just wouldn't obey me.

The evening of the performance finally came in the last week of camp. They'd built a huge pile of wood in the middle of the assembly area, where we were to dance. I gazed out the window of the library as the entire camp trooped in and took their seats. When the bonfire was lit, the sparks shot up into the pale-gray sky like fireworks.

We lined up single file at the door. Mr. West came down the line and gave each of us one of the ceremonial eagle feathers he had made, explaining that they were called coup feathers and were given for bravery against an enemy. I was last in line and couldn't stop thinking about my "enemies" out there. As he handed me my feather, he looked down at me with his deep brown eyes and put a hand on my shoulder. "Don't think about them," he said. "Concentrate on the music, and you will do well."

Trailing the full-feathered war bonnet of Wah-Pah-Nah-Yah, we moved out into the darkness. As the recorded drumming and chants echoed throughout the clearing, we began our first dance, slow stomping one behind the other. We were stalking hunters, praying for the souls of the animals whose lives we must take for food. I closed my eyes to feel the heavy din of the drumbeats, louder and louder. I heard the jingling of the bells on my legs as we chanted and thumped the bare earth. For a moment, I forgot about the faces at the edge of the firelight.

Faster and faster, we danced. Our second dance was the animal dance, where we mimicked the movements of the divine creatures of the forest. I was a young gray wolf, howling up at the black sky, skipping and prancing. And then, without stopping, came the final dance, the victory dance. I was a brave warrior who'd come home triumphant from battle. So hard to keep up with the music now, I was panting. But I was doing it—dipping and swaying in sync with the other dancers, as Wah-Pah-Nah-Yah looked on.

Then it was over. The camp clapped for us as we slowly made our way back into the library to change into our wool shirts and shorts. I couldn't tell whether the applause was real enthusiasm or just the usual politeness. Maybe it didn't matter whether or not they had enjoyed it. I had accomplished something that I was proud of for the first time in my life. I had learned so much from Mr. West, things I wouldn't forget.

After dorm inspection the next afternoon, I sneaked out to the chapel, as I'd often done that summer. I took the long way, a path that wound through the forest for a mile or so around the edge of the camp, a route few people ever took. Shafts of late-afternoon sunlight slanted through the trees, skipping back and forth across the path with the wind. Making my way slowly, quietly, as though I were a hunter, I heard the trill of a hermit thrush, then a veery, the final note of its song echoing as though breathed through a native flute. Most of the calls were familiar to me now—I had learned about the birds here.

I slipped in through the side entrance to the chapel and sat down on the pew nearest the altar. Sunlight shimmered over the mossy stones and birch-bark cross. Even though I didn't believe in Him, it felt as if God were there.

I'd worked so hard with Mr. West but hadn't earned a ribbon. Why didn't they give ribbons for Indian lore? Who decided which activities earned ribbons? Was Indian lore less important than "industries" like tennis? It made no sense to me.

Mr. West was so different from the other counselors. He moved and spoke softly and intently, seeming not to want to waste an effort or breath. Being around him I felt different—somehow more able to just be myself. Jimmy, too, was never loud or obnoxious, the way most of the other boys were. He was unhurried, like his dad, content with who he was and accepting of me.

But whatever it was that I had learned from the two of them, whatever bound me to them, I couldn't take back home. I couldn't imagine my parents wanting to watch me do a Cheyenne dance. I'd be too embarrassed to even put on my costume, with my thin white cotton Jockeys showing on either side of my breechcloth. Jimmy and I had talked about the Cheyenne worship of nature, and how it made so much sense to me, but I couldn't possibly tell my parents that I didn't want to go to church with them on Sundays—that I'd rather be in the woods. They wouldn't understand. Besides, they'd make me go.

Jimmy said he and his dad wouldn't be coming back the next summer. It was too far from Oklahoma, the trip took too long. We talked about staying in touch, but I suspected I would never see or hear from him again.

A wood thrush began singing from a nearby treetop, filling the forest with its sweet melody. I would be back the next summer, I knew. As hard as it was trying to fit in, something made me feel as though I belonged at Mowglis, a feeling I never had at school. Maybe the next summer, I'd grow to be stronger and more confident. Like Jimmy.

BY THE END of my fourth summer at Mowglis, I had thrown myself into nearly all of the camp's extraordinary activities and experiences—nature study, weather forecasting, camping skills, drama, woodworking, and arts and crafts, to name only a few. I'd taken my first classes in photography, and had written articles about our cabin trips and a silly poem for the camp yearbook, called *The Howl*. And the magic of the chapel continued to beckon me when I needed time alone.

I'd become an accomplished swimmer and was one of the only campers to complete the "double full Wainganga," a one-mile swim out to a distant rock in the lake and back to the dock. With practice, I was a good shot with a .22 rifle, earning a progression of NRA medals at the riflery range (but not enough yet to earn a ribbon). I had passed the safety classes for rowing and canoeing, so that I was allowed to take boats out onto the lake by myself. The opportunity to try so many new things was part of what kept me coming back to the camp. Mowglis was the opposite of school, where each year felt duller, more constricted, and more pressured. Nine months of the year were gray. For eight summer weeks, my life played in Technicolor.

I'd paddled for days down fast-running rivers and across wind-blown lakes, sometimes catching fish along the way. Fresh-caught brook trout fried up with bacon over a crackling campfire became a favorite breakfast. I'd hiked all throughout the White Mountains in northern New Hampshire. Some days we simmered in the sun while trekking long hours across an exposed ridge, begging for a breeze; other days we'd freeze in a sideways squall, huddled and shivering beneath our ponchos, waiting for the storm to pass. But I'd grown to cherish being held close by the dense, whisper-still wildness of the forest, as we snaked our way up steep slopes, then finally emerged at the top onto bare rock to a sudden, stunning view of mountain upon mountain etched against a sharp blue sky.

I'd learned to clear trail, load and carry a heavy pack, pitch a tent, build a fire, and cook a meal on it. Once I sliced deep into my thigh while whittling a stick after supper. I had to bite my lip to hold back tears of pain, but I figured out how to staunch the bleeding so that no one would know. The pale-white crescent-shaped scar just above my knee remains to this day.

I'd also learned about the things I was not good at. I lacked the strength to be a skilled archer, and I was too impatient for the meticulous efforts required by woodworking.

And I never took to the constant competitions that pervaded the camp—too much like the sports requirements at

Gilman and Avon. There were softball and capture-the-flag games, tugs-of-war, horseshoes, and an ongoing competition to see which cabin was the cleanest in daily inspection. Points were deducted if a random dust ball was discovered in a corner, or a shirt or blanket lacked precision folds. Occasionally, an especially annoying counselor would show up with a white glove to check for dust.

At the end of each summer, the counselors divided the entire camp into red and blue teams, our allegiances defined by bandannas wrapped around our foreheads for the week. The entire week was crammed with cheers, parades, rallies, skits, and slogans—all at the expense of the other team—but the crew races climaxed the competition. The camp had two seven-person wooden crew boats that had been especially designed with high gunnels for lake rowing by inexperienced oarsmen. We'd practice as cabins, and then we were slotted into four forms according to our rowing ability for the races— from the lowest third, up to the second, first, and racing crews. In my fourth year, I was selected for a boat in the first form. I hated the pressure of the race, the worry of "catching a crab"—putting my oar too deep in the water, not pulling it up and out fast enough, and throwing off the whole boat's rhythm—while the rest of the camp watched.

As I recall, we lost that race. But I took up sculling the summer I turned sixty, rowing in a single. Six months of the year, I row most mornings at our little house on a lake less than an hour from Mowglis. I love the sensation of skimming along the surface of the water, like a skitterbug, always trying to improve my technique. And I prefer competing with myself and don't want or need an audience.

AFTER WE HAD BEEN introduced to various industries in our first summer, the focus of our energy turned to earning ribbons. Much like merit badges, which were developed a decade later by the Boy Scouts, ribbons were evidence of having achieved a level of proficiency in a specific activity. All campers had to earn at least two ribbons in order to "graduate" from Den, the oldest campers' cabin. They were also very public displays of achievement. Earned ribbons were sewn by the camp seamstress onto the gray beanies we wore on all our trips: green for camping, silver for boating, red-white-and-blue for riflery, yellow for tennis, brown for hiking, red for canoeing, golden arrow for archery, black for arts and crafts, and so on.

The ribbons were not easily attained. You might spend many activity periods over several summers working on just one or two. For example, to earn the green camping ribbon, you had to show proficiency in the use of various camping stoves; build and light a fire in the rain; navigate the wilderness using a map and compass; spot edible plants; identify different cloud formations that aid in weather prediction; and learn knots and first aid. You then had to plan a trip and successfully complete an overnight solo expedition with only the most basic of gear: a poncho, some rope, matches, water, and a bit of food.

From my first summer, I'd been intimidated by the idea of having to earn these ribbons. My lousy school grades hadn't helped, and I still thought of myself as uncoordinated. But unlike the tests that I was supposed to study for at school, I always thought these challenges seemed worthwhile. I was willing to try.

I'm not sure why I chose to work on the orange axemanship ribbon. It was considered one of the most difficult to achieve, and I hadn't seen a single one sewn onto any boy's cap. But there was something about the man who taught it—Colonel Alcott Farrar Elwell, the former camp director. He had retired from the directorship years before, but one could see his tall, erect frame and head full of pure white hair striding around the campgrounds most days, with frequent stops for animated conversations with a camper or counselor. He lived next door to one of the camp's ball fields in a small white house he'd named North Star. He was in his midseventies when I began going up into the woods with him during my third year at camp.

Most afternoons that summer, the Colonel and I would walk across the road from camp and hike up to the woodlot. He wore the same gray wool shirt with the blue pocket as the other senior counselors, but he was many years older than the others. His face was weathered and wrinkled from decades spent in the sun. His deep brown eyes conveyed a solemnness and patience that reminded me of Mr. West. I felt respected in the way he looked at me, though I'd done nothing yet to earn it.

First, the Colonel taught me how to carry an axe safely in the woods with my hand gripping the neck between the blade and the handle, blade facing out away from my body, handle straight out in front of me, so that it wouldn't get tangled in brush. He taught me to saw off the tip of the handle's base when I got a new axe. Cut that way, it was less likely to split.

Then he taught me how to sharpen an axe. He explained that the sharper the axe is, the less likely you are to get hurt. A dull blade can bounce back on you. Alternating sides, you file in slow passes from the back of the head of the axe to the blade, to get out the inevitable nicks and to make a nicely beveled edge. At first the thin file handle digs into your palm as you press down on the axe head, but then you learn how to hold it so that it doesn't hurt so much. Next comes the whetstone: you rub the oiled stone in a slow, circular motion from the top of the blade to the bottom. Honing my axe blade every day at the start of our session was painstaking work, but I liked seeing how sharp I could get it—sometimes so sharp that I could cut a piece of paper in half on it.

Learning how to make a tree fall where you wanted it to without it getting caught up in the canopy of another tree was especially daunting. You begin by cutting a V-shaped notch about a third of the way into the trunk on the side where you want the tree to fall. Then you cut another notch opposite the first one, but about a foot above. Cutting the second notch creates a hinge that enables the tree to fall. Once or twice, a tree didn't fall where I'd planned and got caught high up in the limbs of another tree, but the Colonel never appeared annoyed or impatient. He taught me to look at how the tree had broken from the notches to figure out what went wrong.

Then came limbing. I learned to cut off the branches on the opposite side, never the same side, of where I was standing so as to always keep the trunk between the axe blade and me.

Next there was cutting a tree into two-foot lengths. You had to cut a correctly sized notch for the diameter of the tree with a nice forty-five-degree angle. You had to stand in such a way that if you missed the log, the axe head wouldn't gash your leg, and you had to watch for stones hidden in the dirt. Cutting up tree after tree, my sweaty hands got raw and blistered, but gradually they toughened.

Finally came splitting—my favorite. The Colonel taught me that splitting wood when it's green is much easier than when it's dried out. Hit a freshly cut log just so and it would crack into perfect halves, as though struck by lightning. But you had to figure out just where to hit the log, and you needed to have good aim. Hit it the wrong way, and you might break the axe handle.

My hands and back ached from our long summer afternoons at the woodlot. Gnats flew into my eyes. I'd be soaking with salty sweat that poured down my face, making it hard to see. But I liked the *thwack-thwack* of the axe hitting the log and watching the chips fly and seeing my pile grow. And I liked the Colonel's quiet coaching, the way he smiled when I hit one just right. I will never forget the moment he measured, for the last time, the pile of wood I'd been accumulating through the summer and said, beaming, "Congratulations. You've earned your orange ribbon."

I HAD LEARNED who Mr. West was when he'd been introduced to the camp, and when he told us about his tribe. So it's understandable that I wanted to learn about a different vibrant culture when my 1950s school lessons were so vapid. But I knew almost nothing about the Colonel—other than what Mr. Kingsley had told us about his role in Mowglis's early years—and I didn't understand the chemistry between us. Once my parents sold the farm and moved us to the Baltimore suburbs, choosing axemanship made no more sense than Indian lore, yet I'd persisted with him. Why? Some sixty years later, I was curious to learn more about the Colonel. So I got in touch with Nick Robbins, the current director of Mowglis, who invited me to come over for a visit in June 2017, before camp opened for the season.

It was a bright and breezy summer day when I drove over to the camp—the kind of day that was always so thrilling to wake up to when I had been a camper. Nick greeted me warmly as I came into the dining hall, and we sat down to lunch with forty or so counselors and staff who were seated at the same picnic tables and benches where I had wolfed down so many meals. The hall, with its low wood-plank ceiling, waist-high pine siding, and screen windows all around, was unchanged. What had changed, however, was that there are now women counselors. I hoped they had something of a

taming and humanizing influence on the excess of testoster-
one that pervaded the all-male camp when I was there.

Nick looked the part of the outdoorsman that he is, with
his neatly trimmed chestnut beard and a wiry athletic build.
He said he had been involved in summer camps all his life—as
a camper, counselor, and, for the past five years, executive director of Mowglis, whose enrollment had doubled under his
leadership.

After lunch, I asked if I could have some time to walk
down to the chapel. I wondered if it really was the mystical
place that I remembered. But this time I wouldn't be there
alone, as I had on so many other occasions. Nick and Jim Hart,
the director of alumni relations and unofficial camp historian,
wanted to accompany me and know more about my camp
memories. Passing Grey Brothers Hall and the sleeping cabins, I could almost see a younger me racing down the path in
front of us, eager to leap into the lake.

As ever, the chapel arch stood silent sentry in the soft
shadows of the midday sun. The empty pews beckoned me to
sit in the stillness and listen and let go. But I couldn't linger,
not today. I knew that both Nick and Jim were pressed for
time.

Walking back up the hill, Jim asked, "Who were your buddies at camp?"

I smiled wryly. How could I explain? "I studied Native
American lore with Mr. West for a summer, and his son,
Jimmy, and I were friends the year he was here. But I remem-
ber Colonel Elwell most vividly," I answered.

"I can send you a link to the Colonel's dissertation, if you like," Jim offered.

Dissertation? I had no idea that he was anything other than the camp's former director and axemanship teacher—an old wise man with a gravelly voice and a warm smile.

In fact, Colonel Alcott Farrar Elwell was an education critic and a visionary—a kindred spirit. He was the son of Frank Edwin Elwell, a sculptor and museum curator, and Molina Mary Hildreth, born, with his twin brother, Bruce, in Cambridge, Massachusetts, in 1886. Alcott was named for his godmother, Louisa May Alcott. The family spent much of the boys' early years in Europe, but they returned to Cambridge in time for them to finish their middle and high school years in public schools there.

In 1905, two years after the camp's founding, Alcott Elwell was recruited by Mowglis's founder, Mrs. Elizabeth Ford Holt, to be an assistant counselor. He returned nearly every summer for more than fifty years. He was named assistant director of Mowglis in 1914, and became the owner and director in 1925, a year before Mrs. Holt died.

He entered Harvard in 1906, but it took him eleven years to complete his undergraduate degree because he had to take a leave of absence a number of times in order to earn enough money to continue his studies. During these years, he worked as a cook on a geological expedition in Wyoming, as a nurse, and as an automobile mechanic, and he founded a school for boys. In 1917, he entered the army as an officer, trained recruits for the duration of the First World War, and then returned to the Harvard Graduate School of Education, where he completed his master's in 1921 and his doctorate in 1925.

The title of his doctoral dissertation was "The Summer Camp—A New Factor in Education." Like Mrs. Holt, the Colonel was deeply concerned about the impact of growing industrialization and the loss of connection to rural life for children. "This is a time when cities are drawing population from the countryside and confining the individual socially, mentally, and physically to a mechanical existence. . . . The disappearance of the farm in a measure has destroyed the opportunities for personal experience as a phase of education," he wrote. Elwell saw the growing movement to establish "schools of the open" as a logical extension of the New England transcendentalist movement of the nineteenth century: "What Emerson and Thoreau did for the grown-ups of a generation or two ago, the Boy Scouts, Girl Scouts, Camp Fire Girls and Woodcraft League are doing for the children today."

He didn't advocate a "return to nature" for aesthetic or spiritual reasons, however, and he was not interested in creating summer camps as places to entertain kids when school was out of session. Instead, Elwell was deeply concerned about what twentieth-century schooling was doing to children. He argued: "There is a tendency in education to teach the greater proportion of children an outlook of limitation—even of failure, rather than success. Visit some of the public schools and watch. Twenty per cent of the children are learning to be successful, and eighty per cent are learning to be limited—what they cannot do, not what they can do."

Even more fascinating to me, he placed the blame squarely on the demands of the emerging "college prep" high school curriculum and the lecture method of teaching that it encourages. "Schools are circumscribed by the college requirements," he wrote, "even to those who are not going to college at all." Elwell believed, as do I, that a predominantly abstract academic curriculum does not prepare the majority of students for meaningful work, lifelong learning, or active and engaged citizenship. Nor does it help students to stay curious about the world or discover their deepest interests.

The American high school course of studies was essentially created in 1894 by the so-called Committee of Ten, chaired by Harvard president Charles Eliot. These ten men declared that all incoming college freshmen should have completed lessons in specific subjects for a prescribed amount of time. Their unit of measurement for education came to be called the Carnegie Unit. A Carnegie Unit is the amount of "seat time served" in a given class—roughly 120 hours of a class over the course of a school year. The system remains unchanged today, as students have to earn between eighteen and twenty-four Carnegie Units—the number varies state by state—in order to graduate from high school.

However, having the requisite number of Carnegie Units isn't enough to get kids into college. Students' grades in a class are supposed to represent how well they served their time, and students' grade point averages and class ranks are taken as measures of how well they have performed compared with their peers. These numbers still make up the typical high school transcript, which is required in order to be considered for admission by virtually every college and university in America.

In constructing this system, the Committee of Ten deified a kind of academic "scholarship" that allows only a comparatively few students to succeed. The typical bell curve grading system, which is necessary to allow for comparison between students, sorts the kids of a school into a few winners—the A students—and everybody else. Those who get a lower grade are often made to feel as though they are lacking—either lazy or less intelligent, sometimes both. Elwell was troubled by the impact of this scheme on adolescents. He believed that it was "a loss to society" that the "specialized requirements" of a college prep curriculum favored a minority of students, while creating feelings of "inferiority" among the majority.

But the Colonel wasn't merely troubled by changes in the education system. Like other social critics of the 1920s, he was deeply apprehensive about the dog-eat-dog competition and preoccupation with making money that characterized the era. He asked whether "a sense of cooperation can be brought to civilized man before the shadows grow too deep," and, he argued, "one need in life is a new point of view about individual success—from that of taking to that of giving."

Elwell declared that the antidote to increased competition and self-centeredness was play. As I learned from Jean Piaget when I first read *The Moral Judgment of the Child* in my twenties, when children play together, a spirit of "fair play" is developed, and they become less egocentric. Similarly, Elwell stated, "Human beings become more brotherly and thus become play-fellows . . . ever moving towards better cooperation. . . . The time is fast approaching when there must be education for mature play—a landmark along the path of survival, man's first breathing space."

In my own research on how best to develop young people's creative problem-solving capabilities and prepare them for the innovation era, I've explored the role of play, passion, and purpose. Pursuing a purpose—whether social, artistic, or scientific—is, I've realized, a form of disciplined adult play. One of the goals of education must be to encourage a kind of play in school—opportunities to try new things and pursue interests—so that young people can discover their passion and purpose. Without the development of these intrinsic motivations for learning, education is little more than memorization and serving seat time—useless to young people as they go out into today's world.

Around the time that Elwell was writing his dissertation, Sherwood Dodge Shankland was named the first executive secretary of the National Education Association's Department of School Superintendence, an office he would hold for twenty-five years. (The organization changed its name to the American Association of School Administrators in 1937.) In a speech given at Columbia University, Shankland declared that there were "four requirements in the Aim of Education":

1. Knowledge for present need
2. Knowledge for adjustment to change

3. Knowledge of the other fellow's point of view
4. Knowledge that wakes the soul

"Of these, at least three can be taught through the life at camp better than at school," Elwell noted.

At heart, Elwell was asking, *What is the purpose of education?* and *How best can we serve that purpose?* in light of the changes wrought by the industrial era. Much of my life's work has been an attempt to answer these same questions, but at the dawn of the innovation era, with its accelerating changes wrought by the advent of the internet and other technologies. The Colonel found a remarkable answer, one that resonates deeply with me today:

> Summer camps are helping break down the notion that education is mental discipline; that unless the thing is unpleasantly difficult and abstract, it is not education. It is not what we learn but what we utilize that makes up our ability, and camp is helping to create *usable ability* [my emphasis]. . . . Summer camp, instead of supplementing education, *is* education—just exactly as the life of the child is not preparation for life at some future time but all there is of life at the present moment.

A growing number of educators are coming to understand that children's potential can be greatly expanded with effective coaching and opportunities to develop usable ability through classroom projects where they apply what they've learned. Carol Dweck, a professor of psychology at Stanford, describes the role of a "growth mindset"—the idea that we can all improve through effort, and that our capabilities are not fixed at birth. Angela Duckworth, a professor at the University of Pennsylvania, has shown that "grit"—the combination of perseverance, tenacity, self-discipline, and curiosity—is more important for success than the outdated measure of IQ. Taken together, these two ideas are reshaping classrooms around the world. Students *can* be taught that effort matters more than mere ability, and their grit "muscles" *can* be gradually strengthened when they are given assignments they see as worth doing. As they learn to work longer and harder toward goals that they previously thought were unattainable, they feel their success, which bolsters their confidence and becomes self-reinforcing. The job of the teacher should be to develop this potential, rather than having to waste time preparing students for outdated tests and then judging each child's achievement relative to others.

Elwell recognized these truths a century ago. He explained that the purpose of his "school of the open" was to teach:

1. The expectation of success
2. The fearless outlook
3. Undiminished hope
4. The see-it-through desire

"These unfortunately are not in the academic curriculum," he added with evident sadness. "And yet, behind every page of the academic curriculum, their presence or absence determines the issue."

In his concluding paragraph, the Colonel allowed himself to wax poetic: "The School of the Open is a school for simplicity and primitive reality, in which growth is in social ideals and cooperation coupled to better understanding of one's self. The child who can see simply and look into the heart of nature will have a key to the Book of Life—this is Education."

LOOKING BACK, MY SUMMERS at Mowglis certainly taught me to "look into the heart of nature." Equally important, I now see that the camp's emphasis on earning ribbons as evidence of proficiency, along with the scouting movement's merit badge system, contributed significantly to my vision of a high school diploma for the twenty-first century. Rather than being a collection of Carnegie Units, I think a high school diploma should be a certificate of *mastery*—a collection of required and elective merit badges or ribbons that students earn by showing evidence of proficiency in essential skills and content areas.

For example, instead of having to memorize the periodic table in chemistry, or definitions of terms like domain, kingdom, phylum, class, order, family, genus, and species in biology—information that changes, or can now be looked up on a smartphone—I think students should be asked to demonstrate proficiency in the use of the scientific method. All high school students, working alone or in teams, should be required to develop a hypothesis, design and conduct an experiment to test it, and analyze and present the results. And the only grade meted out would be a credit, once the student has shown this mastery.

In working to earn my much-prized orange ribbon, I never took a timed multiple-choice test on the history of axemanship or the parts of an axe. Points weren't taken off when my tree didn't fall as planned, and my work wasn't graded on a bell curve. There was no failure, only learning from trial and error. I simply kept working until I met the prescribed performance standard for the ribbon. I had to demonstrate "usable ability" as Colonel Elwell put it. What matters most is not what you know, but rather what you can do with what you know.

The Colonel didn't presume that he could change the nature of schooling. Instead, his strategy was to advocate for publicly funded summer camps to be set up outside of urban areas for all children. He thought such programs could supplement the months of required schooling indoors and "produce savings of thousands of dollars in expenses of juvenile courts, officers, and houses of correction." And they might well have, but his camps were never established—not in a systematic way.

And just as the Colonel's vision could not transform education, neither could my Mowglis experience altogether compensate for my experiences at school. As a camper, I couldn't possibly realize that what I learned from Mr. West and the Colonel were vital life lessons. Camp wasn't school; I wasn't taking tests or getting grades, so how could I be learning anything?

And yet I was. Mr. West kindled in me a deep appreciation for another culture that translated in later life to a hunger to travel and to study anthropology. Without words, he taught me that it was okay to be different and to identify with others who were different as well. He also exposed me to a completely new way of thinking about religion.

Working with the Colonel in the woodlot, I learned to persevere and take pride in achieving a goal that I had set for myself. I experienced what it meant to develop real skillfulness and mastery for the first time. Were there things he might have said to me then to nudge me toward a life's work that is so strikingly similar to his? It's a question that intrigues me.

Collectively, the lessons I learned at Mowglis did not outweigh the sense of being a failure and an outcast—the main lessons I was taught the other nine months of the year. Eight weeks in the summer weren't nearly enough. Nevertheless, the time I spent at Mowglis gave me a sense of possibilities— in myself and in learning—that I would not otherwise have known. Not until many years, and several colleges, later did I find a place where experiential and book learning came together, where knowledge was understood to come from both the head and the heart.

THREE

A Radical Education

RANDOLPH-MACON WAS A TINY MEN'S COLLEGE PASTED onto the edge of Podunk, Virginia, about an hour north of Richmond, capital of the Confederacy. There was nothing remarkable about the town (it was actually called Ashland), and the campus was just a random collection of old brick buildings linked by paved paths. The buildings, lawns, and trees were worn and wilted in the hot, late-summer sun. Some of the dorms, like the one where I lived, were newer, but they had all the charm of a run-down, single-story motel on some dusty back road. There was no forest or field nearby to explore, just flat stretches of dried dandelion-and-crabgrass lawn dotted with a few forlorn trees. The place felt sterile and alien.

The only reason I'd gone to college was because that's what every kid I knew did when they finished high school. What kind of reason was that? But, then, what were the alternatives?

The alternatives, my father told me, were the army or pumping gas.

I thought college would be different, that we'd have stimulating studies and probing discussions. But no, it was just one lifeless lecture after another, and tests you had to memorize a bunch of crap for—much of it the same stuff I was supposed to have memorized in my high school classes (but hadn't). I couldn't settle down to study. Nothing made me curious. Nothing inspired me to want to learn.

I had imagined college as a place where there'd be a lively social scene, and that I'd meet lots of fascinating people. Wrong again. I'd blindly chosen a single-sex school in a redneck town because I didn't know enough to research schools and to apply to several. No one had told me. And just as at Avon, the kids at Randolph-Macon were mostly jocks. We were put through a series of fitness tests in our required freshman physical education class, and when I ended up near the top of the class, the coach who oversaw the tests asked if I would try out for one of the varsity teams, but I wasn't interested.

I said no thanks to frat life, too. I went to a couple of rush parties and watched packs of guys try to get drunk on "near beer"—3.2 percent alcohol, the only stuff they sold in town—while listening to the Beach Boys' *Surfin' USA*.

I had spent many hours working on my writing with Mr. Edwards at Searing, and I had this idea that I wanted to become a novelist. But I'd gotten an F on my first essay writing assignment in my freshman English composition class. I wrote about a quote from Thoreau: "Our life is frittered away by detail." I gave as examples all the facts you learn and forget in history and the superficial conversations people have around the dinner table. I couldn't believe the comment Mrs. Greenberg wrote on my paper: "Expository writing is an anathema to you. Your first paragraphs are rotten. They were as boring to read as they obviously were for the writer to write."

"Mrs. Greenberg, your English class is boring beyond belief, and it's frittering away my life," I wanted to write back. But I didn't.

Thank God for Bryan and Judi. Without them, I would have spent way too much time alone. Bryan was a tall, lanky senior with a scraggly goatee, and Judi was his wife. A guy I was rooming with from Avon had made friends with them the previous year and introduced me to Bryan and Judi soon after I got to campus. They lived across the street from my dorm in one of the few cottages for married couples. With her sweet southern drawl and easy smile, Judi was a wonderfully gracious host, and she was always inviting me over for dinner.

Bryan's passion was folk music. He played the guitar and had recently taken up the Autoharp. He introduced me to Pete Seeger and the Weavers, the Carter Sisters, Mississippi John Hurt, Dave Van Ronk, Woody Guthrie. And there was this new young guy he was crazy about: Bob Dylan.

I didn't like Dylan's voice—it sounded to me as if he were singing through his nose—but the lyrics, they were pure poetry. After dinner at Bryan and Judi's, we would sit on the floor of their living room drinking cheap wine and listening to records. When they put on "The Times They Are A-Changin'," the song had incited a heated discussion. The Reverend Martin Luther King Jr. was on the news most nights, and the Civil Rights Act, outlawing discrimination in employment and public places, had just passed. I thought that was a sign of real progress, but Bryan vehemently disagreed. He pointed out that three young civil rights workers—Michael Schwerner, James Chaney, and Andrew Goodman—had been murdered by the Mississippi Ku Klux Klan over the summer. Bryan had been raised in rural Virginia, and laws weren't going to change people's beliefs or behaviors, he'd said.

"A Hard Rain's A-Gonna Fall" soon became my favorite Dylan song. A mother asks her boy where he's been, and he describes all the lies, hypocrisy, and injustice he's encountered in his journeys. Late one evening, while listening to the song for about the twentieth time since I'd first heard it, I recalled a day with my mother, soon after we'd moved off the farm to our house on the golf course in the Baltimore suburbs. I'd gone with her to drop off some laundry.

She'd pulled the car onto a cratered lane lined with shacks—small, rickety wood buildings perched precariously on crumbling cinder blocks, with paint peeling from the clapboards and sheet metal rusting on their roofs. Partway down the street, my mother stopped the car in front of one of these cabins, waited a moment, then gave the car horn a tentative toot. A white-haired black woman with a deeply wrinkled face stepped out from a ripped screen door, wiping her hands on her apron. She came over and took the heavy wicker basket, piled high with dirty laundry, from the backseat of our station wagon. "Be ready first of next week, ma'am" was all she'd said. Mother nodded.

Across the street, I saw a couple of kids about my age kicking a ball around. They wore torn T-shirts spotted with sweat. One of the boys turned and stared at me. Hot as it was, I remember winding up the car window and looking down at my lap until we drove away.

I didn't understand why I'd looked away, or how I could have just sat there quietly, not saying a word to my mother about what had happened. As I thought about it now, as a college student with Dylan echoing in my head, my cheeks burned. I'd grown up in a lily-white world of privilege and knew nothing of how most people lived. How could people so close to our big brick house on the hill be living like that? Why hadn't I spoken up when, later that year, some kids at my middle school said blacks shouldn't be allowed to attend classes with us?

Listening to this music, and talking late into the night with Bryan and Judi, I began to awaken to the world around me. On the nightly news, I'd seen civil rights workers pulled off burning buses and beaten, and cops hosing and clubbing peaceful protesters. I'd observed these events in passing, as though through the windows of a moving train. But now, what had merely been TV footage and music lyrics was all around me. I realized that I'd come to a college where the only black faces I saw were those of the janitors. That there were no blacks in the church my parents attended or at the country club where they golfed. That real poverty was just half a mile from my house. And it all suddenly felt very confusing—and wrong.

Why was I going through the motions of attending lectures where I didn't listen to a word, then procrastinating about doing my assignments night after night? Why was I still pretending to try to learn the things that the "adults" had decided were important, but which weren't important to me? What was the point of college anyway? To prepare me for some "normal" job, like being a lawyer or a banker or a businessman? Those were things that I could never imagine myself doing.

Bryan said he was thinking of dropping out, even though he was a senior. College wasn't going to help him become a folk singer. It wasn't going to help me become a writer, either. What I needed was to learn something about the real world and write about it. It was December, so somewhere warm. Florida, maybe?

I made a plan, with all the impatience and bravado of adolescence, to do something meaningful. I would drop out, hitchhike south, find a job, and write a novel.

LIVING IN A CRAMPED STAFF DORM behind the Fort Lauderdale Beach Hotel wasn't the life I'd imagined when I fled Randolph-Macon. They deducted money from my paycheck for my housing, and all I got was a top bunk with squeaky springs and an army surplus blanket. But I was making good money as a room service waiter and could scrounge meals from the kitchen staff, so I had few expenses. And I had time to write every night. It was only journaling by flashlight, but writing regularly was honoring the promise I'd made to myself when I dropped out of college. It helped keep alive my hope that I might become a real writer someday.

After a month, I had enough saved to buy a used 80cc Yamaha motorbike. I was set free. On my days off, I rode around Fort Lauderdale, feeling the wind and warm sun on my face. I often hung out at the busy seaport, where I watched men scurry along the docks while tall cranes unloaded cargo ships from around the world. Someday I would go to sea—but on a small fishing boat, in search of tuna or sailfish or marlin, as had Hemingway's Old Man. I hungered for what I imagined to be the "writer's life" of experience and adventure.

Often I'd go walking on the beach in front of the hotel. It became my new Piney Run, my chapel in the woods. I loved following the line where the lapping waves last left the sand, feeling the damp squish beneath my bare toes. And then, when the next wave slipped in, the water swirling around my ankles and back out into the foam. After the sun had streaked the graying sky with bands of pale orange, I'd stroll slowly back to the dorm and try to capture the moment in my journal.

By the end of January, though, I'd grown exasperated with dorm life, of having to ingratiate myself with the hotel's managers and the rude and demanding guests. This wasn't what

I'd dropped out for. I was in a hurry to get somewhere—where, exactly, I didn't know.

I'd found a little coffeehouse in the low-rent district and hung out there on my nights off. I rented a room at the back and got a job flipping burgers at a Royal Castle franchise for ninety-two cents an hour in take-home pay, plus all I could eat. It annoyed the hell out of me that they took a chunk of money out of my paycheck for "uniform rental," so I figured out a way to make the miserable salary go further: I'd take the ten-hour graveyard shift that nobody else wanted, beginning at eight o'clock at night. That way I could get two of my three meals a day on them.

Or what passed for meals. The house specialty was an overcooked, paper-thin, greasy burger, dressed up in a fluffy white bun and decorated with all the mustard, ketchup, and pickles you could desire. Customers paid fifteen cents for this treat. Add the Castle coffee or birch beer, with fries on the side, and you were a king or queen for half an hour—maybe a little more if you stretched the meal out, as many did. Torn and tattered bits of white, brown, and black humanity shuffled through the doors all night long—people whom I would never otherwise have met: drunks, prostitutes, and folks who had to scrape out their pockets to find enough change to pay the paltry bill.

Each dawn at the end of my shift, I would slowly weave my way back to my room on my motorbike, shower off the skillet's spittle, and collapse on my unmade bed. I had no energy left for writing. I'd wake up at three in the afternoon, grab some coffee and a donut at the bodega across the street, and meander back to the Castle, wishing I were going somewhere, anywhere, else. Six days a week. This was no writer's life. It was barely a life at all.

I scoured the want ads for another job until one caught my eye. A guy was looking for somebody to work on his sixty-five-foot sailboat. Excited, I called up. He told me the boat was in dry dock, and its steel hull needed sanding and painting. He'd pay a dollar fifty an hour to start. "Would I be considered for crew once the boat was ready?" I asked. I still had my dream of going to sea, chasing and catching experiences worth writing about. "Sure, sure. Absolutely," he said. I gave my week's notice the same day.

When I pulled up to the address he'd given me, I found a rusted hulk of a boat, propped up with timbers in a tumbledown, corrugated tin shed. There was no cabin, no decking; just the metal hull and keel.

"Is *this* the boat?" I asked, thinking that maybe I'd made some mistake.

"Yup."

He led me up the ladder on the side. Peering down from the top, I saw that the boat had been gutted, and the length of the interior was crisscrossed with scaffolding and dimly lit with a few bare lightbulbs hung from wire. He explained that my job was to sand off the thick crust of rust on the walls of the hull. He showed me where the supplies were stored and then sped off in his Mercedes convertible, promising to check in on me from time to time.

For the first few weeks, I actually did quite a bit of work. But the more I sanded, the more rust there seemed to be to sand. Lying on my back on the scaffolding, I'd often fall into a catnap, half listening for the crunch of the convertible's tires rolling into the gravel lot. One day in April, the owner caught me sleeping. I told him the fumes had got to me. He believed the excuse the first time, but not the second, and I found myself unemployed.

It was just as well. I'd had my fill of a state without seasons, of working for minimum wage. I'd told myself I'd dropped out of college to get a "real world" education, and I did, sort of. I'd seen for myself how many people were struggling to scratch out a life. I'd come to understand what it was like to mark time in a dead-end job and barely get by—even though it was only for a few months, and help was never farther away than a phone call home. Working at the Castle had deepened my sense of outrage at the disparities I now saw all around me—inequities that seemed to be determined mostly by the color of a person's skin. I wanted to learn more about the roots of injustice in America. I wasn't going to learn it by staying here.

But most of all, I'd realized that I wasn't going to become a writer in the ways I'd fantasized—by zigzagging my way around the city on my motorbike, wandering along the beach, flipping burgers, and journaling in what little spare time I had. If I wanted to be a writer, then I needed to go back to school. I needed a good teacher, like Mr. Edwards, and I longed to discuss novels and ideas with like-minded people. I missed my late-night conversations with Bryan and Judi; they'd helped me make sense of what I was starting to see. I now understood that I couldn't go it alone.

It was spring up north—my favorite time of the year. I decided to try school again. But it couldn't be Randolph-Macon. I'd find a college that was co-ed, where I could live off campus and be free, as I had been in Florida. This time, I'd *choose* to go to college instead of merely going because it was something I was supposed to be doing.

I ENDED UP ENROLLING at Richmond Professional Institute, today known as Virginia Commonwealth University, for the fall semester of 1965. I chose it because it was urban—I'd had it with isolated schools in the middle of nowhere—and near my friends Bryan and Judi. The sprawling downtown Richmond campus had a gritty feel; it consisted mostly of older mongrel buildings that had been retrofitted to serve as classrooms. Many of the students had jobs and were seeking professional certifications. But RPI was also well known for its art school, and so it attracted a more hip and diverse student body than I'd met at Randolph-Macon. Or anywhere else, for that matter.

With the remnants of my savings from Florida, I rented a tiny, one-room studio apartment a few blocks from the center of campus and bought another used motorcycle, a more powerful 250cc Yamaha. I decorated my walls with posters of my favorite folk singers and filled my bookcase with volumes of poetry and novels.

I'd started reading some of the Beats—Allen Ginsberg, Lawrence Ferlinghetti, Gary Snyder. I especially liked the work of Kenneth Patchen. His *Journal of Albion Moonlight* was written in stream of consciousness interspersed with poems and drawings, and described a young man's disillusionment at the dawn of the Second World War. I loved what he said about why he had to write: "If ecstasy, to celebrate the moment; if agony, to staunch the bleeding."

Back then I related to the world first through feeling and intuition—and I still do, to a great extent. Events and experiences that I was seeing and hearing were "teaching" me in ways that tedious classes and lectures hadn't, but I needed to write about these experiences in order to try to figure them out. Through the act of writing, feelings and thoughts are melded in ways that make meaning, and I felt at the time that writing about my childhood would help me grapple with questions that nagged at me. So, soon after moving into my apartment, I set to work on a coming-of-age novel. I wrote most mornings and had a stack of eighty typed pages done by the time classes officially started in September. Even with classes, I would keep at it, I told myself. And this time I would study every day and not procrastinate.

But once the semester started, I quickly became demoralized. The required freshman courses, the texts, the lectures—

everything was the same. The only noticeable differences were the larger lecture halls and the women in them.

Most of my fellow students sat silently taking notes during the dreary lectures. Listening to the same old stuff, I grew impatient. After a few weeks, I couldn't stand it any longer. I raised my hand in the middle of my ancient history class, interrupting the professor's droning monologue. Seemingly caught off guard, he actually called on me. "I don't understand why we only study the kings and their wars. Why don't we learn about how ordinary people lived then?" I took the risk of confronting him because he was young, and I thought he might actually listen.

"Come see me after class," he replied curtly. Then he picked up his lecture right where he'd left off.

I had received a 91 on the first test of the semester, so I figured he knew I wasn't just trying to slack off. But I wasn't prepared for what he would tell me in our meeting.

"You don't understand" was how he'd started. It was something about being untenured, about having to strictly follow the course syllabus he'd been given to teach. Yeah, he was right, I didn't understand. And it wasn't the only thing about this "institution of higher education" that I didn't get.

During the first week of school, a couple of guys had been handing out flyers from the sidewalk near the school's administrative building. Curious, I took one. It was titled "Could Jesus Get into RPI?" Apparently, the previous May a student had been expelled for refusing to cut his long hair. Then in

September, three seniors—honors students—were denied re-admission because they had grown collar-length hair, side-burns, and goatees over the summer. These guys and some other students had formed a group called Students for Individual Rights, or SIR. They were taking the students' case to the courts and needed to drum up support.

I went to one of their first meetings that fall and volunteered to help. Over several afternoons, I stood on a busy street corner in the center of campus and tried to hand out a pamphlet on academic freedom. Very few kids took it. Or if they did, they'd take one look, ball it up, and toss it in the street. One student even asked me if I was a commie. I stared at him, incredulous. My hair wasn't long, I didn't have a beard. The pamphlet even quoted Francis Keppel, the former U.S. commissioner of education, for Christ's sake.

At the next SIR meeting in October, a young woman—her name was Gail—stood up and introduced herself. She was from a new group called the Virginia Students Civil Rights Committee (VSCRC). In the summer, they had sponsored a "Freedom Summer" in southern Virginia, modeled after the one in Mississippi the previous year. The goal was to desegregate public facilities like lunch counters and register more black people to vote. Blacks were 50 percent of the state's population, but only 18 percent were registered. Civil rights workers had tried to get that number up by offering transportation to county registrar offices. But then the registrars started to keep random, unannounced working hours. I had no idea that voter registration was such an issue. But it was what she said next that shook me.

As Virginia civil rights groups became more active during the summer of 1965, the Ku Klux Klan reacted aggressively. Klansmen from North Carolina recruited their Grand Klokard, a man called Marshall Kornegay, to serve as Virginia's Grand Dragon and ignite a white resistance in the state. He'd organized a big Labor Day rally just outside the town of Victoria; thousands of people had attended. Kornegay had incited the crowd by screaming that Martin Luther King was a communist, and that President Johnson and the Supreme Court were imposing racial mixing on America just like Soviet dictators. The Klan ended their rally by burning a sixty-five-foot cross. Gail said it had lit the night sky for hours.

She held up one of the brochures the Klan had given out in Victoria and read: "Make Virginia a hell on wheels to the New York, communistic, racial agitators who seek to use our peaceful Negroes in their filthy 'Black Revolution.'" She was looking for volunteers to help launch a boycott of white-owned businesses in Victoria that refused to put a sign in their windows saying they denounced the Klan and its message.

Excited by the idea of really doing something, I signed up. But after the meeting, as I walked along a dimly lit street back to my apartment, I was shivering. It wasn't the cold, I realized. I felt frightened in a way I'd never been before. Gail had said, "You understand, there may be violence. Rock throwing . . . or worse."

The following morning, after my last class let out, I fired up the Yamaha and headed to Victoria along a country road that wound through dusty fields of late-harvest tobacco. I couldn't imagine what it was like to pull and pick and haul those heavy, broad leaves with a blazing summer sun beating down, day after day. Worse than any work I'd ever had to do.

It was midafternoon when I found myself stuck behind three or four slow-moving cars with a straight stretch of road ahead. I was eager to get to Victoria, and so I downshifted and jammed open the throttle all the way—thrilling at the surge of power beneath me as the bike leaped forward. I passed the first car, then the second. Suddenly there was a dark pickup truck turning left at the head of the line of cars, directly in front of me. I slammed on the brakes—too late, I knew. I remember skidding and then the sound of crunching metal.

Next thing, I was coming to, my helmet off, sitting under a tree. My whole body hurt, and I had an excruciating headache, but there was no blood. A cop was standing over me, ticket book in hand.

"You okay?" he asked. I nodded.

He gestured over to a stooped black man in coveralls standing off to one side of the road. "No turn signal on that pickup. You want to press charges against this nigger?"

I shook my head, and the cop left. What the hell was I getting myself into down here?

I surveyed the damage on my bike. Aside from a few scrapes along the side, the only problem was the bent front fender. I wrestled it back as best I could and rode on.

Eventually I arrived at the address on the edge of Victoria where I was supposed to stay the night before starting to work on the boycott the next morning. When I stepped onto the porch, an elderly black man opened the front door, nervously scanned the street, then urged me inside.

The man introduced himself as Samuel and showed me into the small living room. He said things were getting tense in town, and they were grateful that I had come. White men had started cruising up and down Main Street, sometimes with the barrels of rifles and shotguns sticking out from their car windows.

He invited me to sit down while he helped his wife put on dinner. It seemed every inch of the room was taken up by the sparse furnishings: a tan couch covered in transparent plastic took up one wall, and a dark wood coffee table squatted in the middle of the floor; a La-Z-Boy chair was planted in one corner, and a small glass display case was wedged into the other. Hanging above the display case was a series of framed photos of a boy, each at a different age, all the same face.

The stiff plastic crackled as I took my seat on the couch. I'd never been in a black person's house before. I felt like a foreigner in their world. They both seemed nervous, too. I wondered if they'd ever had a white person sleep in their home.

After a simple supper of beef stew that was mostly gravy, I was taken to my bedroom. It was their son's, Samuel told me. He was in the army, fighting in Vietnam.

Early the next morning, Gail came by to pick me up in her

battered VW bug. I felt queasy. Was it the breakfast grits, the exhaust fumes drifting up through the rusted-out floorboards, or the looming danger? Neither of us spoke on the ride to town.

For the next two days, I stood on a street corner in the town's three-block-long dilapidated "shopping district," handing out a flyer that declared: "Negroes unite: don't spend a nickel to support cross burners and race haters!" And just as Samuel had warned, cars and pickups full of white crackers cruised by from time to time, sometimes yelling threats like "Go back to where you came from, you commie bastard!" My morning nausea gave way to a taut knot in my stomach.

At the end of the first day, our group of five volunteers—Gail, a black guy, two other white guys, and me—met at "Freedom House," a small shack the Virginia Students Civil Rights Committee had rented on the outskirts of Victoria. One of the men kept lookout at a window covered in burlap while Gail reported on the success of the boycott. Businesses were losing $400 to $500 every weekend that volunteers came to town. This was a lot of money in this part of the state. About one quarter of the black people in Victoria earned less than a thousand dollars a year, she said, and they worked mostly in menial, tobacco-related jobs. The school dropout rate for black students was around 70 percent—double what it was for white kids.

Gail and the others appeared to be in their midtwenties yet were already veterans of the civil rights movement. I'd expected they'd talk about the movement, but after our short economics lesson, they turned to the topic of Vietnam. The two white guys were members of a group called Students for a Democratic Society (SDS), which had sponsored the first protest against the war in D.C. that spring. They'd dropped out of college and were worried about being drafted. One gave me a copy of the organization's founding document, the Port Huron Statement. "It's much more than just a civil rights struggle," he'd said. "Read this and you'll understand what I mean."

The two days passed without violence. Back at my apartment late on Sunday, I flopped onto the bed, more exhausted than I'd ever felt in my life. As the fear and adrenaline slowly drained from my still-sore body, I began to realize that I could have been killed there. They could have just fucking shot me, and the cops probably wouldn't have done a thing.

BEFORE HEADING OUT TO CLASS the next morning, I took a look at the booklet the SDS guy had given me. The first page began: "We are people of this generation, bred in at least modest comfort, housed now in universities, looking uncomfortably to the world we inherit." They sure got that right, I thought. I skipped my first class so that I could read the whole thing.

Like a manifesto, the Port Huron Statement portrayed "events too troubling to dismiss"—experiences I'd lived:

First, the permeating and victimizing fact of human degradation, symbolized by the Southern struggle against racial bigotry, compelled most of us from silence to activism. Second, the enclosing fact of the Cold War, symbolized by the presence of the Bomb, brought awareness that we ourselves, and our friends, and millions of abstract "others" we knew more directly because of our common peril, might die at any time.

I was transported to that moment outside the dining hall at Avon, gazing at the stars at the start of the Cuban missile crisis, afraid that we were all going to die. Then I was shuffling through the dark hallway of my middle school, staring at the large yellow-and-black triangular FALLOUT SHELTER signs on the wall. I was following a teacher's instruction to "duck and cover" under my flimsy desk during one of our regular drills. I was reeling at the impact of a giant mushroom ball of fire billowing up into the atmosphere in slow motion during a TV documentary. My generation had lived with this fear all our lives. And we thought it was normal.

We had also been brought up to believe that segregation was normal, too—if not by law, then by custom, something that was not to be questioned. Segregation wasn't normal, I now knew, and there was no such thing as "separate but equal." The behavior of the Klan and the cops in Victoria wasn't normal, either. Adults had jury-rigged this crazy, screwed-up world, and then they called it "normal." The more I read, the more outraged I became.

A lot of young people read the Port Huron Statement and felt the same way. On its fiftieth anniversary, the historian Michael Kazin wrote a tribute to the document in *Dissent* magazine. He called it "the most ambitious, the most specific, and the most eloquent manifesto in the history of the American Left." It was all of those things, but it was also much more than that to me. The Port Huron Statement helped me, for the first time in my life, begin to make sense of a senseless world. After years of failure at school, I'd come to believe that the Mole had been right: that there was something fundamentally wrong with me and that I was, and always would be, a "fuckup." Now I realized that maybe it was the world my generation had inherited that was fucked up, not me.

The statement gave me hope, too. "Men have unrealized potential for self-cultivation, self-direction, self-understanding, and creativity," the authors wrote. "The goal of man and society should be human independence: a concern not with image of popularity but with finding a meaning in life that is personally authentic." I started to believe that I could construct a fulfilling future that was fundamentally different from my parents' conformist, country club life.

I filled out the SDS membership card at the back of the pamphlet and mailed it in with my check on my way to classes later that morning. I knew I had to do more, though. There was a big demonstration against the Vietnam War coming up in a few weeks, cosponsored by SDS. But if I was going to march, I decided that I needed to know why.

I found a short history of the origins of the war by an

independent journalist, Robert Scheer. It recounted how, after a hundred years as colonists, the Vietnamese had succeeded in driving the French out in 1954. To end the war with the French, the Vietnamese had been forced to accept a temporarily partitioned country, with one government in the north, led by Ho Chi Minh, and one in the south, led by Ngo Dinh Diem. Elections were supposed to be held in 1956 to determine who would lead the reunified country. Everyone was certain that if the reunification elections had been held, Chairman Minh would have won in a landslide. The U.S. government had colluded with Diem to prevent the elections from happening.

President Johnson described the conflict as a struggle "to contain Communist aggression." But Scheer's account, and several others that I picked up as I tried to educate myself about Vietnam, argued that it was a civil war. Ho Chi Minh might have been a communist, but the newspapers and evening newscasts conveniently left out the fact that he had lived in the United States for a while and was fond of quoting the Declaration of Independence. He was a nationalist before he was a communist.

As I studied Vietnam, I couldn't stop thinking about all the "dead history" I had been told to learn for no other reason than it was on a test. The Peloponnesian War, the Saxon War, the Crusades, the Hundred Years' War, the Wars of the Roses, the Franco-Spanish War, the Anglo-Spanish War, the Nine Years' War, and on and on and on. Toppled kings, puffed-up generals, and "important" battles and dates all jumbled together, none of it making any sense whatsoever.

But what I was learning about Indochina was helping me to understand forces shaping history and affecting the lives of real people. It was a living history that gave meaning to actions and events happening in the world, right now. And it was the first time in my life that I'd decided to really study something on my own. I now knew why others were demonstrating, and I knew that I had to as well.

Gail was driving up to D.C. a couple of days before the march to attend a conference at the Institute for Policy Studies, a New Left think tank that had recently been set up by a couple of ex–Kennedy administration guys and had quickly become a hub of activism. I got a lift from her and went to the conference, too. The people at the conference were debating the need to combine the antiwar and civil rights movements into one larger resistance. It felt incredibly heady just to be there, as if I were in a war room helping to develop a plan to fight an enemy.

And the march itself was thrilling. Tens of thousands of college-age kids as well as older people assembled together, holding protest placards high and parading around the White House, chanting, "Negotiate Now!" and "End the Bombing!" Later, at the Washington Monument, Carl Oglesby, the new SDS president, made a plea to the older generation: "Help us build. Help us shape the future in the name of plain human hope."

We were more than 30,000 strong, the *Washington Post* reported the next day. It was more than twice the number of people who had marched in the first antiwar protest, held in the spring. But the paper also included a depressing report on General Westmoreland's request to President Johnson to increase the number of U.S. ground troops in Vietnam—from 150,000 to 400,000. Had we protested for nothing?

When I got back to campus, there was a letter waiting for me from the Office of the Dean of Students. The dean wanted to see me, right away.

I GAVE MY NAME and the dean's secretary frowned. She motioned me to sit on a bench against the wall and picked up the handset of her phone.

"Wagner's here" was all she'd said.

I had missed a few classes, but I was still doing okay, so it couldn't be about academics. The machine-gun clickety-clack of the secretary's typewriter and the metrical ticktock of a clock, somewhere out of sight, made my minutes of waiting feel like hours.

The secretary's intercom finally buzzed. She looked up from her typewriter and said in a steely voice, "You can go in now."

I walked into a large, oak-paneled office. The room was dominated by a life-sized portrait of what seemed to be a Confederate general mounted on a gray horse that hung on one wall. Robert E. Lee, I assumed. Opposite it hung another massive painting, this one maybe of a Civil War battlefield, with lines of soldiers facing each other, little sparks of fire erupting from their guns.

Flanked by the paintings, the dean's massive mahogany desk was planted in front of a wall of windows with the drapes pulled back, so I had to squint to see him in the bright sunlight. It felt as if I were a prisoner about to be interrogated under a blinding lamp.

He had a folder in front of him. "Sit down, son," he said with barely a glance at me as he pointed his pen to a straight-backed chair beside his desk.

I tried not to stare at him as he studied the papers in the folder, but I couldn't help noticing how his ample belly struggled against the confines of his pin-striped blue three-piece suit. I wondered how those vest buttons could still do their job under such a strain.

The dean finally looked up. Setting his large black-framed glasses on the desk, he leaned far back in his chair, clasped his hands together around his girth, and slowly twiddled his thumbs while he rocked back and forth. His face puckered into a scowl as he stared at me, long and hard.

Then he spoke: "Son, we know all about your communistic, homosexual drug activities." His frown grew deeper as he continued to rock and stare.

What the fuck? It wasn't true. Yes, I'd tried pot a couple of times. Most of the kids in the movement had. But that was it. And I was practically living with a girl, an art student at the college, and I definitely wasn't a communist. I believed in democracy. I couldn't wait to vote.

"S-si-sir, I'm not a communist," I stammered. But then I realized that not saying anything about the other two accusations sounded like an admission of guilt.

The dean waved his hand dismissively. "Get out of my office," he barked.

I stumbled back to my apartment, shaking with fear and anger. How did he know about the pot? Or was he just guessing? Did he have spies on the campus? But then they would have known about my girlfriend, too. The dean and the school disgusted me. I couldn't stay here. I couldn't stand to spend another minute in the heart of "Dixie"—the land of the Klan and racist cops and adults who couldn't be trusted.

At the conference before the march, I'd met a tall sandy-haired man in his late thirties by the name of Bill Higgs. He'd told me he was a lawyer heading up a civil rights lobbying initiative in D.C. and was seeking full-time volunteers to work for him, and that I should give him a call if I was ever interested. So I called and asked if he was still looking for help. He was, and he could offer seventy-five dollars a month, plus free room and board at his house on Capitol Hill. The prospect of going to work with Higgs meant that I could be a part of something larger, doing something useful for a change.

GOING HOME FOR CHRISTMAS after dropping out of RPI had been a mistake. My dad and I had argued for four days. First, it was the war. He didn't want to hear anything from me about its history. He said my opposition was just

cowardice—that I should enlist because I wasn't going to college anymore. Then he blew up because I refused to dress in
a jacket and tie for dinner, and we all ate in silence. Later,
when I made the mistake of telling him that I was thinking
about a career in social work, he'd sneered, "Jesus, that's
worse than being a male nurse." My younger brother and sister stayed out of the way, glad that I, and not them, was the
target of my father's tirades, while my mother wrung her
hands and looked on helplessly, cowed by his rants. I couldn't
tell whether or not she agreed with him.

Heading to D.C. on my motorcycle a few days later, I was
relieved to be out of the oppressive atmosphere of my parents' house. But I felt deeply saddened, too. I couldn't stop
seeing the grim, distressed looks on their faces when I'd announced my decision to drop out of college yet again. My
parents had given up on the idea that I'd make something of
myself, I was sure. They'd probably decided, like the Mole,
that I really was just a fucked-up kid. From my first days of
school, they'd received one bad report card after another.
Then they were told that I wasn't allowed to return to Gilman. And now, for the past two years, they'd seen me flit
from one thing to another, over and over—running away from
Avon, dropping out of Randolph-Macon, popping off to Florida, suddenly back home, then into and out of RPI just as
quickly. My life was chaos. How could I explain these choices
and changes to them when I didn't fully understand them
myself?

The coming year—1966—would be different. I was going

to stop reacting and start acting. I wanted to accomplish *something*. I wanted to move forward with a sense of purpose, even if my purpose wasn't going to make my parents proud.

When I got to D.C., Bill Higgs welcomed me into his small run-down row house. It looked like he had furnished it entirely with Salvation Army castoffs. "It's not much, but it's only five blocks from the Hill," he'd apologized. I was to sleep downstairs in what used to be the study.

Over dinner, Bill told me how he'd come to be in Washington. He'd grown up in Greenville, Mississippi, graduated from the University of Mississippi, and then earned his law degree from Harvard in 1958. He'd returned to Jackson, Mississippi, to set up a law practice, where he became notorious for taking on civil rights cases that no other white lawyer in the state would touch. His most famous client was James Meredith, whom he'd helped become the first black student to be admitted to Ole Miss in 1962.

When he began housing out-of-state civil rights workers in his home, he'd started getting death threats. Then, early in 1963, he was put on trial for some kind of trumped-up morals charge. While he was out of state to accept an award, an all-white jury found him guilty in absentia, and he was sentenced to six months in jail. Bill could never go back to Mississippi, so he'd come to D.C., where he'd help draft key provisions of the landmark Civil Rights Act of 1964.

The next day, Bill put me to work. O. Roy Chalk, a fat-cat capitalist who owned the D.C. transit system, had announced a fare increase from twenty to twenty-five cents. People in the capital who worked menial jobs in restaurants and office buildings—most of whom were black—relied on the buses to commute to work, and an extra five cents in fare each way was going to hurt. Marion Barry Jr., then head of the D.C. chapter of the Student Nonviolent Coordinating Committee (SNCC), had called for a one-day bus boycott for January 24, just a week away. My assignment for the week was to ride my motorcycle up and down the major bus route along Benning Road, stopping in different neighborhoods to hand out flyers detailing the plans for the boycott.

The day was meticulously organized. People who usually rode the bus would be offered free car pools and alternate bus service to and from their jobs. There were four major assembly points, forty-five neighborhood substations based in shop fronts and churches, and hundreds of volunteer drivers. More than twenty churches donated "Freedom Buses" for the action.

The morning of the twenty-fourth dawned sharp and cold. I returned to Benning Road and gave people waiting at bus stops directions to the closest place to find a free ride. I whooped as I saw one empty "Chalk bus" after another go by.

That night, the *Evening Star* reported that the boycott had been more than 90 percent effective on Benning Road. The next night, the paper estimated that 130,000 bus riders had participated in the boycott. In response, the transit system rescinded the fare increase.

My next job for Bill was my own idea. Just after the U.S. bombing of North Vietnam had resumed and intensified, Senator J. William Fulbright of Arkansas, chairman of the powerful Foreign Relations Committee, had begun to hold hearings on the history and conduct of the war. Some of the hearings were televised. I watched as Secretary of State Dean Rusk told the committee that the prospect for peace would disappear if America didn't stand up to the communists, and Fulbright countered that the conflict did not involve the vital interests of America and could easily be a "trigger for world war."

It was astounding to hear one of the most respected senators—and one from the South, to boot—question the war on national TV. It lent legitimacy to the protests against the war. We weren't just a motley collection of radicals making trouble outside the mainstream. A widely respected senator agreed with us.

"What if we got some buttons printed up that said FUL-BRIGHT FOR PRESIDENT?" I wondered aloud as Bill and I sat glued to the tiny black-and-white TV in his living room one drab February day.

"That's brilliant, Tony!" he replied with a big grin.

One week later, I began to walk around Capitol Hill, going in and out of Senate and House office buildings, proudly sporting the enormous blue-and-white FULBRIGHT FOR PRESI-DENT button pinned to my shirt pocket. And I had handfuls of buttons to give away—I'd gotten hundreds of them made up. You could tell how they felt about the war as soon as they spied my button. People would stop and stare. Their faces would become animated with either a glower or a smile. I asked everyone I saw if he or she would like a button; most said no. But I made sure to leave a few prominently displayed on the reception desk of every office I visited.

Not long after I'd handed out the last of my buttons, I received a letter from my local draft board—official notification that because I was no longer a full-time student, I had been reclassified to 1-A, "Available for Military Service." I thought I'd eventually get this notice, but I'd figured it wouldn't come for many months, or maybe that they'd lost track of me.

I'd heard some kids talk about going to Canada, but that seemed like a cop-out. Trying to get a medical deferment for some nonexistent ailment felt futile. My family doctor wasn't going to make up something. And I was sure the army doctors would see through any efforts to act crazy, the way some guys were doing.

But I knew the Selective Service System allowed members of traditionally pacifist churches, such as the Church of the Brethren, the Mennonites, and the Quakers, to file for conscientious objector status and do two years of civilian service in lieu of military duty. I had grown up as an Episcopalian— hardly an antiwar church—and I no longer believed in God. But through my years of roaming the forests, fields, and streams on the farm, of meditating at Mowglis's chapel in the woods, I had come to feel a deep reverence for nature—for all life—and couldn't imagine killing someone.

Would I defend myself if I was attacked? Would I have fought in World War II, as my father had? Was I the coward he accused me of being? Deep down, was I simply terrified of coming home in a body bag? These questions haunted me. I wasn't sure I had any honest answers for myself, let alone for my draft board. Defend myself? Yes. But kill another human being in the process? No. And who knows what I would have done if I'd been called up in 1941. My childhood fantasies of flying a Spitfire in air-to-air combat as my dad had done were nothing like the reality of piloting helicopter gunships to strafe peasants in the rice paddies of Vietnam.

Despite my self-doubting, I began to wonder if I might qualify for conscientious objector status. Bill suggested I research recent court cases to see if there had been any relevant rulings, and I began plowing through his piles of law journals. Then I found it: *United States v. Seeger.*

In 1965, the Supreme Court had ruled that conscientious objector status could not be reserved only for people who believed in a supreme being. Individuals whose views on war derived from a "sincere and meaningful belief which occupies in the life of its possessor a place parallel to that filled by the God of those admittedly qualified for the exemption" might also qualify. I thought it was a long shot, but I set to work composing a letter to my draft board describing my spiritual beliefs and citing the court case.

I didn't have to wait long for a reply. The standard form came back about a week later, saying that my request for "CO" status had been denied. There was a box that I could check to appeal the decision and request an in-person hearing, and I sent the form right back. I didn't have much hope, though, and spent my nights awake in bed, tormented by the idea of being shipped off to Vietnam.

As the date for my appearance before the draft board drew closer, I worried about how to convince them that my beliefs were "sincere and meaningful." Whom could I ask to write a letter of support? I thought about the people who might jump at the chance to make sure that I *did* go to Vietnam: the Mole, the dean—even my dad, who probably thought that war would finally make a man of me. He was always demanding that I should "straighten up and fly right." Presumably because that's what he'd learned to do in his war. Who else was there? Bill could argue the legal case, but I didn't think that a civil rights lawyer from D.C. would impress my draft board in Reisterstown, a rural corner of sprawling suburban Baltimore County. My board would almost certainly be made up of farmers and small-shop owners.

Then I had an idea. All through high school, when I was home on vacations, I had continued to attend the small Episcopal church near our home. It was a beautiful old brick structure, dating back to 1740. I loved the throaty hum of the organ and the deep hues of the stained-glass windows, and I was intrigued by the Sunday school discussions after services. The hymns, prayers, and sermons didn't speak to me, but the rector, the Reverend Henry Rightor, was a lovely man. He had a soft Arkansas accent, a gentle smile, and bright blue eyes—as well as a beautiful daughter, whom I had taken to the movies a few times. When I came to the house to pick her up, he was always gracious, inviting me in and asking how school was going.

I decided to go up to Baltimore a few days before my draft board appearance and talk with him. I felt he was my only hope.

Knocking on the front door of the rectory, I began to worry that my visit would be a waste of time. What if Reverend Rightor didn't think I was sincere and refused to help? But he greeted me with a smile, placing a friendly hand on my shoulder as he guided me to his study and asked about my work in Washington. Then we sat down on his couch, and he listened intently, nodding occasionally, as I explained the nature of my spiritual beliefs. The fact that I never mentioned God didn't seem to bother him at all. At the end of our conversation, he said that he would be glad to write a letter to the draft board on my behalf.

Three days later, with a fresh haircut, suit, and tie, I stood in front of the three men seated at the table in the one-room office of the Selective Service in Reisterstown. They each seemed to be studying two pieces of paper—one I recognized as a copy of my original letter; the other, I hoped, was a testimonial from Reverend Rightor.

Eventually, an elderly man seated in the middle looked up, as if noticing me for the first time, and said sharply, "So why can't you serve in Vietnam as a medic?" I knew that one option they had was to classify me "1-A-0," which meant that I would be assigned to Vietnam in a noncombatant capacity, and I was ready for the question.

"Sir, medics and other noncombatants must go through the same basic training as other soldiers, where they learn how to fight and kill. I respect people who do that, but my beliefs prevent me from being one of them." I was shaking as I spoke.

The man looked to his colleagues on either side and asked if they had any questions. Both shook their heads. "We'll let you know our decision in a few weeks," he muttered, dismissing me with a wave of a hand as he turned his attention back to the papers in front of him.

WHILE I WAITED for the draft board's decision, Bill had an important new project to keep me occupied. He had teamed up with Julius Hobson, a black activist. When Hobson wasn't stuck working at his day job as a statistician for the Social Security Administration, he headed up an organization called Associated Community Teams (ACT). Hobson had been organizing demonstrations for nearly twenty years—demanding better-paying jobs, fair housing, and more black sergeants in the D.C. police force.

In 1964, wearing his trademark fedora and smoking his ever-present pipe, Hobson had driven all over fashionable Georgetown with cages full of large rats, which he said he'd trapped in the ghetto. He'd threatened to set them loose if authorities did not deal with the infestations plaguing poor neighborhoods. Lately he had taken to telling the press, "You may not like my protests, but if you ignore me, and Stokely Carmichael and Malcolm X come to town"—referring to the leaders of the emerging Black Power Movement—"you'll wish you had listened to me, instead."

Now Hobson was suing the D.C. public schools for discriminating against black students. He'd asked Bill if he would prepare the lawsuit, and Bill had tasked me with researching the school district's policies.

Ever since *Brown v. Board of Education* in 1954, public school districts around the country had been mandated to integrate. I discovered that the D.C. school system, like many others, had found a way to work around this requirement by crafting an ingenious new system for segregating students. Depending upon their test scores and previous achievement levels, students were placed in one of four rigid academic tracks: honors, college, general, and basic. This tracking system had been implemented in D.C.'s high schools in 1956 and then expanded to include junior high schools and elementary schools in 1959.

In practice, nearly all the white kids were placed in the top two tracks, while the overwhelming majority of black kids were placed in the bottom two. In the D.C. school system—and today in school districts where tracking still exists—kids from economically disadvantaged backgrounds often get placed in the bottom tracks because they lack vocabulary and basic reading skills. They fall behind on these measures because the adults in these families are struggling to work multiple jobs and don't have the luxury of reading to their children at bedtime, or of taking them to museums on the weekend. And they cannot afford to hire a tutor (as my parents had done for me) to help their kids catch up. Poor reading skills inevitably translate into lower test scores and grades. And kids who get stuck in the lower tracks drop out far more frequently, have little to no chance of going to college, and typically get nothing more than a minimum-wage job when they leave school.

Back then, I knew nothing of the pernicious effects of tracking or the impact of poverty on learning. Nor did I realize how destructive tracking is, even in predominantly white suburban schools. It would be years before I was to see the emotional damage that tracking does to kids' self-esteem and motivation to learn. It took even longer for me to begin to understand how much harder it is for educators to teach students in an untracked, heterogeneously grouped classroom. The research I did for Hobson's court case gave me my first glimpse of some of the most pressing challenges educators face in public schools today.

For Hobson, though, the problem of tracking was not just an academic matter. It was deeply personal. He had attended the Tuskegee Institute and Columbia University before his career as a government bureaucrat and activist. And he *did* read to his children and take them to museums. Yet his daughter, an intellectually curious and capable girl, had been dumped into the lowest track at her junior high school. That's when he'd decided to sue.

We unearthed compelling evidence that the tracking system was a de facto racial segregation system, but because Bill had been disbarred in Mississippi, he wasn't allowed to

practice law anywhere. So he called up an old friend—a lawyer from New York City by the name of William Kunstler.
Kunstler was a nationally known civil rights and civil liberties
lawyer who served on the board of the American Civil Liberties Union. The two of them had met when Kunstler helped
defend the Freedom Riders in Mississippi in 1961. Recently
Kunstler had been all over the news for agreeing to take on
the defense of Jack Ruby, the Texas nightclub owner who had
fatally shot Lee Harvey Oswald.

Perhaps it was because I knew how famous he was, but
Kunstler seemed larger than life when he strode into Bill's
living room for our first meeting about the lawsuit. He had a
big head of dark unruly hair, an oversized pair of glasses
perched at the top of his forehead, and a booming voice,
which demanded that you sit up and pay attention. Being in
the room while Bill, Hobson, and Kunstler argued law and
strategy was electric.

Kunstler had a passion for poetry, and he and I hit it off
talking about literature after one of these legal strategy sessions. When I told him about my struggles with the draft
board, he invited me to "take a break from the movement"
and visit his family's home in suburban New York for the
weekend. I eagerly accepted.

My dinner with Kunstler; his wife, Lotte; and their daughter Jane in early April was like none I'd ever experienced.
First, they talked about the day's news. The Soviets had just
launched the first lunar probe, and now their satellite was
orbiting the moon and sending back signals. Kunstler turned

to Jane and asked if she still thought Kennedy's promise of sending a man to the moon was a squandering of resources.

"Absolutely," she replied. "Instead of spending all that money to send men to the moon, we could be rebuilding our ghettos."

"But what about the goal of scientific advancement?" Lotte asked.

"What good is science if too many people in our country live in poverty and go hungry every night?" countered Jane. "First it was Vietnam, and now it's sending men off to the moon. We have problems at home we need to take care of."

The lively give-and-take went on throughout the leisurely meal. They seemed to genuinely enjoy talking to one another and lingered at the table. I was struck by how Kunstler and Lotte encouraged their daughter to express her views. How different it was from the angry arguments and bitter silences at my family's dinner table, night after night.

As we sat in the glow of their living room fireplace after dinner, Kunstler recited Dylan Thomas poems, and then a few of his own. The warmth of the embers, the lyricism of his voice, and the rhythmic cadences of the poetry quieted the churning and whirling in my head for long moments. But then I began thinking about the draconian choices in front of me when the draft board denied my appeal, as I was sure they would. Why couldn't I have stuck it out in school, like most other kids, and held on to my student deferment?

Sensing the change in my mood, Kunstler stopped reading and asked what was bothering me. It all came spilling out: how there seemed to be no place for me in school, what the Mole had said, how I'd run away from Avon, how I'd dropped out of college, not once but twice, and now how I was afraid I'd be drafted.

When I told him of the dean's accusations, Kunstler roared with laughter. I let myself smile. Why couldn't I have been born into this family? Maybe they would have understood my struggles with school. Maybe they would have believed in me.

"There are some interesting new options for colleges now," Kunstler reassured me. He went over to a pile of brochures that Jane, a high school junior, had stacked on a table in the corner. He shuffled through them, then walked back and handed me a stapled, mimeographed booklet with a blue construction-paper cover. "Friends World Institute" it said in plain black letters.

The contents of that simple booklet—and the decision that I subsequently made to apply to this experimental school—changed the course of my life.

FOUR

Study Tour

AS MY TRAIN TO WASHINGTON SWAYED AND RATTLED down the tracks, I pored over the brochure Bill Kunstler had handed to me after dinner. I couldn't quite believe what I was reading: "Friends World Institute wishes to attract students who seek the challenge of a college program dedicated to the development of their potential for creative and constructive living in an increasingly interdependent world." A school dedicated to the development of one's creative potential? Incredible. I honestly hadn't thought about my potential since I'd spent that morning skipping classes to read the Port Huron Statement.

Friends World had been founded just a year earlier, in 1965, by a group of Quakers attempting a "new experiment in world education." They were in the process of seeking accreditation as a four-year college. The curriculum consisted of studying social problems, rather than traditional subjects, and students moved to a different part of the world each semester to learn about the particular issues of that region. I'd wanted to learn about other cultures since my summer with Mr. West. There were daily seminars, but no formal exams and no grades. Instead, students kept a journal of their learning. I already did that. There were also regular meetings where students and faculty dealt with community concerns together, instead of adults just telling kids what to do. This was just like the system at A. S. Neill's Summerhill that had intrigued me from the moment I first read about it. It all sounded too good to be true.

As soon as I got back to Bill Higgs's house, I completed the admissions form and put it in the mail. In my application essay I explained how, at my previous colleges, I felt "my studies consistently interfered with my education." Mark Twain was supposed to have said that, and I borrowed the quip. But the next statement was all my own: "I want to learn, not memorize, and relate, not regurgitate."

A woman from the admissions office called a week later. I listened, my heart pounding, as she explained that a group of students from Friends World was going on a study tour to Greenbelt, Maryland, a suburb on the fringe of the Capital Beltway. Would I be available to go to their campsite for an interview with the director of the North American Center? I had no idea what she meant by "study tour," but I was excited—and nervous—about my upcoming interview. I was also curious to know what kinds of kids would go to this experimental school.

Half a dozen or so students were unloading duffels from three VW buses and beginning to set up tents when I rode my Yamaha into their campsite a few days later. I didn't see a teacher anywhere, and so I introduced myself to a pretty young woman who was unpacking pots and pans from a cardboard box. She was dressed in a denim skirt and a white peasant-style blouse with puffy short sleeves and red embroidery across the front. Her wavy, dark brown hair cascaded halfway down her back.

Connemara was her name, and she told me that her class of nineteen had come to Greenbelt to learn about urban planning and consumer cooperatives. She explained that the entire town had been carved out of tobacco fields by the federal government in the 1930s as part of the New Deal. The immediate goal was to relieve the housing shortage because of the increased numbers of government workers, but the planners also wanted to demonstrate how a community might be better organized. All the major retail stores in town were co-ops, and every resident owned a share—and had a say in how the stores were run. Connemara told me that Morris Mitchell, the president of Friends World, believed the school's students needed to experience for themselves how promising social experiments like Greenbelt worked, that is, to learn not just from reading books but by taking study tours. This one was her first.

Speaking with a quiet, firm voice and looking at me intently, Connemara seemed so sincere, so mature—and so very different from other women my age. Before college, she'd gone to a Quaker boarding school on a farm. She said she'd dropped out of a college where she'd been studying weaving in order to come to Friends World and learn about alternative approaches to education, such as Montessori, a name I'd never heard before.

By now students had finished setting up their tents, and several wandered over to help prepare supper on some camp stoves. To help keep tuition low, Connemara explained, students usually camped out on these trips. They did regular chores back at the campus as well.

Connemara led me over to one of the tents and introduced me to the director of the college's center in North America, a middle-aged man dressed in rumpled khakis and a blue work shirt named Arthur Meyer. As I told him about my previous college experiences and work with Bill on the lawsuit against the D.C. public schools, he nodded reassuringly. I was exactly the kind of student Friends World was seeking to attract, he said.

Traveling the world; having great discussions with interesting, like-minded students; learning about new ways of solving social problems—my head buzzed as I left the campsite. I couldn't wait to be a student again. This time it would be different. And I hoped that I'd see Connemara again, too.

The next few weeks were an emotional roller coaster. One minute I was elated, the next I was crushed. I whooped with joy when I received notice from my draft board that I'd been granted conscientious objector status. Then I read the rest of the letter, which stated that I had to report to Virginia in less than a month to start my two years of alternative service as an orderly in a mental hospital. Two years of having my life on hold, spending my time cleaning toilets and mopping floors, was how I pictured it. A few days later, I eagerly tore open a letter from Friends World and, after learning I'd been accepted, rushed off my request to the draft board for a student deferment. It took them only a week to notify me that my appeal had been denied. Furious and with tears in my eyes, I shredded the form into a hundred tiny pieces. But then it suddenly occurred to me that, since Friends World was a Quaker college, the draft board might let me fulfill my alternative service there.

The college readily agreed to the idea and, surprisingly, so did the draft board. The Selective Service System regulations stipulated that a conscientious objector's alternative service should be a hardship, and they must have reasoned that making me move all the way to New York would be more of a sacrifice than working closer to home. They didn't know—and didn't have to be told—that I'd be a student, too.

And so in June 1966, I said good-bye to Bill Higgs, thanked him profusely for all I'd learned from him, sold my motorcycle, and made my way to Mitchel Field, in Westbury, Long Island, where the college had leased some abandoned air force barracks for use as dorms and classrooms. Before our seminars started in September, I was to work as an administrative assistant at a small estate nearby, called Harrow Hill, which had been donated to Friends World to serve as the college's "world headquarters."

My job consisted of running the mimeograph machine, stuffing envelopes, and licking stamps for the college's newsletters, fund-raising appeals, and brochures—tedious but necessary work. I spent my solitary evenings poring over a novel Bill Kunstler had recommended to me—James Joyce's *A Portrait of the Artist as a Young Man*. I was totally caught up in Stephen Dedalus's stream of consciousness. Stephen was a kindred spirit coming of age, even more so than Thomas Wolfe's characters had been in high school. Like me, Stephen was struggling against the oppressive confines of school, parents, and the church. Like me, he "was destined to learn his own wisdom apart from others or to learn the wisdom of others himself wandering among the snares of the world."

The high point of the summer came a week or so after I started when Morris Mitchell invited me into his office. It was a small room, made smaller by floor-to-ceiling bookcases bursting with their contents. Morris was seated in a deeply creased, overstuffed chestnut-brown leather chair surrounded by seemingly random stacks of papers and magazines. He was a large man with broad shoulders. His thick, bushy eyebrows were a stark contrast to his thinning white hair. Sun streamed through the window and lit his craggy face as he motioned for me to take a seat in his chair's twin, positioned across from him. I felt insignificant as all five-foot-ten of me sank into it.

Morris quickly put me at ease, congratulating me for having taken the initiative with my draft board, and for my stance as a conscientious objector. "I was director of a camp for conscientious objectors for a period of time during World War II," Morris said in his deep, commanding voice. He had this odd habit of rolling his two thumbs in circles as he talked. Later I learned that he had been severely wounded and gassed in the trenches as a young lieutenant during World War I, and the thumb rolling was one consequence. The other effect of the war was his becoming a pacifist and a member of the Society of Friends, or Quakers, as they are commonly called.

"We want our graduates to become agents of social change," he told me, in what felt like an orientation to the aims of the college. "And we want to equip our students with an understanding of the emerging, creative forces that, if implemented at scale, have the capability to dramatically impact many of the world's most pressing problems."

I nodded my assent. I didn't know what creative forces he was talking about, but I was eager to learn.

MUCH LIKE ALCOTT FARRAR ELWELL, with whom I'd learned axemanship at Mowglis, Morris Randolph Mitchell was an education visionary. But unlike the Colonel, who believed that the worst effects of schools could be ameliorated through summer camp experiences, Morris sought to fundamentally transform the experience of learning in schools.

Morris was born in Georgetown, Kentucky, in 1895. His father, Samuel Chiles Mitchell, was an educator—first a history professor and then a college president and a trustee of a foundation whose mission was to improve the education of black students growing up in the South. His mother, Alice Virginia Broadus, was the daughter of a preacher and university president.

So from an early age, Morris was exposed to discussions about education and social justice. But he had a problem: he disliked school and was frequently disruptive. He was asked to leave two schools—one public, one private—before finally graduating from high school in 1912. He then attended a succession of three colleges, moving as a student each time his father took a new position as president. He interrupted his studies to enlist in the army during World War I and then, at the end of the war, returned to complete his degree in 1919.

Morris suffered from what we would today call post-traumatic stress disorder (PTSD) as a result of his war experiences. He was told by his doctor that he needed peace and quiet to heal, and so after graduation, Morris moved to Marston, North Carolina, where, with help from his brother, he built a cabin and planted peach trees. With little to do in the winter, he took a job as a teacher in the neighboring town of Ellerbe to supplement his meager income.

In 1925, Morris published an article titled "Mine Own People," about his experiences in Ellerbe and used both a pseudonym—Benjamin Harrison Chaffee—and a fictional name for the town—he called it Federal—when his article was published in the *Atlantic Monthly*. That was likely because of his decision to honestly and vividly describe the malnutrition, diseases, overwork in the fields, and physical abuse suffered by this poor community's children. He was appalled at what he saw. At the end of the article, he declared his commitment to education: "My anger turned into solemn resolve. I would never forsake these starving people. Education would henceforth be my religion."

As a teacher without any training, Morris made things up as he went along in Ellerbe. He began by asking his class of a dozen students to go out into the community to learn more about some of the common diseases and malnutrition from which the town's people suffered. Students then returned to the classroom to study how these problems could be solved, learning basic literacy, math, and science along the way. Some years later, *Reader's Digest* sent a journalist named Robert Littell to report on how Morris had transformed Ellerbe's school:

> I saw a class spending one of its periods giving blood tests to a neighbor's chickens and another which went outdoors to study Caesar and fight battles with Helvetians in North Carolina's sand. I saw an arithmetic teacher's classroom, in which the children were about to start a bank with money printed by the school press. . . .

Morris's students did not learn math by doing problems on worksheets in class, then doing more of the same at home, and finally taking a test. They learned math by creating and using currency and then conducting financial transactions through the school's bank with their fictional money. His students learned by doing.

This hands-on, problem-based approach to learning proved so successful in its first year that many children who hadn't been attending school were enrolled, and his little school grew large enough to require hiring three additional teachers. The community built a new school building and then, four years later, added eight more classrooms.

Morris took two years' leave of absence from his position at Ellerbe for graduate study in education at Peabody Teachers College, where he received his doctorate in 1926. As a student there, he encountered the philosophy of John Dewey. According to Morris, Dewey's writings were a revelation and a confirmation: "Dewey put into theory the things I had been doing in practice." Morris sought out Dewey to be his mentor, and spent a year studying with him at Columbia University.

Neither man thought that what passed for education in their time, or in ours, for that matter—memorizing the content of textbooks and taking predominantly factual recall tests—had any lasting impact on student learning. They observed that the things students studied for tests were quickly forgotten and contributed very little to their development of essential skills, or to their understanding of basic concepts. Instead, students had to actively encounter and investigate their immediate world, just as Morris had asked his students in Ellerbe to do. The teacher was a coach and guide, rather than the keeper and conveyor of a seemingly endless supply of mostly useless information.

Dewey and Mitchell both believed that the goal of education should be to prepare students to be independent thinkers and actors in a democracy, not mere automatons who followed orders. But Morris took this idea much further than Dewey. Radicalized first by his war experiences, then by his encounters with poverty in Ellerbe, and finally by the Great Depression, Morris undertook his own "study tour" to Scandinavia and Russia in 1937. From these ventures, and as a result of an attempt to establish a utopian, cooperative community on a thousand acres he'd purchased in the town of Macedonia, Georgia, Morris grew convinced of the importance of social planning and the co-op movement as essential counterbalances to unfettered capitalism. He believed that students needed to understand and embrace these concepts in order to save the world from the ravages of war, poverty, racism, and environmental catastrophe.

Morris seemed to be always searching for a place where he would be free to put his theories into practice. Throughout the 1930s and '40s, he never stayed for more than a few years at any given teaching or administrative position. Then finally, in 1950, another Dewey disciple, Carmelita Hinton, asked Morris to start a teacher education program. Fifteen years earlier, Hinton had founded the Putney School, in southern Vermont, the first co-ed boarding school in the United States. The school was widely seen as a leading light in the progressive education movement. Now Hinton wanted to steep future teachers in Dewey's beliefs and practices. She gave Morris carte blanche—within a tight budget—to develop a brand-new approach to preparing future educators for the classroom.

Over the next fourteen years, the Putney Graduate School of Teacher Education became the proving ground for many of the ideas that Morris would later apply to learning and teaching at Friends World. Study tours were at the heart of his curriculum. Students visited sustainable woodlots in rural Vermont, settlement houses in New York City, and the Highlander Folk School in Tennessee, where civil rights activists and labor union organizers were trained. Morris called these "places of quiet revolution," and his students were his budding revolutionaries.

As an international, interracial, co-ed group traveling in the South, his students frequently encountered prejudice. Once, in Georgia, some white men in a truck threw manure on two students as they were walking along the road. After the experience, Morris asked the students: *What would make a man do something like that? What are the forces of the community that may have influenced his behavior? How did it make you feel?* He constantly encouraged his students to reflect on their experiences as a way to gain a deeper understanding of a person, a problem, or an idea.

In 1964, the Putney Graduate School merged with Antioch College and, at the age of seventy-one, Morris was headed back to Georgia, where he planned to spend his remaining days farming. It was then that he got the call from a group of Quakers who wanted to create a new kind of college.

Friends World had been the brainstorm of George Nicklin, a psychiatrist and prominent Quaker in New York who had experienced the horrors of World War II as a young soldier. For years Nicklin had lobbied and cajoled fellow Quakers to establish a college dedicated to peaceful coexistence, and by 1963, sufficient money had been raised to run a pilot project— an international summer program for the children of UN delegates. The program proved popular, and the Committee on a Friends World College set out to recruit a founding director.

When the committee interviewed Morris for the job, he offered them a much bolder vision for the college than what they'd been imagining. Rather than merely having an international group of students study together, Morris advocated for setting up campuses around the world, one each in North America, Latin America, Western Europe, Eastern Europe, Africa, South Asia, and East Asia. Eventually, he said, students from all seven regions would enroll at their regional campus, then rotate from campus to campus each semester as they completed their college education. After seven semesters of immersion in regional problems and possible solutions, students would return to their home campus in their final semester to research and write a thesis on a problem of particular interest to them.

Morris was hired by the Quakers, and he and his family moved to Harrow Hill in the summer of 1965, just a few months before the first class of students arrived. From the beginning, he faced significant logistical challenges turning his idea for a world college into a reality. First, with the college's very limited resources and tiny staff, he had great difficulty managing the network of regional centers. Morris and his deputy, Ruth Mary Hill, hired local staff who were sometimes unqualified (and occasionally untrustworthy). The locations and arrangements for the regional centers changed frequently. And because of the cost of tuition and lack of scholarship aid, very few students enrolled through the college's regional centers outside North America.

But as I consider it now, the more serious challenge was a fundamental contradiction in Morris's stated goals for the school. Morris believed education was the means by which each individual's unique capabilities are best developed and most fully realized, and that real learning was a process of active discovery. Yet he was also convinced that the world was imperiled and could be saved only by educating his students about the importance of a handful of ideas and institutions that he considered to be indispensable in any effort to create a better world. So Morris dragged students on tours of projects dating from the New Deal, more than a generation removed from our lives. He thought a visit to Greenbelt would prove the benefits of co-ops and planned communities; that a tour of the Tennessee Valley Authority would provide an outstanding example of regional development that could and should be replicated anywhere. Morris couldn't help himself: he handed us both the problem and the solution—his solution.

Where he saw revolutionary practices, his students saw only the outdated and ordinary: stores and tract homes in suburban Maryland, a collection of big, ugly dams throughout Tennessee. For many of us, Morris and his ideas were too old to be relevant. This was the 1960s, after all, when a growing number of youth had embraced the mantra "Don't trust anyone over thirty." Most of us had been drawn to Friends World by the other visions spelled out in the college's brochure: individual autonomy, self-fulfillment, and—as we interpreted it—freedom from oppressive schools and authorities.

The tension between these two opposing forces had a significant impact on the early years of the college and its students. Like others, I was caught in the maelstrom of these years. But at the same time, my life was transformed by the opportunities to learn that Friends World offered—and that I seized.

OVER THE SUMMER, I'd been living in a room in one of the small officers' cottages at the former barracks at Mitchel Field that Friends World had taken over. On the first day of classes in September, the rest of the students—a total of forty, with nearly equal numbers of men and women—joined me, unloading their stuff in their assigned rooms in the cluster of renovated bungalows. The barren compound was surrounded by tall wire fencing and overrun with weeds, but no one seemed to notice. We were too caught up in conversations, getting to know one another.

In the afternoon, we gathered in the seminar room for introductions. Almost every student had previously gone to another college and dropped out. Like me, they were here for a different kind of education. I had finally found some kindred spirits who weren't just characters in a Joyce novel.

Morris came over from Harrow Hill in the evening to greet our group. That night I tried to capture the gist of his welcoming words on the first pages of my official student journal: "He frightened us, warned us, 'WE MUST'ed us, loved us, hoped for us. . . ." I was a bit dumbfounded by all his declaratives and didn't really understand what he was saying, except that he had very high expectations. Afterward we sang civil rights and folk songs.

Classes began the next day. The first semester was to be an introduction to problems at the individual, neighborhood, city, regional, national, and global levels. In reality, we were fire-hosed with lectures about the ills of the modern world. Guest faculty arrived every morning to dispense their expertise on a topic. Week one, it was the individual and society—the challenge of families, problems of communication, the need to stay physically and spiritually healthy, dealing with sexuality and identity. Perhaps if we'd had a week to explore each of these topics, and time for more in-depth discussions, things might have been okay. But the deluge continued, relentlessly. Over the next few weeks we heard talks on automation, concepts of labor, worker alienation, arbitration, conciliation, mediation, Black Power, white thinking, urban blight, rural poverty, the destructive pressures of modern society. We heard from avowed Marxists one day, Quakers the next, our heads spinning with questions of who and what to believe, and no time to figure out anything. There was a field trip to the Port Authority in New York City—why?—and a quick tour of the United Nations headquarters because "world government" was on Morris's list of must-haves. And one night, Morris delivered what felt like a sermon on cooperatives. He portrayed them as a "magic elixir" that would instantly cure all the excesses of capitalism.

Then, abruptly, we were tackling global issues. Wednesday was "How can we begin to understand hostility and war between nations?" Thursday, "A conversation with the Ford Foundation." Friday, "How can we begin to understand the problems of developing the human and material resources of the poverty-stricken majority of mankind?" with a guest lecture on Africa—the entire continent—in the afternoon. By Saturday morning we'd moved on to "How far has India been able to develop her human and material resources?" The following week, we studied the history of the cold war, the Cuban missile crisis, the dangers of nuclear weapons, the fallacy of "mutually assured destruction" as a defense strategy, and failures in arms control, failures in disarmament.

We were drowning in information. And almost all of our seminars focused on problems; very few were about solutions, except for the ones doled out by Morris himself. Everything about the experience was overwhelming. A growing number of students stopped doing the recommended readings. Then they began skipping the seminars—and their assigned jobs in the kitchen and dining hall as well. The majority of kids were smoking pot. Some were experimenting with LSD. One had a mental breakdown and went home.

At the community meetings, faculty and administrators pleaded with students to take more personal responsibility, while students complained that the readings and seminars were boring or—worse—irrelevant. They were sick of hearing about the problems of the world. I quickly grew tired of everybody's blather.

I didn't smoke pot. I attended seminars and tried to keep up with at least some of the reading. I took the faculty's side in our community meetings. The result was that I found myself increasingly isolated from most of the other students in the very place where I'd thought I'd finally fit in.

I dealt with my growing disillusionment and loneliness by throwing myself into a challenging academic project that offered me a chance to study solutions, not just problems: a simulation of a conference on India's development over the coming decades. We signed up to be in one of four groups. Three were mock delegations—one from India, one from China, and one from the United States—that would research and present a development proposal to the fourth group of students, who were to play the part of distinguished Indian political and business leaders. Their role was to listen to the three presentations and ask the delegations tough questions. I volunteered to head the Chinese delegation and plunged into readings about India's problems and the Chinese communists' approach to the development of so-called Third World countries.

I relished writing my speech, and I had a blast tracking down copies of Chairman Mao's Little Red Book in a Greenwich Village bookstore so that we could hold them high when we marched into the room and read some authentic quotes as part of our presentation. I began my remarks to the Indian dignitaries with a bit of bravado. "The peoples of China hold the concept of self-reliance to be the single most important factor in a country's development. This obviously means that foreign imperialists must be ousted from your country before any real developmental progress can take place." I then argued that the massive $450 million deficit in India's most recent five-year plan was the result of an overreliance on foreign investments and loans—investments and loans that had never materialized. The more I learned, the more excited I became—not because I was drawn to the Chinese point of view, but rather because we were finally studying a problem in some depth and investigating a range of possible solutions.

In lieu of grades, the college's academic transcripts featured narratives, written by a faculty adviser, about your progress. My adviser wrote:

"Tony Wagner has done outstandingly well in all his studies during the past semester. He has planned his time carefully, read extensively and critically and shown a remarkable capacity for sustained hard work. In his Journal, he has achieved a superb integration of life and learning, politics and poetry with excellent style and economy."

Was he really writing this about me—the same Tony Wagner who'd been asked to leave middle school, run away from high school, and dropped out of two colleges? For the first time, I felt real pride in my scholastic accomplishments.

In spite of the squabbles at community meetings and my feelings of social isolation, I had finally found a school that fit *me*.

OUR BUS ARRIVED in Mexico City after nightfall. We'd been told we had a few full days of orientation seminars in the capital before we would move on to Cuernavaca, an hour to the south, to begin our studies. I was eager to explore, and so early the next morning I set off on foot from the Friends Center where my class of students was being housed. I made my way along the grand boulevard of the Paseo de la Reforma, following the steady, bustling flow of people babbling in tongues I couldn't understand—not just Spanish, but also indigenous languages. Vivid green-and-yellow taxis streaked by, honking their cacophonic, multinote horns, seemingly for no reason, or perhaps just for the pleasure of hearing the noise they made.

On every corner there were brown-skinned women sitting on blankets, their waist-length black braids shining in the bright sunlight, dressed in long dark skirts and blouses smocked with red, orange, lime, and fuchsia flowers. Their wares spilled out before them onto the sidewalk: shining silver bracelets and earrings, painted earthen pottery, hand-sewn cloth dolls that looked like miniatures of the infants that nearly every woman kept tightly wrapped in a rebozo against her back. They looked up at passersby, entreating in wide-eyed but dignified silence.

The acrid smell of burning charcoal and barbecued meat filled the air. All along the street, male vendors offered up enormous flour tortillas filled with dripping, steaming beef or chicken. Others hawked paper cups overflowing with succulent pineapple, mangoes, strawberries, and fruits that I'd never seen before. I watched and figured out that they'd concoct a milk shake with an egg and the fruit of your choice. Some of the men were dressed in stained and mismatched Western-style shirt and pants; others in the traditional campesino white pants and shirt, their heads sticking through the slits in their rainbow-colored serapes. Regardless, they all wore the same style of sandal, made of leather thongs stapled to recycled bits of car tire.

Eventually I made my way to the vast Chapultepec Park—even larger than New York's Central Park—in the heart of the city. There men carrying enormous bundles of helium-filled balloons and great armfuls of fragrant flowers plied their trade. Families were picnicking, their children laughing and tumbling in the lush green grass, while lovers strolled the paths arm in arm. It seemed as though everyone was smiling, touching, holding hands, childlike. Thousands of unseen birds sang strange songs from the canopies of tall trees, and high above the city, the snowcapped volcanoes Popocatépetl and Iztaccíhuatl stood sentinel against an ocean-blue sky.

My stereotype of a "developing country" was one of filth, poverty, and suffering—and I would certainly see some of that in Mexico. But at this moment, I was stunned at how different the city was from what I'd been expecting. I had never been in a place that felt so sensual. Both viscerally and physically, I felt as though I were being swept along by a gentle wave of soft, innocent caresses.

After getting my fill of people watching, I slowly made my way up the long hill to the castle situated above the park. Before the revolution in 1910, it had been the home of a succession of viceroys and emperors sent by Spain to rule the peasants. Now it was a history museum. As with the rest of Mexico City, the museum astonished me.

In room after room, I was confronted with intensely pigmented, life-sized murals that seemed unbound by the two dimensions of the walls. I hadn't seen such animated art since first encountering Mr. West's paintings of scenes from Kipling's *Jungle Books* at Mowglis. But these paintings had a very different intent: they depicted the history and suffering of the Mexican people over the centuries. Fierce Aztec warriors tore the hearts out of their rivals and placed them, as a ritual offering, on a stone altar. Horse-mounted, gun- and sword-wielding, metal-clad conquistadors kicked and whipped the natives. A group of top-hatted tycoons presided, tight-lipped, over a naked peasant's lynching, as some priests looked on impassively. A bare-breasted woman struggled against the massive

manacles on her wrists, almost leaping off the wall, so reso-
lute was she in her resistance to the white men in the background.

And then came the scenes of revolution: phalanxes of peasants sporting sombreros and crisscrossed bandoliers; blackened, bombed-out earth on which men and horses lay dying,
abandoned cannons strewn beside them; and the smiling,
triumphant pride of the mestizos marching to victory through
the streets and fields of tall corn and carrying the new flag
of Mexico. The Mexicans, ancient and modern, exuded raw
power and determination, even when they were half naked
and vulnerable to the world. The Europeans wore scowls on
their pallid white faces, and they always had a sword or gun
or whip at hand.

This was like nothing I had ever seen in an American museum. I'd picked up an information brochure in English when
I came in, and now I read it eagerly, trying to understand who
would paint this forcefully, and why.

The paintings were primarily the work of three muralists: Diego Rivera, José Clemente Orozco, and David Alfaro
Siqueiros. They had been revolutionaries and believed that
art should be for all the people—not just the rich—so they
had created murals on many of the public buildings in the
capital. They also believed that an important purpose of art
was to help the Mexican people understand their history and
heritage. White conquerors had turned proud people into
slaves, and these artists wanted to help their fellow Mexicans
to reclaim their identity and dignity.

I sat on a bench outside the castle in silence, piecing together what the murals meant to me, enthralled with the idea of art having a collective consciousness. We'd been told that our semester in Mexico would consist of three months of Spanish-language immersion and seminars on Latin America, after which we'd have a month for an independent study project. I now knew how I would spend that time: I'd learn more about these remarkable artists.

A FEW DAYS LATER, we arrived at the Centro Intercultural de Documentación (CIDOC). Set high on a hill overlooking the city of Cuernavaca, in a large white hacienda surrounded by flower gardens, CIDOC was an extraordinary place to study. Its genteel, aristocratic appearance belied the progressive thinking inside its walls.

CIDOC had been founded by a Catholic monsignor named Ivan Illich, who had been born in Vienna. He had attended the University of Florence and then the Pontifical Gregorian University in Rome, where he became an ordained priest. He went on to earn a doctorate in history from the University of Salzburg. After graduating, Illich volunteered to be a parish priest in one of New York City's poorest neighborhoods, Washington Heights, where many newly arrived Puerto Rican immigrants lived. At the age of thirty, he'd been appointed vice rector of the Catholic University of Puerto Rico, but he was expelled a few years later because of his vocal criticisms of the church's stand on birth control and other social issues.

Illich then traveled throughout Latin America before settling in Mexico and establishing CIDOC in 1961.

The monsignor was a constant paternal presence at the center, always introducing scholars to students gathered on the porch for lunch and engaging in intense one-on-one discussions in the halls. Though he no longer wore a priest's cassock or clerical collar, he invariably dressed in crisp white shirts and well-creased dark pants, which added to his natural aura of seriousness and service. Once in a while I saw him break into a toothy smile, but I don't recall ever seeing him laugh.

The monsignor's goal was to better prepare missionaries, clergy, nuns, and development workers for their assignments in the region. He knew the importance of learning to speak the native tongue of those you were serving—he himself was fluent in six languages—and the school's intensive Spanish-language program was considered the best in Mexico. But he was even more concerned that many of the people who came to work in Latin America arrived with an attitude of superiority and condescension toward the poor. They felt they were doing God's work by spreading the Gospel to heathen peasants who lacked both religion and an appreciation of the Western way of life. "Industrial hegemony"—the psychological domination of indigenous cultures by industrial societies—is what the monsignor called it. And so at CIDOC he sought to create "a center for de-Yankeefication."

Intellectuals from across Latin America came to CIDOC to give lectures and debate alternative approaches to their countries' futures. There were talks on the "real" history of Latin America—a history of conquests by Europeans that led to their enslavement of native populations. There were lengthy discussions of the problems of Western-style economic development in the Third World that mainly served the interests of the rich. There were debates about the ways in which the Catholic Church's theology of unquestioned obedience to authority subjugated peasants. There were arguments about the extent to which the American CIA had helped to overthrow popular leaders in Latin America who were leaning toward socialism. Several times while I was there, speakers pointed to the postrevolutionary improvements in health and education in Cuba, and a few people who worked at the center seemed sympathetic to the aims of Fidel Castro's regime. One was rumored to have fought at the side of Che Guevara.

Having focused so much on the problems of American racism and the Vietnam War, I hadn't seen the extent to which our economic system "conquered" other countries by creating an insatiable market demand for all the stuff we manufactured. This "cultural imperialism" was manifested, I began to realize, in the huge billboards that hovered above the streets of Mexico City selling cars, booze, and cigarettes. Everybody in the advertisements was having a good time, but they all had white faces. The billboards weren't selling only the "American way of life," but also the idea that whiter is better. I now understood why the muralists whose work I'd seen in the castle had strived to create art to tell their own people's stories.

While I found the seminars more enlightening and engaging than any classes I had previously attended, I struggled to stay alert through the three hours of daily language drills, which involved listening to a recorded Spanish phrase or passage through headphones, then trying to repeat what I'd heard into a microphone, with a teacher listening in and occasionally correcting my pronunciation. I couldn't make myself spend time memorizing grammar and vocabulary in my dark little room after class. I wanted to be out in this new world, "learning by doing."

So what I lacked in book time, I more than made up for in street time. I rode the bus nearly every day to downtown Cuernavaca, where I took pride in practicing my Spanish in cafés and in the huge open market. I'd greet folks with a warm *Muy buenas tardes*, and then bargain for a pineapple or a pair of huarache sandals, or a serape I'd been eyeing. Talking back and forth, accompanied by a volley of frowns, nods, and smiles, seemed to serve an important social function for the sellers and buyers. I relished these negotiations in my new language.

After three months, I was fluent enough to start work on my independent study project, "The Arts as a Tool for Social Change in Mexico." I interviewed Mexican artists and writers, students and intellectuals. I visited museums and attended plays. One was a Latin American variant of the Hans Christian Andersen tale "The Emperor's New Clothes." Afterward, the director told me he'd adapted the play to teach Mexican children that people in power were often fools.

The high point of the project was an opportunity to talk with David Alfaro Siqueiros. An avowed Marxist, Siqueiros had fought in the Mexican and Russian revolutions as well as the Spanish Civil War, and in 1920, along with Diego Rivera, he had launched the Mexican muralist movement. In 1960, he had been jailed by the government for publicly criticizing the country's president. Most recently, he'd donated the entire proceeds of his Lenin Art Prize—$25,000—to the North Vietnamese.

CIDOC had arranged for a few students to receive a tour of Siqueiros's studio south of Cuernavaca. Shortly after we arrived, Siqueiros joined us, dressed in paint-crusted pants, polka-dot shirt, and a hat that was an odd hybrid of business-man's fedora and cowboy's ten-gallon. After greetings and in-troductions, he led us to his workshop, a sprawling, brightly lit warehouse with murals in various stages of completion hanging from every wall and surrounded by ladders and scaf-folding.

He was working on a new mural, *The March of Humanity*, which, he explained, would take four years to complete and would be the largest in the world. He gestured at a couple of panels—a few men standing in front of a factory, defiant; an-other of muscled men tilling crops in the fields. "They are saying that the land and industry of Mexico belongs to the people of Mexico."

The next panel we approached was stunning: a volup-tuously beautiful naked peasant woman, with jet-black hair cascading down to her waist and flowers at her feet. "There is a story behind this picture," he told us. I half expected an anecdote about one of his many legendary lovers. "A friend had a painting of an aristocratic woman dressed in fine clothing. When he was away, I painted this and hung it in his house where the other one had been. He came back and demanded to know what had happened to his painting. I told him that I had taken it out to be cleaned." A mischievous smile crept across his face.

Near the end of the visit, I screwed up the courage to ask Siqueiros a question.

"Sir, why have you been so involved in political movements?" I said hesitantly.

"I am not making pretty pastry. I am creating art. But art that is for the people. That's why I prefer murals. . . ." The great painter paused for a moment, gazing at the work around him. "But sometimes painting is not enough. That's why I had to go fight in Spain in 1936."

My independent study project and visit to Siqueiros's studio helped me to appreciate even more deeply the importance of the arts as a tool for social criticism and consciousness. They also served to fuel my burning but vague ambitions. *What might I create that could have an impact? How could I make a difference?* Writing a novel felt as far away as a trip to the moon. I didn't even know where to begin. I had taken a painting class in Cuernavaca and quickly discovered that I had no talent. I couldn't even draw. Maybe I could transfer to a film school. But I had one more year of alternative service to complete before I could transfer anywhere.

At the end of the semester, the college asked me to stay on in Mexico for another six months to help with a variety of administrative chores, instead of moving on to the school's European center in London. I didn't mind spending a second semester in Cuernavaca—I loved the people, the food, the landscapes—but with all the work they wanted me to do, I would be only a part-time student. It felt as though I were being asked to put my life and my learning on pause. And in many ways, I was.

It was the fall of 1967, I'd just turned twenty-one, and my year in Mexico was almost over. My class had moved on without me, and I hadn't really connected with any of the kids from the incoming class during their semester in Mexico. Like many in my class, they seemed more interested in the quality of the freely available marijuana than in learning about the country, and they offended Mexican sensibilities with boys' hair that was too long and girls' skirts that were too short. It was a solitary few months.

It was during this time that I reread *The Art of Loving* by Erich Fromm. I'd first come across the book during my introductory semester at the Mitchel Field barracks, and the book had made such an impression that it was one of the few— along with *A Portrait of the Artist as a Young Man*, of course— I'd brought with me to Mexico. In it, Fromm describes love not as something mysterious that you passively "fall into," but as a part of a daily practice of living—requiring a person to develop his or her capacity for care, respect, responsibility, and knowledge. He also argues that self-love is the opposite of arrogance or egocentrism, and that in order to actively and truly love another, you must first develop care, respect, responsibility, and knowledge for yourself. Ultimately he argues that the goal of life should be to develop oneself fully as a human being by living with balance and discipline, including the practice of meditation, exercise, reading, and listening to music every day.

There hadn't been much love in my family growing up, and I had never thought about what it meant to cultivate my capacity to love. I was captivated by the idea of striving to grow in new ways, to be more fully human. I'd been going to Friends World's optional Quaker worship meetings and experienced the power of their silence, and I was intrigued by the notion of meditation as a discipline. I tracked down several books about Zen Buddhism and began to practice sitting in silence for twenty minutes a day, attempting to calm a mind preoccupied with questions about the future. My future.

Sitting alone on a stone bench in CIDOC's rose garden, I was struggling at yet another attempt at meditation when Monsignor Illich walked up and sat down silently beside me. Though I'd been in Mexico for nearly a year, we'd barely spoken. He often seemed to be in another, more important world.

"Tony, you seem troubled," he finally said in a quiet voice.

How did he know? I didn't even think he knew my name.

He looked at me attentively, waiting for me to speak. "It's

just that, well, my time in Mexico is almost up, and I'm really not sure what I'm going back to." I started tentatively, not sure that I should be bothering him with my personal problems.

"I have heard from my faculty adviser in New York. . . . There is kind of a crisis at Friends World right now. Lots of students have left the program, and the ones who have stayed want more flexibility. They don't want to have to move to a different center every six months, and they're demanding more time to pursue their own projects."

"What do *you* want?" the monsignor asked.

"I'm not sure. . . . I mean, I think I want to stay with the college, but I don't want to be around kids who aren't serious about learning. And I guess I want the freedom to create my own independent study program. But I don't know if I could pull it off. . . ."

I stopped talking and stared at my feet.

"Go on," he said gently.

"I guess I just don't know if I have enough self-discipline and, well, self-confidence."

"Tony, have you met God yet?"

What did God have to do with anything? I was confused by the monsignor's question and didn't know how to reply.

Finally, I said, "I used to pray—or I believe it was a kind of praying—in a little chapel in the woods at summer camp. But then . . ." Could I tell him the rest? Would he lose respect for me if I did? "But then . . . I stopped believing that there was a God."

The monsignor smiled slightly. "I'm not talking about a Divine Presence in the sky. I'm talking about the God within."

"I . . . The Quakers talk about God in that way. But I just never . . ."

"He's there in you. But you have to make time and space to discover Him."

The monsignor put a hand on my shoulder. I turned to meet his gaze. He lingered for another moment, then rose up and walked away.

Though not yet certain of what he'd meant, I felt blessed.

TWO DAYS LATER, I was on a bus to Tepoztlán, a small village of about five thousand people nestled at the base of Tepozteco Mountain, sixteen miles west from Cuernavaca. It was said to have been the birthplace of Quetzalcoatl, the feathered serpent god widely worshipped by the Aztecs. There were other sacred associations, too. High on the cliffs rising above the town stood the ruins of an ancient temple built in homage to Tepoztecatl, the god of pulque, a drink made from the pulp of the maguey cactus that is Mexico's oldest alcohol.

I was on a pilgrimage to the temple in search of God. My God. But first I had to get there.

One thing I'd learned about Mexicans is that they will always give you directions with total certainty out of politeness, even when they have no idea which way is right. I'd successfully negotiated the chaotic bus terminal in Cuernavaca, finding the right bus only after practicing my Spanish on five people.

Though their bodies resembled big yellow American school buses, the local Mexican buses were each a unique work of art. Their sides were decorated with bright bands of color, their bumpers festooned with paintings of flowers, the space above the windshield filled with either a mural or a religious sentiment. The bus to Tepoztlán declared in large letters over the windshield JESÚS EN TÍ CONFÍO—"Jesus, I trust in thee."

The driver, who had crucifixes and rosary beads hanging from his rearview mirror, drove as if he were sure that Jesus would take care of him. We screeched around mountain curves, lunged down steep ravines, and passed plodding trucks on blind turns in a journey that was part deathtrap, part circus.

A circus broke out every time the bus came to an abrupt halt for a hand-waving knot of peasants by the side of the potholed black tarmac road. Each stop was like that act where the performers amaze you with how many people they can cram into a VW bug. As women and children piled on, men pulled and tugged scruffy suitcases, battered cardboard boxes tied with twine, burlap bags of grain, and wooden crates of squawking chickens onto the bus's roof, then squeezed themselves in next to their families, three or four tight on the torn vinyl seats meant for two. Once the seats were overflowing, the men stood in the aisles or hung off the back of the bus. I was amused by these roadside shows, but then the bus would start to back up, and I'd be terrified again, hanging on, white knuckled, to the seat in front of me. Finally, miraculously, everybody and everything made it to Tepotzlán intact.

I stopped briefly in the center of town at the Gothic-style gray stone church, built by Catholic missionaries shortly after the time of Hernán Cortés. Pushing against the massive wooden door, I found myself in a long, high-arched space, lit by shafts of sunlight streaming down through stained-glass windows. The altar at the far end was framed by four massive white columns. Behind the columns, there were two murals—one on each side of the altar—depicting a solitary man dressed in robes and bathed in orange light, reaching up, beseeching the sky, it seemed. On the altar itself stood a five-foot-high statue of the bloodied Jesus, nailed to a cross and wearing His crown of thorns. The sharp sweet scent of incense filled the air. Close to the altar, an older woman, dressed in black and with her head covered, genuflected on the bare terra-cotta floor in front of one of the plain wood pews. Her God might be here, I thought as I walked out, but not mine.

In the long shadows of the late-afternoon sun, I made my way slowly down the dusty cobblestone street that led away from the village and toward the mountain. The road quickly turned to dirt as it wound its way past fallow fields. It was late in the fall, harvesting was over, and the rainy season would soon begin. After walking for half an hour or so, I found the path I was looking for, which led steeply up through and out of the forest—two thousand feet to the temple above. The straps of my canvas rucksack dug into my shoulders and my shirt was soaked through with sweat as I scrambled up the rough, rock-strewn trail. But now the sun was setting, the blue above turning to gray as the air chilled.

It was dusk when I reached the cliff where the crumbling stone pyramid was perched. I retrieved a flashlight from my pack and slowly made my way past the wooden lean-to where I'd planned to spend the night. It was a simple temple, resembling three stacked square stone boxes, each one a little smaller than the one beneath, protruding about thirty feet into the sky. I climbed a set of stairs that led from the base to the very top.

Shivering, I sat down and looked out into the gathering darkness. Far across, on the next mountain range, I saw the faintest trace of a pale-red sunset, while below me, Tepoztlán's few lights flickered like fireflies on the valley floor. Above, an effervescent blanket of shimmering stars was spreading out across the crystal-clear, ink-black heavens. I pulled a jacket, some water, and a couple of stuffed and dripping tortillas wrapped in foil from my bag. Mole poblano—chicken smothered in a spicy sesame, cinnamon, and chocolate sauce, my favorite Mexican dish—had never tasted so good, I thought as I ate, gazing out into the night.

A solitary owl called out. *Whoooo*. Who indeed. I was more alone now than I had ever been. More alone than I ever was at Mowglis's chapel in the woods, where I could still hear kids' faint voices from the lake. Strangely, I didn't feel lonely, though. And I'd anticipated feeling afraid, up here all alone, all by myself. But I wasn't.

What I felt was an odd calmness as my mind slowly ceased its chattering. It was this stilling of my thoughts that I sought in meditation, yet almost never found.

So was this what the monsignor had meant? *Was this the God within me?* Maybe so. What I did know was that, at this moment, I felt a kind of quiet confidence for the first time in my life. I was emerging from the misshapen cracked cocoon of my childhood, and I would soon spread my wings.

Mariposa, Spanish for butterfly. I smiled. I would find my way.

FIVE

Learning for a Reason

THE SPRING OF 1968 WAS A BRUTAL TIME TO BE AN IDEAL-
istic young American who believed in nonviolence. First,
Martin Luther King Jr. was gunned down in April, and the
ghettos in Washington, D.C., Chicago, Baltimore, and dozens
of other cities erupted in furious flames. Students turned
angrier and more confrontational, as more than one million
boycotted classes and took over buildings to protest the ever-
escalating war in Vietnam. Then Robert F. Kennedy, who said
he was seeking the presidency in order to end the war, was
assassinated in June. I was stunned and horrified. I believed
King and Kennedy were leaders who could take us to a better
"promised land." "America the Beautiful"? Not anymore. We
were a country being torn apart.

With all that was happening, I didn't see the purpose, after

I completed my alternative service, in traipsing around the world to the college's other regional centers with a bunch of kids who weren't serious about learning. Spending just six months in each center meant that I would, at best, gain only a very superficial understanding of the region's culture. I had spent a full year in Mexico and knew I still had so much more to learn. I was also keenly interested in tackling what I now considered to be America's number one export: the growing cancer of the consumer society. People in poverty were exposed to constant marketing, urging them to buy things on credit that they didn't necessarily need and certainly couldn't afford. They'd been convinced that having more of these things would somehow magically cause them to have "a better life."

That was a lie, I knew. Having lots of material goods didn't make my parents or their friends any happier. In fact, it seemed to me that there was more satisfaction in daily life and a greater sense of community in some of the small rural villages I'd visited in Mexico than in the well-heeled suburban community where I had grown up. And it upset me deeply that America—the world capital of consumerism—was working so hard to sell the rest of the world on the manufactured idea that they needed to buy more of *our* stuff.

I believed that young people in the United States should lead the way in forging a different life path—a life based on creating and learning, rather than on consuming. The problem was that much of my generation—kids I'd met at Friends

World and elsewhere—seemed lost and angry. Too many had turned to drugs for entertainment, claiming that smoking pot or dropping acid was a revolutionary act, a way to make peace and love instead of war. In reality, few of them were peaceful or loving.

An essay I'd read by Erich Fromm about the difference between a rebel and a revolutionary had helped me understand what I was observing. The kids around me sought "freedom from" oppressive families and institutions and conformist pressures. They were rebelling from a prescribed way of life that they found stultifying, but they didn't have anything to take its place—except for drugs.

Fromm wrote that the true revolutionary was a person who sought the "freedom to" develop himself and work toward a more sane and just society. First and foremost, pursuing such a life required real self-discipline. From my experiments with meditation and in trying to make more time for reading and writing, I had begun to see just how hard it was to live more intentionally. Drugs were so much easier.

What would a community and a culture look like that supported individuals' strivings for growth and self-development? What kind of education would help people realize themselves more fully?

A few months before I completed my alternative service with Friends World, I began to talk with my faculty adviser about the possibility of creating an extended independent study program to pursue these questions. He worked with me to create a long reading list of books on philosophy, religion, and psychology and to develop a study proposal to present to the full faculty. I wrote that I would take courses at the so-called free universities that were cropping up in large cities, enroll in weekend seminars for human development, and visit communes. In the second and last year of my independent study program, I would focus on writing my thesis—a requirement for graduation—but my thesis would take the form of a novel that would attempt to synthesize and integrate all that I had been learning. I titled my proposed independent study program "The Poverty of Affluence."

I wasn't the only student who'd decided to petition the college for an independent study program. After we'd first met at the campsite in Greenbelt two years earlier, Connemara and I had stayed in touch. We'd corresponded faithfully and spent time together on our few vacations in the United States between our semesters studying at different Friends World regional campuses. We'd reunited in May 1968 at Mitchel Field, and we were now a couple. Connemara was in her final year at Friends World, and she also longed to be free of the distraction of other students as she began work on her thesis on new approaches to education. And so she, too, developed a proposal to research the work of Rudolph Steiner, founder of the Waldorf schools, and Maria Montessori on her own.

We told our advisers that if our proposals were not accepted, we might drop out of Friends World. The faculty considered us to be two of the college's most serious students, and our plans were approved. Thus, Connemara and I became test cases for a student-designed studies program completely outside of the college's regular curriculum. We'd still keep a journal, we'd check in monthly with our advisers via the mail, and we'd return to campus at the end of each semester for a review of our work. Otherwise, we were free to study anywhere and however we wanted.

While I was in Mexico, I'd met a psychoanalyst named Michael Maccoby, who had been trained by Erich Fromm, and I'd started talking with him to try to make sense of my unhappy childhood and miserable adolescence. Maccoby had also given some lectures at CIDOC on anthropological research he'd done with Fromm in Mexican villages, and he had written articles about education. So when Maccoby told me he was taking a position at Stanford, I suggested to Connemara that we move to San Francisco. I could continue to meet with Maccoby, and she could ask him to serve as her thesis adviser, which he did. And so we set off across the country on our extended independent study tour.

Independent learning—or what now goes by the name "personalized learning"—is all the rage in education these days. Schools that pride themselves on innovative approaches offer students opportunities to "learn at their own pace" on a computer or choose from a "playlist" of software programs. But these approaches are almost always designed to walk students through the same prescribed academic content, with the only "personalization" being in how fast students go through the material or in what order they complete units of study. This approach to personalization, while sounding progressive, does nothing to develop students' curiosity, self-discipline, or initiative. Even worse, students in such programs often work in isolation for much of the day, with few opportunities to learn with peers or from teachers.

The program that Connemara and I had created for ourselves could not have been more different. We designed our proposals around questions and topics that deeply interested us, and our program required us to take initiative and to develop real self-discipline. We knew that we'd have to seek out mentors who could help us learn, as well as opportunities to learn with peers. But first we had to find a home.

We arrived on the streets of San Francisco not knowing a soul and without a place to stay. I bought a newspaper, got a roll of dimes, and started calling the phone numbers in the classified ads for places to rent. Everything was taken. And so we resorted to cruising the streets in search of a FOR RENT sign in a random window.

Amazingly, we found one within about an hour. We knocked on the door of the stately gray Victorian house near the crest of one of the city's famously steep hills and were shown the two-room apartment with a tiny kitchen on the top floor. The view was spectacular—west to Golden Gate Park and the ocean, north to the red girders of the bridge, and beyond to the hills of Marin County. As I wrote the check for our first and last months' rent, I asked the landlord for the address.

"Don't you know?" He laughed. "This is 964 Ashbury Street. Haight Street is just three blocks down the hill."

The previous year, there had been a "Human Be-In," where thirty thousand hippies had gathered at Golden Gate Park to hear poets Allen Ginsberg and Lawrence Ferlinghetti, comedian Dick Gregory, and many others, alongside rock bands that would later become famous—Jefferson Airplane, the Grateful Dead, Big Brother & the Holding Company. Free food had been handed out by a commune called the Diggers. The crowd had also consumed enormous quantities of LSD, and roared their approval when Timothy Leary advised them to "turn on, tune in, and drop out." Sometime shortly after the event, someone had proposed that 1967 should be the Summer of Love, and Haight-Ashbury became its epicenter. More than a hundred thousand "flower children" had descended on the Haight. They'd established communes, crash pads, meditation centers, yoga classes, free food distribution sites, medical clinics, and free schools for their children.

Now, one year later, the Haight was anything but the utopia that its recent immigrants had sought. It had become a kind of hippie shopping mall and a place where kids came to get stoned. Storefront after storefront hawked hippie clothes and "essential" accessories, from beads, incense, sandals, bell-bottomed jeans, and tie-dyed T-shirts to psychedelic posters that glowed in the dark, "trippy" disco balls with strobe lights, and marijuana grow bulbs. There was a "head shop" selling drug paraphernalia on every block. Kids in their teens and twenties with filthy clothes smoked dope and dropped acid openly on the street. Steps away, panhandlers begged for money. Drunks lay sprawled across the grimy sidewalks.

The so-called counterculture had become just another version of America's consumer society. This was not what Connemara and I had come for.

STILL, THE NEXT NINE MONTHS was a time of exciting exploration. I took time to learn the rest of the city, delighting in riding the open streetcars to the end of the line, their bells clanging as we sliced through thick blankets of fog. I went to lectures at the local Zen center and talks around the Bay on alternative lifestyles.

In addition to her research on new approaches to elementary education, Connemara had begun to work as a volunteer teacher at a local free school. She told me that the founders had been inspired by A. S. Neill's *Summerhill*. Curious, I went one morning with Connemara to visit the school. I wanted to see if it was anything like what I'd imagined when I read the book after high school.

As we walked into the dimly lit room of the church basement that housed the school, I saw a dozen or so kids, ranging in age from perhaps five to ten, yelling and running around, throwing things and arguing. In one corner, I saw a boy concentrating hard on building an elaborate wood block bridge, before it was quickly kicked over by another kid.

"Hey, fuck you!" he cried as he threw one of his blocks at the back of the retreating intruder.

Two girls were fighting over a pile of dress-up clothes in another part of the room. "I was here first," one whined. She yanked a dress out of the other girl's hands, tearing a sleeve in the process.

"Where are the teachers?" I asked Connemara.

"They're probably drinking coffee and chatting upstairs. They believe kids should be free to do whatever they want, without adult interference," she explained. "They say the kids will work things out if they are left alone."

I could barely hear Connemara over the shouting of the kids, who continued to run wild around the room. I left as she was attempting to corral the most disruptive of the boys.

This couldn't have been what Neill intended. There wasn't any learning going on. I didn't see even a single book. Maybe the unfettered freedom for kids that Neill espoused wasn't the answer. Neill wrote about the idea of giving kids "freedom, but not license." But were there any boundaries?

At the time, I was puzzled and decided to read some of Connemara's books on Montessori education, which she said offered a more structured approach to learning than Neill's model, while still giving kids lots of independence. Born in Italy in 1870, Maria Montessori trained as a physician and, over time, had developed a method for teaching young children that involved setting up "learning stations" with carefully selected materials, and then letting kids choose from among them. There was a reading corner, a corner for playing with blocks, a painting corner, a dress-up corner, and so on. Montessori teachers were trained to observe and to quietly intervene in order to help children expand their learning or choose a new activity based on each child's interests. There were already thousands of Montessori schools all over the world, but almost all of them were for elementary-age children.

All of Connemara's books about progressive approaches to education focused on younger children, as Montessori had done. Thinking back to my high school experience, I wondered how a Montessori education would work for teenagers. Would it work to give students opportunities to choose the experiments they wanted to do for science or research a period in history that especially interested them or read novels that interested them for English? What about math?

I didn't have time then to pursue these questions, but I put them in a new "Education Issues" section of my journal. I turned my attention now to the question I'd posed as the topic of my thesis: *What would a society, or a way of life, look like that was not based on consumption?* I read books on sociology and psychology, histories of utopias, guides to Zen, novels and poetry, and used my daily journal entries to document and reflect on what I was learning.

Memories of Mr. West's fascinating lessons in Native American lore had influenced the books I'd put on my self-styled syllabus. The first book of anthropology that I chose to read was *Ishi in Two Worlds* by Theodora Kroeber. Ishi was the last surviving member of his Northern California tribe. He had hidden from European and American settlers for forty years before emerging from the wilderness in 1911. Fortunately, he was befriended by the anthropologist Alfred Kroeber (Theodora's husband), who protected Ishi and then spent the next several years, until Ishi died, learning about the tribe's way of life.

Theodora Kroeber's depiction of the California Native Americans' character and culture helped to confirm what I had sensed in my visits to villages in Mexico—namely, that one could live simply, without all the modern conveniences. In fact, doing so provided what I considered to be a high quality of life:

> The California Indian was an introvert, reserved, contemplative, and philosophical. He lived at ease with the supernatural and the mystical which were pervasive in all aspects of life. . . . The ideal was the man of restraint, dignity, rectitude, he of the middle way. . . . Life proceeded within the limits of known and proper patterns from birth through death and beyond. Its repetitive rhythm was punctuated with ritual, courtship, dance, song, and feast, each established according to the custom going back to the beginning of the world. . . .

Was it possible to live such a life today? What did it mean to be "of the middle way" in twentieth-century America? I kept track of all my questions in my Friends World journal.

Helen and Scott Nearing's book *Living the Good Life* provided some answers. The Nearings had fled New York City in 1932, at the height of the Depression, and homesteaded in

Vermont for the next twenty years. They built a house and outbuildings from the stone they found on the property and grew most of their own food, adopting a vegetarian diet. What I loved most, though, was their portrayal of "the good life," which every day included four hours of manual labor and four hours of intellectual and artistic pursuits—playing music, writing, or reading. This was strikingly similar to Fromm's description of a balanced and disciplined life in *The Art of Loving*.

Taken together, these three books—*Ishi in Two Worlds*, *Living the Good Life*, and *The Art of Loving*—shaped my thinking about what kind of life I aspired to live, a life that was radically different from my parents'. Connemara and I talked about the idea of moving to the country after she'd completed her thesis. We'd heard about a Quaker boarding school in rural Canada, and thought about applying for jobs teaching there, once I'd completed my degree. I could imagine myself teaching high school English, but in a way that would be very different from how I had been taught. Earning a living as a teacher would also allow me more time to write and to travel.

Inspired by the Nearings, I began to seek my own version of "the good life" through a more disciplined approach to writing and reading. And for the first time since dropping out of Richmond Professional Institute, I took some formal classes. It was proving hard to learn on my own, without the benefit of any mentoring and discussions.

The first class I took was a workshop on lyrical writing taught by Robert Leverant. A dropout from some name-brand

East Coast college, Robert was about thirty years old, with wild curly hair and a scruffy beard. He mostly made his living as a picture framer but pursued his passion for writing by teaching occasional classes.

I enjoyed his workshop, so after it was over, I asked Robert if he would consider doing a weekly writing tutorial with me. He agreed and, much like Mr. Edwards back in high school at Searing, encouraged me to experiment with diverse writing forms. But, different from my high school experience, Robert also suggested books and authors for me to explore, and our weekly meetings grew into a lively give-and-take, as well as a time for me to get feedback on my work. We'd trade stories from Sherwood Anderson's *Winesburg, Ohio*—his favorite—and Ivan Turgenev's *A Sportsman's Sketches*, which was a new-found favorite of mine.

Robert was also an excellent photographer. He exhibited and sold his work at the many arts-and-crafts fairs in the Bay Area. In his apartment, he had a small workshop where he framed his photographs of nature using beautiful, rough-grained woods. My experience studying the Mexican muralists had awakened an appreciation for the visual arts, and I would admire Robert's photos before each writing lesson. Finally, late in 1968, I went downtown to a pawnshop and bought my first camera—a used 35mm single-lens reflex Pentax—and asked Robert to teach me photography in addition to writing.

One day, instead of reviewing the contact sheet of my latest photographs, he announced that we were heading out to the San Francisco Museum of Modern Art. I hated abstract art, but Robert prodded me to stand in front of canvas after canvas of blobs of color and shape until I began to see the patterns of composition in them and point them out to him. Only then did he call my attention to the movement in each image—where one's eyes were taken, and how this abstract work shared principles of composition with the muralists I loved. It was an astonishing experience of immersive learning.

Looking back, I would never have gone to that museum by myself or come to a deeper understanding of composition on my own. A good teacher, like Robert or Mr. Edwards or Colonel Elwell, sees what a student needs in order to take learning to the next level and acts as a coach, offering the right combination of pressure and support. That's what Robert had done when he took me to the museum that day.

With a more trained eye and my camera in hand, I hiked the sweeping hills surrounding Mount Tamalpais, in Marin County, where the sweet smell of tall grasses brought back my days of haying on the farm. I ambled through the Muir Woods, staring up in awe at the towering redwoods, and walked atop the rocky cliffs of Point Reyes Peninsula, sniffing the salty air, as wave after giant wave crested, rolled down, and thundered onto the rocks and pebbled beach below. Looking through the camera's lens, I saw the world with fresh eyes. Much like when I was writing, the hours I spent taking photographs passed like moments, sand slipping through my fingers, disappearing with no beginning or end. I knew I would always spend at least some portion of my life working to create things of meaning or beauty.

I didn't think I would ever earn a living as a writer or a photographer, but in the winter of 1969, I volunteered to do a photo essay for *Freedom News*—one of the area's alternative newspapers—to document how human activities were destroying the natural beauty of the San Francisco Bay. I spent days tracking down images of the plastic bottles and oil pools that pockmarked the primal wetlands, of broad swaths of land cleared for electric transmission towers that marched their way down to pristine shorelines, of housing developments carved like deep scars into unspoiled natural habitats.

Yet my sense of accomplishment at seeing my photographs printed in the special supplement of the paper quickly gave way to feelings of frustration. It was one thing to document the ways in which man was destroying the environment, but what were we—what was *I*—actually doing? I threw myself into reading *Our Plundered Planet*, *Silent Spring*, and *The Population Bomb*, and as well as books that pointed to a lifestyle that was more in harmony with nature—*A Sand County Almanac* and *The Forest and the Sea*.

But reading didn't feel like enough, and so I signed up for two courses at the University of California extension school: Conservation of Natural Resources and Introduction to General Ecology. The first time I walked into one of the classrooms, I was sure I'd made a mistake in enrolling. I could taste the chalk dust in the air, and my body tensed in resistance. The place looked and smelled like too many others where I'd had bad experiences. But I quickly realized that taking conventional classes to seek answers to *my* questions was very different from my past life as a student. Because I was interested in what we were studying, I was able to listen more actively to the teacher's lecture, naturally sorting out and retaining the information that was most useful to me.

Both classes helped me to understand nature's delicate web of interrelationships. They were also much more relevant to everyday life than the high school biology and chemistry science classes I'd been forced to take. Why were those classes required, but not ecology? Who decided what was required to take? More questions for the expanding education section of my journal.

As the year wore on, I became increasingly upset by the craziness of many of the organizations that marched under the umbrella of the New Left. The widely televised riots in Chicago around the Democratic convention sickened me, and I was infuriated by the antics of Jerry Rubin, Abbie Hoffman, and their group of "yippies," who turned political protests into pot-fueled clown shows that revolted the middle class. Public dope smoking and confrontational encounters with police weren't going to end the war or gain us allies, nor would they create a more just and equitable society.

That spring, I took part in a different kind of demonstration at Stanford. We were protesting the university's sponsorship of the Stanford Research Institute, which was doing extensive classified research for the Department of Defense. We had a simple slogan: "Research Life, Not Death." "Research cancer cures and solutions to poverty, not ways to make napalm deadlier" read one flyer. Our peaceful demonstration had drawn a large crowd—not just the usual long-haired and bearded twentysomethings, but also families with kids in tow—and I felt as though the spirit of our efforts was more like that of the early civil rights and antiwar protests—affirming, not hostile.

I sat down to write in my journal about the connection between what I'd seen at the demonstration and what I had been learning in my classes. As I wrote, it occurred to me that presenting the idea of social change as necessary to save the planet had the potential to be much more persuasive to people than the angry and ideological rhetoric that had become so common.

My journal entry turned into an open letter to the New Left, then evolved into a manifesto. "The most fundamental question today is whether or not life will continue on this planet," I wrote. "We may debate economic alternatives until we become cold and numb, but the undeniable ecological reality is that an unlimited, infinite growth economy—the economy of spiraling, mindless 'progress'—cannot exist in a limited *finite* environment for very long." In place of angry protests, I proposed that we do things like create miniparks in vacant lots, and I urged that all high school science classes incorporate some study of the physical environment—past, present, and future. I ended with a call to action: "There is only one earth! We must all direct our attention towards limiting its population, ending its exploitation, cleaning it up, and generally making it a fit place to live."

I called it "The Ecology of Revolution" and sent it off to an influential New Left publication in New York called *WIN Magazine*—WIN stood for "workshop in nonviolence." A few weeks later, I read the acceptance letter with shaking hands. It was my first published piece of writing. It was eventually reprinted in two anthologies, *Ecotactics: The Sierra Club Handbook for Environmental Activists* and a college reader, *The Pollution Papers*. I couldn't believe it.

There was a magic to the way things had suddenly come together in my year of independent study. Driven by a wide-ranging curiosity, my constant scribbling and my seemingly random readings, workshops, and classes had combined into something that I hadn't planned or anticipated. I had written an article to influence others, and it was being read by many thousands of people. I began to feel a sense of a mission and purpose in my education. Rather than write a novel for my Friends World senior thesis as I'd originally proposed, I decided to write a real thesis—about the impending environmental crisis.

CONNEMARA'S THESIS WAS ACCEPTED in the spring of 1969, and she received her Friends World diploma in the mail. In June we were married at the San Francisco Quaker Meeting, where we had been attending services throughout the year. Immediately after the wedding, we packed up my Volvo and headed back east. We wanted to live in the country, and my faculty adviser had encouraged me to pursue my newfound interest in ecology through an internship at a demonstration woodlot in East Barnard, Vermont, called Hawk's Hill.

On the way, Connemara and I made a detour to attend the War Resisters' International tricentennial conference at Haverford College in Pennsylvania. It was the centennial year of the birth of Gandhi, and the theme of the meeting was "Gandhi's Heritage: Liberation and Revolution." Having felt alienated from the hippies, yippies, and other assorted political types in the Bay Area, I hoped to find a community among this group of people who opposed war in any and all forms. I was also curious to see to what extent the organization's members were thinking about the ecology crisis. But the keynotes and small group discussions mostly focused on the need to resist the Vietnam War. There was nothing on the agenda about the environment.

I saw an opportunity to change this at the closing plenary session. I raised my hand to speak, and the moderator actually called on me. My knees like jelly, I got up in front of the hundreds of people who had gathered for the conference and briefly explained the connection I saw between the war machine and the plundering of the planet, and I proposed that the WRI form an ecology commission. Much to my surprise, my motion was immediately passed, and I was asked to chair the new body.

The most important moment of the conference for me, though, was a chance to talk with Narayan Desai, the son of Gandhi's personal secretary. Desai had grown up in Gandhi's ashram, and had become one of the young leaders of the Indian Peace Brigade. He agreed to meet with three of us in his room late one afternoon, near the end of the conference.

Sunlight poured through the open window of the cramped dorm room where Desai sat on the bare wood floor hunched over a small portable spinning wheel. In his midforties, he was dressed in a plain, white, loose-fitting jacket and pants that looked like pajamas. We were invited to sit on the floor beside him. For the entire conversation, his eyes stayed focused on the thin, uneven thread in front of him, which emerged, almost by magic, from a lump of coarse cotton he held in one hand while he turned the crank of the spinning wheel with the other.

He explained that he was spinning a type of cotton, called khadi, a practice Gandhi had urged the Indian people to take up as an act of resistance against the British colonial government. If the people had native-made cloth for their clothing, they could boycott British-made imports and move one step closer to independence. The spinning wheel soon became a symbol of Gandhi's independence movement; it appeared in the center of the movement's flag.

But Gandhi didn't advocate spinning khadi only as a political act. Desai told us that it took inner spiritual and psychological preparation to remain nonviolent in the midst of hysterical mobs, that patience was necessary for true revolution. He still spun cotton to practice patience: the thread was always breaking.

For the past year, I had been around all sorts of people who called themselves revolutionaries, but none of them was any-thing like Desai. So I asked him what he meant when he talked about "revolution."

He stared out the window into the warm afternoon light for a long moment before he finally responded in a quiet but firm voice. "Revolution is the dynamic process of transform-ing individual virtues into social values."

How, I wondered, could such a revolution happen? A whole generation wasn't going to just start meditating or go to seek the God within at the top of some Aztec temple on their own. I thought about the many ways in which schooling prepared us for the status quo: learning to obey authorities, trying to fit in, learning to comply, doing mindless work, ac-cepting ready answers, never questioning.

What if, instead, school prepared us *for* revolution—not the "revolution" of the druggies or the kids who taunted the cops in the streets, but the kind of revolution Desai was talk-ing about? It was in that room, sitting cross-legged and mes-merized by an emerging thread, that I began to think about teaching not just as a way to earn a living, but as a means to contribute to a better society.

WHEN WE GOT TO VERMONT, Connemara and I found a hundred-year-old farmhouse to rent halfway between East Barnard, where I was going to work on the woodlot, and Han-over, New Hampshire, home of Dartmouth College. The plain wood clapboard house sat on a rise overlooking a large beaver pond and surrounded by deep forest and rolling hills. The land reminded me of Noon's Delight but was much wilder. There were no cows—only deer, grouse, and a very occasional bear. The nearest neighbor was a long mile down a rutted, dirt track.

Connemara set to work on her weaving loom, and I began commuting to my day's work in the woods. Managing a good evergreen woodlot requires regular pruning of the trees, selectively thinning out the smaller ones to allow the healthiest to grow, and conducting periodic harvests. All of this work cannot be done without a network of grass roadways, so my first job was to clear the downed and overhanging trees and the accumulating brush from the roads.

I loved being in the woods again: the filtered sun warming my face, the perfume of the pines, the way they whispered in the wind, the familiar feeling of the axe in my hands as I deftly felled and limbed small trees. I laughed out loud early one September morning as I delivered the first cut into a bowed silver birch and was showered with huge wet drops from leaves still cupping the rainfall from the night before.

But after several months of working in the woodlot every day, I realized that I was much more interested in the sociology of the ecological crisis than in the science. I wanted to know more about how we'd gotten into this mess and what we could do about it. As much as I enjoyed it, I decided to quit my internship at the woodlot, and cut a different path, one through books and paper. Lines from *Portrait of the Artist* came once again to mind. Stephen Dedalus "was destined to learn his own wisdom apart from others." It seemed that I was, too, yet again.

My faculty adviser back at Friends World was understanding, and he continued to offer encouragement, reading suggestions, and feedback, but I was essentially on my own. Every morning after an early breakfast, I'd take my coffee up to the tiny spare bedroom that was my study and plunge into my reading and note taking. After lunch, Connemara and I would strap on our wooden snowshoes—for the fields were now buried in a blanket of white—and set out across the windy and snow-swept hills. As we walked, I'd be distilling disparate thoughts into a set of ideas for my thesis.

Even though I'd written many pages only of notes, I began to feel a growing sense of confidence that I'd likely complete my thesis by the end of the 1969–70 academic year. I needed a plan for what I'd do once I'd graduated. So I turned my attention to getting into a graduate school, with the goal of becoming a certified teacher.

I was hoping to go to the Antioch-Putney Graduate School of Education—the master's in teaching program that Morris Mitchell had established in 1964. Having dropped out of two colleges, and with a Friends World transcript that had weird course titles and no grades, I thought I wouldn't get in anywhere else. Then Michael Maccoby encouraged me to apply to the Harvard Graduate School of Education. I laughed when he made the suggestion, thinking it was a joke, but he was serious. Maccoby had earned his doctorate in psychology at Harvard, and he suggested I meet with one of the professors with whom he'd studied—the sociologist David Riesman, author of a widely praised book on American character, *The Lonely Crowd*.

Early in the new year, I drove to Cambridge to meet with Riesman, who cordially offered to write a letter on my behalf. With this bit of good news, I set to work completing the applications. I opened my essays by quoting Narayan Desai's definition of revolution as "the dynamic process of transforming individual virtues into social values" and explained how I believed teaching was the best way to realize this goal. But by the time I'd dropped my applications in the mail, I couldn't help but think I'd wasted my time—and Riesman's—with the Harvard effort. I should have stuck to my original plan and just applied to Antioch-Putney's program.

I then set to work in earnest finishing my senior thesis. Running seventy pages, it was an elaboration of four articles that I'd already had published on the contradiction between a consumer-driven capitalist economy, fueled by infinite growth and planned obsolescence, and the all-too-finite limits of the environment. But my critique wasn't just economic. I wrote that our acquisitive society—one where people measured the worth of their lives by how much they possessed—was spiritually bankrupt. We had to create an economic and social system focused on the full development of human potential, and transforming education was the first step. Rather than schooling kids to be passive consumers, we needed to develop young people's capacity to think critically and to create.

I had been too busy with my thesis to think much about my grad school applications until one snowy gray day in March, when I trudged out to the mailbox and discovered two envelopes—one from Antioch-Putney and one from Harvard. Returning to our kitchen, I sat down and opened the one from Antioch first. Thank God, I was in. I had a plan for the future. Then, almost perfunctorily, I opened the one from Harvard and read, "I am delighted to inform you that the Committee on Admissions . . ." My loud shriek echoed through the house, and Connemara came running. With a gigantic grin on my face, I showed her the letter.

Later that night, I called my father, whom I hadn't spoken to in months, to tell him the news.

There was a long silence before my father responded. "Harvard?" he said incredulously. "The Harvard Graduate School of Education?"

"Yes, Dad. Harvard."

He couldn't believe it. And neither could I.

I mailed my thesis to my adviser at Friends World in late April, and we began preparing for the move to Massachusetts. We'd loved living in the country, but as we hunted for apartments in Cambridge, we realized how eager we were to go to ethnic restaurants, concerts, and lectures—cultural experiences that we missed from our time in San Francisco.

Then in early May, our enthusiasm curdled into anger and then turned to terror when we heard the news about the Kent State massacre. Four unarmed college kids protesting the Cambodian bombings had been murdered by Ohio National

Guardsmen. Nine others had been wounded. Living in rural Vermont and participating in our weekly silent vigils to protest the war on the Hanover village green, we'd felt righteous—and safe. Now it seemed that no one who opposed the war was safe. I tried to push these thoughts out of my mind as we finished packing our things.

The Harvard program began in July. My stomach was in knots throughout the first two days of orientation. All of the other students in my cohort, I discovered, had gone to elite colleges, and they seemed so much smarter and more self-confident than me. I was sure that the only reason they'd let me in was because of David Riesman's letter.

Immediately after orientation, my anxiety gave way to disillusionment. Every morning, my cohort and I drove out to the suburbs to a public middle school where seventh- and eighth-grade boys and girls were enrolled in a summer school enrichment program. We were divided into small groups of five or six, with each group assigned to a "master teacher" and eighteen or so middle school students. The master teacher's job was to teach demonstration lessons and supervise us as we took turns planning and teaching classes. In the afternoons, we returned to Harvard for lectures on "The Psychology of the Learning Process," followed by small group discussions.

My first disappointment was with my so-called master teacher, whom I'll call Fred. He'd taught social studies for a few years before quitting teaching to return to Harvard for his doctorate. He foisted slick slide shows, film clips, and "innovative" games onto the kids in a pathetic attempt to engage them, but the actual material he taught was far too dry and factual. The students openly displayed their impatience and boredom, whispering and passing notes the minute Fred turned to write something on the blackboard. I couldn't imagine how this guy was going to help me become a good teacher when it was my turn to get in front of them.

The afternoon lectures were also a bust. In the first place, it was ridiculous to try to lecture us after our long mornings of observing, planning, and teaching lessons. We could barely keep our eyes open from exhaustion, and we were stressed out by the experience of being thrown into teaching on day one. Then there was the content. The assumption of many of the lecturers appeared to be that it was the teacher's job to graft a motivation for learning onto otherwise disinterested students. One psychologist advised routinely lying to students. "So when little Johnny picks up that paintbrush in first grade," he said, "you lie to him: you tell him what a great artist he is."

I was outraged. Later, in our small group discussion, I objected vehemently to his advice, arguing that students are naturally curious and have an intrinsic interest in learning. You didn't have to trick them by giving them false feedback. Several members of my group laid into me. One asserted that children, if left to their own devices, wouldn't learn the "important" things—the things adults understand they need to know. Another told me that I was expecting too much from kids to be self-motivated. I was shocked and sickened by their condescension.

When my turn came to teach to our class of kids, I decided to take a big risk and gave them a choice of different projects they could do, all related to Native Americans. I remembered how fascinated I'd been by what I'd learned from Mr. West about the Cheyenne way of life and how much I'd learned from reading *Ishi*, and I thought these eighth graders might enjoy learning about another culture through some hands-on experiences. No more droning, or film reels that broke halfway through.

Borrowing from Montessori, I created different learning corners in the classroom. One cluster set to work creating a model village, based on a written description that I gave them. Another played with crushing maize into flour, and two girls took the sticky mess home and came back the next day with a baked bread of sorts. A couple of boys did their best to make bows and arrows. (I set strict limits on their not trying to shoot them until after school—and then only aiming at trees, not people!)

I felt a huge wave of relief when my three days of teaching were over. The kids had seemed engrossed, and while their projects were pretty mediocre, there hadn't been any major screwups. Maybe a modified Montessori approach to middle and high school could work. Still, I worried about what my master teacher, Fred, and the other graduate students in my group would say when we met to review my classes.

Fred started by asking me what my learning objective had been. That was easy. I explained that I'd wanted the kids to gain an appreciation for different aspects of Native American culture. "But what about the content?" Fred pressed. "The geographical distribution of the different tribes, the American government's policies toward Native Americans, and so on? Don't you think you should have taught some factual information?"

My face burned. Being chastised in front of my classmates was humiliating. Maybe I should have done more "real teaching," as the others had. But then another student in our group piped up. "Yeah, he should've included more content in his lessons, but the kids didn't give Wagner any behavior problems." Fred ignored the comment.

In his final evaluation at the end of the summer, Fred wrote, "Since Tony strives for free and full development for himself, he also seeks that for kids, so that the parameters of the teaching situation do not extend to the full range of public schools." Was that obfuscating Harvard-talk for saying that I cared too much about kids? Yes, I was committed to nurturing students' curiosity and creativity, and I wanted them to have the kinds of learning experiences in schools that I wished I'd had. But did that mean that most schools wouldn't want me as a teacher? The veiled critique in the assessment haunted me.

I was relieved to get out of Fred's classroom when the summer program ended, and absolutely elated when, at the end of August, the letter came from Friends World informing me that my thesis had been accepted. My diploma was in the envelope as well—number twelve from the college. Out of three classes totaling more than a hundred students who had started at the same time as me or the year before, only eleven others had managed to finish and earn a degree.

I'd done it. I had essentially created a college education that fit my interests and ways of learning, and I had succeeded where most others had not.

In September, my classmates were each assigned master teachers in suburban schools to work with for the academic year, but I didn't want to risk getting another "Fred" and so persuaded the director of Harvard's teacher-training program to let me instead seek out my own master teacher. I found a social studies teacher at Brookline High School who taught at a school-within-a-school set up for kids seeking more of a say in their learning. The students could choose different projects in some of their courses, and there were weekly community meetings where students and teachers sounded off about concerns. I was both pleased and relieved when this teacher, whom I'll call Allen, agreed to work with me.

During my year-long practice teaching, I had to take classes, too, though now I had my pick of courses—anything offered throughout the university. But I felt increasingly anxious as the start of the semester approached. How could a two-time college dropout survive in rigorous academic classes at Harvard?

It didn't take long to find out. Except for one required class on teaching methods, where there were endless lectures on what history teachers needed to cover and how to choose the right textbook, I thoroughly enjoyed the courses I selected. There were no quizzes, no final exams, nothing to memorize and regurgitate, only papers to write.

One standout course was taught by an aging, eccentric anthropology professor. There were only four of us in the class, and it met once a week for three hours in the evening. For reasons that were never clear to me, the professor was obsessed with different theories of history—why events happened. He would lecture us for the entire three hours, and everything he said went right over our heads. But he gave us a research assignment—an analysis of one thinker's theory of history—that turned out to be the most difficult academic challenge I'd ever undertaken.

I did it to myself, though. For my paper's subject, I chose Karl Marx, not because I thought of myself as a communist, but simply because I wanted to understand the work of a man who had so influenced the world and was quoted by so many of my peers. I had no idea how hard it would be to understand and then to explain in writing such a complex theory of history. But as I dug more deeply into his work, I discovered a side of Marx that none of my New Left acquaintances seemed to know. Beneath all the rhetoric, and long before he became a revolutionary, Marx was a humanist and philosopher. The goal of his revolution was to liberate the human spirit from the mechanized oppressiveness of the looming Industrial Revolution. "The free development of each," he wrote, "is a condition for the free development of all." Yet the quote of his that most struck me—and came to guide me in my work for many decades—was about how to be effective in creating change: "To make the frozen circumstances dance, you have to sing to them in their own melody."

It wasn't just the poetry of Marx's words that spoke to me.

It was the idea that fundamental change begins with *under-standing*, with listening carefully and closely to the "melody" of the status quo. When I became a full-time teacher, I looked for opportunities to "sing" to my students in their own melody—to try to deeply understand each student's interests and aspirations. This was equally important when, later in my career, I interviewed business and community leaders and tried to translate what I'd learned from them into a language—a melody—educators could understand, for my book *The Global Achievement Gap*.

David Riesman's course, American Character and Social Structure, was another great intellectual experience. From the nineteenth-century classic *Democracy in America* by Alexis de Tocqueville to contemporary works in sociology and anthropology like *The Levittowners*, *Street Corner Society*, and *Tally's Corner*, he immersed us in the study of the diverse cultures and communities that make up America. The class—with a total enrollment of more than a hundred—was divided into small sections of about twelve students for weekly discussions. Mine was led by a teaching assistant named Jay Featherstone. Jay's artful and engaging way of teaching was truly masterful.

A round-faced man with a ready smile, shaggy eyebrows, and wavy, dark hair that often flopped into his face, Jay was in his midthirties when I first met him. He had earned his undergraduate degree at Harvard, and he was rumored to have been working for some time on a PhD thesis about John

Dewey, but for the past few years, he had been earning his living as an editor for the *New Republic*, where he'd published numerous articles on education. Now he had a year-long fellowship at Harvard's new Kennedy School of Government.

Jay believed that the art of teaching required constructing the conditions for thoughtful conversation and reflection among students. He never lectured and would often start our discussions by simply asking, "So what did you think of this week's reading?" Beyond that, he rarely spoke in our section meetings, and when he did, it was to throw out a thoughtful or penetrating question. He wasn't looking for a "right" answer, though—only to make us think more deeply. "So what similarities do you see between the lives of the Italians in *Street Corner Society* and the African American street corner culture in *Tally's Corner?*" he'd asked. When we students were universally repelled by the description in *The Levittowners* of American's first large-scale tract-home development, Jay pushed us to consider a contrarian point of view: "Can you think of some reasons why so many people said they enjoyed living there?" He always showed respect and interest in what we had to say, often nudging us to better explain or defend a point of view. Like Mr. Edwards, Jay modeled an approach to teaching and learning that I aspired to emulate.

For my forty-page final paper for Riesman's course, I decided to analyze how schools shaped a child's social character, and I described the ways suburban public schools were changing as America seemed to be evolving from a blue-collar industrial economy to a white-collar knowledge economy. "Old" urban schools had chairs lined up in rows, with teachers barking commands like factory foremen, while in "New" suburban schools, kids often sat in circles, and teachers cajoled kids into learning with competitions, acting more like midlevel managers in a corporation. I concluded that, though suburban schools appeared more relaxed and informal, they nevertheless contributed nothing to the development of students' real interests, or to their capacity to think critically. A different model was needed, I argued.

In his comments on my paper, Jay wrote: "The most fascinating and original part of this paper is your extended contrast between the Old and the New education. . . . Your point that schools are changing, but that the changes are problematic themselves is new and convincing." He singled out my conclusion, where I advocated for a fundamentally new approach to education, for special praise: "Part IV, 'Active Education,' is one of the best and most succinct statements of humanistic education I've read." Jay then went on for three single-spaced typed pages detailing the strengths and weaknesses in my observations and argument. He finished with a note of encouragement: "A stimulating introduction to a work in progress. I can't tell you how much I have enjoyed you and your contributions to the section."

For the first time in my life, I felt deeply affirmed as both a thinker and a writer. A teacher whom I respected highly had described ways in which my work had been "fascinating and original." I was beginning to discover my capacity for scholarship and a love of challenging learning experiences.

Despite my worries at the start of the academic year, the lowest grade I received in my for-credit courses was an A minus. All of the writing I'd done as a student at Friends World had prepared me better than I'd imagined. I had proved to myself that I could "do" school, and do it well. But it was in Jay's other class, which I took for no credit, where I learned the most.

At the time, the Kennedy School of Government offered a series of semester-long noncredit seminars on various contemporary issues. Jay's was on current issues in education. We read a book a week for his class, all of them written by progressive educators: John Holt, Herbert Cole, Jonathan Kozol, George Dennison, Sylvia Ashton Warner, and others. Every class erupted into a lively discussion of questions provoked by the readings and by Jay, questions that continue to be central to my work: *Are there different ways to be a good teacher? What is the best way to know whether one approach to teaching is better than another? What is the right balance between introducing students to new material versus letting them choose what they want to learn? Will a progressive approach to learning in high school be an adequate preparation for college? How must schools of education change to better prepare future teachers?*

Jay also introduced us to what became one of my most cherished books on education—Elwyn Richardson's *In the Early World*. Richardson taught white and Maori children in a one-room school in rural New Zealand. He believed that all children have "a gift of seeing clearly and a talent for expressing their vision with truth and power. . . . It is there in all children, I feel, but it will not come to the surface unless it is recognized and developed."

Trained as a scientist, Richardson taught students to be close observers of their immediate natural environment—the habits of the bees that lived near the school, or the structure of a fly's wings. He then urged them to express themselves creatively, capturing their observations in artwork. The kids worked in clay, linoleum prints, and woodcuts, as well as different forms of writing and drama. A student might first do a woodcut depicting a wing, and then write a poem about flight to explore the theme further. In daily class discussions, Richardson encouraged his students to criticize their own and one another's work, and over time they developed the ability to pick out details in a painting or particular lines in a poem that were especially powerful or original. Students began putting out a monthly school magazine, choosing the best art and writing to publish in it.

Richardson's approach to teaching self-expression was an important influence on me when I later became a high school English teacher. However, at this time, I planned to teach social studies. Caught up in the upheavals of the 1960s, I believed that one of the most important roles for a teacher was to expose students to new ideas that might help them to think more critically about their world. I hadn't yet figured out that a teacher can accomplish the same goal through discussions of literature. Nor did I then understand the value of teaching writing as a means of understanding the world and oneself—despite how critical this had been to my own metamorphosis from failing student to Harvard master's candidate. And so, when my turn finally came to plan and teach a full curriculum unit for the social studies class at Brookline High, where I had been observing all year, I decided to teach Eric Fromm's *The Sane Society*. Fromm had offered me a profound new way of understanding the world, and I wanted to give my students a similar experience.

My choice of Fromm was influenced by having read Paulo Freire's *Pedagogy of the Oppressed*, not for any class but on my own. Freire was a Portuguese educator and philosopher who taught literacy to Brazilian peasants. Rejecting what he called the "banking" method of education—treating students as empty vessels to which "deposits" of knowledge must be made—Freire taught adults to read and write by engaging them in discussions of subjects that were emotionally charged for his learners, such as "power" and "authority," and the people and institutions that shaped and constrained their lives. I wanted to see if I could expand my high school students' consciousness of their world through dialogue, as Freire had done with his adult students.

For my weeklong unit, I wanted students to understand what Fromm called "the pathology of normalcy." I assigned them the first two chapters of the book as homework. Both chapters began with a question: chapter 1 asked "Are We Sane?" and chapter 2, "Can a Society Be Sick?" Each day, I arranged students' chairs into a circle and, following Jay's model, tried to kick off a class discussion by asking them what they thought of a quote from the book that I'd written on the board. Blackboards, I'd come to realize, didn't always have be instruments of torture.

The first day, I'd neatly chalked up a quote I thought would get things going: "We . . . have created a greater material wealth than any other society in the history of the human race. Yet we have managed to kill off millions of our population in an arrangement which we call 'war.'" The students dutifully read the quote and raised their hands to condemn wars in general and Vietnam in particular. Blinding flash of the obvious. I lacked the experience to ask a good, provocative Jay-like follow-up question like "Was it wrong to go to war against Hitler?"

The class "discussions" went on like this for the next four days. I grew increasingly impatient. On the last day, out of desperation, I asked my students: "What does the 'pathology of normalcy' mean to you?" Fromm had described the concept in chapter 2.

Not one hand was raised. The silence that greeted my question totally unnerved me. They'd read about this concept in Fromm's book, so I didn't understand their lack of responsiveness.

I quickly moved to the next question on my prepared list: "Are we sane?" More silence.

After an agonizing minute or two, one boy tried to help

me out by offering, "Well, I guess that depends on what you mean by 'sane.'" After a week of discussions, I'd assumed the kids had gotten Fromm's basic idea that there are norms for judging the sanity of a society. Had they learned nothing?

Exasperated, I jumped to what I believed to be my payoff question: "What would a society that was more sane look like?" No hands, just fidgeting and glances at the clock.

I dismissed the class early.

And I thought that being a good teacher was easy: just ask great questions like Jay's. But the kids had been as bored in my classes on Fromm as they had been in Fred's back in the summer.

Part of the problem—easy to see in retrospect—was that I had not checked to see if students had even understood the complex material I'd given them to read. Most probably didn't. In fact, the material wasn't even appropriate for high school kids. And when I posed a question where the students' silence might have been taken as an indication of thoughtfulness, I swiftly rushed to the next question on my prepared list, without giving them sufficient time to reflect or to offer an opinion. I had not really learned the importance of "wait time."

My master teacher, Allen, had popped in a couple of times for a few minutes, and then disappeared. He'd evidently decided that my week of teaching meant more free periods for him. But I didn't need him in the room to tell me that my first foray into teaching high school had been a disaster. Worse, I had no clue then what I should have done differently.

. . .

DESPITE THE WORKLOAD AT HARVARD, Connemara and I found time to explore the rich cultural opportunities available in our Cambridge. I was entranced by my first introduction to early Renaissance music at a performance by the New York Musica, whose artists danced, played, and sang in period costume. Judith Jamison's electrifying athleticism with the Alvin Ailey American Dance Theater was my first experience of ballet. But it was a lecture in the spring of 1971 by an Italian social activist named Danilo Dolci that had the deepest influence on me.

Known as the "Gandhi of Sicily," Dolci began advocating for the poor in southern Italy in the 1950s. He used hunger strikes, sit-down protests, and nonviolent demonstrations to call attention to the extreme poverty of the region and the close connections between the Mafia and the government. Memories of my conversation with Narayan Desai were still vivid, and so I was eager to hear Dolci speak about his activism.

As Connemara and I walked through Harvard Square toward the church where Dolci was to speak that evening in April, we saw sickening evidence of how the antiwar movement had turned away from nonviolence as a strategy. Virtually every glass storefront in the square was boarded up, having been smashed by rioters, with slogans like END THE FUCKING WAR, OFF THE PIGS, and FREE THE BLACK PANTHERS spray-painted onto sheet after sheet of plywood.

The church was packed. And the audience, which consisted mostly of students, seemed to pay close attention as Dolci described his tactic of the "reverse strike," in which he encouraged unemployed peasants to work for no pay, repairing impassable Sicilian roads. They had all been arrested for obstructing the thoroughfares, but their cases had gained national attention, and the government had been pressured to step in to improve the roads. The story was riveting.

Then, at the end of his talk, he shared how, every year, he took a few weeks to go to Urbino to study and play recorders with his family. The mood in the room shifted. Radicals were incensed. One yelled out, "How could you do that with all of the suffering around you?"

Dolci replied calmly, "What is the revolution for—if not for music, if not for beauty?"

Maybe, I thought as we made our way home that night, I should spend less time trying to point out all the evils of society to my future students and spend more time helping them to find the things in their lives that give them meaning and joy.

I SOMETIMES WONDER what would have become of me if I had not learned of Friends World College from Bill Kunstler. I doubt that I would've tried a conventional college for a third time. I had felt so burned by my high school and two previous college experiences that I was convinced I would neither be happy nor succeed in any place called "school." Friends World provided a stark contrast by enabling me to discover and pursue my own real interests. I understood this to be a necessary ingredient to learning by the time I started the master's program at Harvard, but I hadn't yet translated my Friends World experience into a philosophy of teaching. I was missing a key element.

The most fundamental lesson of my Friends World experience was learning that having an interest wasn't enough. You also have to develop the muscles of self-discipline and concentration needed to pursue your interest and deepen your knowledge and understanding. Interests are frequently discovered through exploration—a kind of play. If the interests are genuine, they can become passions over time. But self-discipline and concentration are required to sustain these passions and enable them to deepen to a sense of purpose. Without these capabilities, intrinsic motivation can take you only so far. You need to persist over time in order to experience growing satisfaction in your own evolving mastery of an art form or intellectual inquiry. This satisfaction deepens your interest, which in turn strengthens discipline and concentration, until you start to feel satisfaction in practice and study, too. It is an upward, mutually reinforcing spiral.

The freedom that Friends World offered its students was double-edged and difficult. Most students couldn't cope and left. Connemara and I took a big risk when we sought to create our own independent study programs. To succeed in an environment with few external demands or constraints, we had to develop self-discipline, and we had to learn to focus—to concentrate. In my last two years at Friends World, I'd sought good teachers and people who inspired me as I pursued my interests in ecology, writing, and photography. The more discipline I gained, the stronger my writing, acquisition of knowledge, and intellectual inquisitiveness became, which in turn motivated me to continue developing my self-discipline.

Then there was Harvard—a decidedly mixed blessing. I'd discovered that I could master challenging intellectual content in a rigorous academic environment—but only when I could choose my courses and assignments. Regular opportunities for collaborative inquiry and discussion were also vital to my learning there. When all of these elements were in place, I thrived.

However, my required education school classes were a complete waste of time. The professors who lectured us were poor models of effective teaching and contributed little to our development as teachers. I wondered if any of them had ever actually taught in a high school. And my so-called practice teaching had taught me absolutely nothing about how to be a teacher. There, my motivation, self-discipline, and good intentions weren't enough. I lacked coaching and useful, regular feedback—things that all good teachers give to their students. But I didn't know that. Not yet.

Throughout my last semester at the Graduate School of Education, I was also busy researching job opportunities. Inspired by Desai and Dolci, I no longer sought to retreat to the countryside and teach in an exclusive private school. I now wanted to try to make a difference in public schools, where progressive teaching practices were few and far between. The challenge was to find a public high school where there would be at least some receptivity to my ideas on education, as well as the freedom to experiment.

At the time, a few suburban school systems, like Brookline's, had begun to establish school-within-a-school programs for high school students seeking more of a say in their education. I heard somewhere that such a program had been established at Walter Johnson High School, in suburban Montgomery County, Maryland, just outside of Washington, D.C. The previous year a group of tenth graders had marched into principal Donald Reddick's office, sat down on the floor, and declared that they were going to drop out if they could not learn the things that most interested them. So he set the kids loose, creating a totally unstructured independent study program for them.

I wrote to Dr. Reddick and expressed an interest in working in what had come to be called the Project in Education, or PIE. He replied instantly, saying that he would be delighted to have me join the program. It took months for my job application to work its way through the bureaucracy of the Montgomery County Public Schools—which had more than 120,000 students—but by early May, I had signed a contract and made plans to move to Bethesda, where Walter Johnson was located. I didn't bother sticking around for graduation.

I was twenty-five, married, credentialed with a master's in

teaching from Harvard, and about to start my first real full-time job—things that were supposed to mean I was a "grown-up." But I didn't feel like a grown-up inside. Though I had lots of ideas about what education should be, when it came right down to it, I had no idea how I was going to learn to be a good teacher, someone who could engage a class with great questions and make a difference in the lives of students. Someone like Jay Featherstone.

SIX

Mastering My Craft

BUILT IN 1956 TO FEED THE EXPANDING POSTWAR SPRAWL in what had once been endless cow pastures, Walter Johnson was the quintessential suburban high school. Housing developments spread out in every direction from the campus, yielding an enrollment of about eighteen hundred students. Connemara and I had found a brick ranch to rent about four miles away in one of the older developments, where the houses were much smaller and less expensive.

Feeling both eager and anxious, I stepped through the main entrance for the first day of faculty meetings at the start of the 1971–72 academic year. Eager to begin my career as a teacher. Anxious about meeting my students and trying to figure out how I was going to work with them. I belatedly realized that I should have visited the school before accepting the job. I had no idea what my students were going to be like, what would matter to them.

I made my way down the hall a short distance to the door marked OFFICE and walked in. Directly in front of me there was a long counter, and behind it, three secretaries busy clickety-clacking away on their IBM Selectrics. One finally looked up, asked my name, and then directed me down a corridor to the principal's office. I was struck by the layers of secretaries and the rabbit's warren I had to navigate to get there.

Don Reddick soon emerged from his inner sanctum. Very tall and tanned, he was nattily dressed in a charcoal suit, crisp white shirt, and striped blue tie. His graying hair, which was trimmed in a slightly moplike early-Beatles style, covered the tops of his ears and softened an otherwise imposing figure.

"Great to have you here, Tony," he said with a big smile and a comfortable handshake that made him seem more teddy bear than grizzly. "I just know you'll make the program work for the kids."

On the first day of classes, I got my first look at the rooms designated for the Project in Education program—two tiny former guidance counselor offices with a small seating area adjacent that appeared to have been furnished with castoffs from the town dump: two torn and tattered tan couches, a couple of lounge chairs with frayed arms, a stained brown rug, and several ragged psychedelic posters Scotch-taped to the windowless beige cinder-block wall. The ceiling's fluorescent tubes were off, the only light coming from a standing lamp in one corner. The room felt cavelike.

As my eyes grew accustomed to the dim lighting, I began to make out eight students sprawled across the chairs and couches. Long hair on both the boys and the girls, and everybody dressed in hippie clothing, they were a disheveled bunch. I introduced myself as Tony—a studied effort to be accessible—and began chatting with the two students who looked up and appeared halfway interested in the newcomer.

They quickly filled me in on the disaster of the previous year. Four teachers—one each for English, history, science, and math—had been cajoled by Dr. Reddick to work with the students on an independent study project of their choice. But according to the kids, the requirements were too rigid, and they soon stopped going to the meetings with their teachers, who really didn't want to meet with them anyway. When everything fell apart, the students were assigned to regular classes, but they'd rarely gone.

This year, I was the only teacher assigned to PIE. Students would earn English and social studies credits with me, but they'd have to go to regular classes for their other academic subjects, and they were clearly dreading it. One boy said that he couldn't wait "to get out of this shithole."

What was I going to do with these demoralized kids? And with the forty or so others who were theoretically enrolled in the program but didn't even bother to hang out in the PIE room? It appeared to me that the independent study program and its students were teetering on a precipice. The kids whom I met that day seemed as though they'd drop out at the slightest provocation. If they did, this education "experiment" would be deemed a failure and terminated. I felt furious with myself for not having asked more questions before taking the job.

I put out word that I wanted to meet with every student who was supposed to be enrolled in PIE. I suggested that we set up a regular conference schedule, where I'd meet with each student once a week for a half-hour conference to develop their independent study proposal and discuss their progress. They seemed to warm to this idea, and I was soon meeting regularly with forty-five kids, who ranged in age from fifteen to seventeen. I established the basic requirement that in order to earn an English or social studies credit, students had to come to the weekly conferences and do a combination of reading and writing for a minimum of six hours per week, but that what they read and wrote would be entirely their decision.

The PIE students were a diverse bunch. Some were musicians, ballet dancers, drama geeks, gymnasts. They wanted a more flexible schedule, freedom to read what interested them, and the opportunity to pursue creative assignments. I encouraged them to experiment with a variety of writing genres—just as Mr. Edwards had done with me at Searing. With these motivated kids, I was mostly a cheerleader, sometimes a coach. They were far too busy to hang out in the PIE room. The main challenge was getting them to take their writing as seriously as their other pursuits.

The students who camped out in the PIE room for most of their day were an altogether different challenge. Judging from their glassy, bloodshot eyes, many were coming to school stoned. They attended their math and science classes sporadically and, half the time, "forgot" about their conferences with me. When they did come, they usually didn't have very much work to show me.

With this group, I had to start much more slowly and be more experimental. I encouraged them to keep a journal, as a way to begin working on their writing. Each week, at their conference, when I'd ask what they were interested in reading, often the reply was a vacant stare or vague answer—"novels" or "books about World War II." When they proposed a general topic, I'd suggest a reading to get them started. At their next conference, I'd ask them about the reading and request that they share one entry from their journal.

Gradually I realized that with this group, as well as with the growing number of "in-school dropouts"—kids who were referred to PIE by the guidance counselors because they came to school every day but never attended classes—my job was to listen carefully and conscientiously for sparks of interest. Once I discovered a spark, I'd kindle it—to affirm the interest, no matter what it was—until it ignited into something that resembled real learning. Sometimes it would take several months for a student to reveal a topic that she or he really wanted to learn about. In order to share something that mattered to them, these students had to trust that I would take them seriously.

I remember a lean and lanky boy—I'll call him Mike—who hung out with the jocks near the gym all day. In our initial conferences, he would slouch down in the chair next to my desk, stretch out his legs, and shrug his shoulders when I asked him what he was interested in learning. It was months before he began to talk about his passion for cars. Finally, when he realized that I was actually listening to him, he told me that he wanted to read about the difference between carbureted versus fuel-injected engines. We went over to the library together, and I helped him find some books. With my regular feedback, Mike eventually wrote a lucid paper on the topic and, after graduating, sought training as a mechanic.

Guidance counselors also sometimes referred students to me who they thought had learning disabilities. "Sally" was one such student. She was a twelfth grader, and I was told that she had difficulty reading and writing and couldn't function in a regular English class. She appeared for her first conference dressed in neat jeans and a prim print shirt, signaling that she was no PIE kid. As she sat down next to my desk, her dark eyes darted around the room, like those of a cornered cat, and her shoulders were practically touching her earlobes. When I began to talk with her about her previous English classes, she looked away and half whispered that she just couldn't stand all the pressure. Her face softened noticeably and her shoulders dropped when I told her that she would be able to read the books she wanted to, and that there would be no tests or deadlines. The same went for the writing assignments, I said.

The first book Sally read at my suggestion was *Of Mice and Men*. She took her time with the novel, but she loved it. Afterward she wrote a good paper on the question I'd posed to her about the ending: Did George do the right thing when he killed his best friend, Lennie? She liked the challenge of trying to tackle a question that didn't have a right or wrong answer. It did not take too many months before Sally came to enjoy reading and writing for the first time in her life and—most important—to do so competently.

Partway through the year, Sally confided in me that her parents wanted her to get training as a CPA because she got good grades in math. "But just because I'm good at it doesn't mean I actually like it," she said.

From some of her journal entries, I learned that she loved crafts and working with her hands, and so I mentioned a crafts college in New England that might interest her. She applied, was accepted, and ultimately managed to persuade her parents to allow her to go. But Sally came back a year later to say that she had decided to become an architect instead. She attended a local community college for a semester to earn the grades and credits that she needed to get into an architecture school, where she flourished.

Mike and Sally weren't the only students with whom I started to experience a sense of success as a teacher. By the end of my second year as the PIE teacher, the program's enrollment had grown noticeably, and I was especially proud of my two years of work with a young woman whom I'll call Jane—one of the scraggly kids I'd met in the PIE room on my first day.

Jane wore her stringy blond hair unfettered, hanging halfway down her back. Her thin, delicate arms peeked out from the sleeves of her motley collection of tired tie-dyed T-shirts, every one of which topped a pair of torn jeans. But what set her apart from most of her peers were the red bandanna she wore knotted around her neck and her cowboy boots.

I'd often observed Jane cocooning in the corner lounge chair of the PIE room, secretively scribbling away in a small notebook. Yet she'd come to our first few one-on-one conferences with no work in hand. Rather than chastising her for not bringing any writing, though, I simply wondered what she wrote when she was in the PIE room. "Oh, just some stuff," she said, blushing. "You know, poetry and stuff."

"I'd love to see some of your work," I replied gently.

The next time we met, Jane came clutching scraps of paper with phrases and images scratched on them in pen. Reluctantly, she offered a couple of pieces to read. I tried to encourage her by pointing out several striking lines, and then urged her to consider combining some of her especially vivid images of nature into a finished poem.

That semester, Jane completed several drafts of poems, and it became clear that she had some talent as a poet. As the year went on, I heard from her teachers that she'd also begun to attend her math and science classes more consistently and to turn in assignments. But it was not until near the end of the year that she finally acquiesced to my nudges to try *revising* her poems, doing multiple drafts and honing her language with each version.

It was during this time that I began to realize how many of

my PIE student regulars were socially immature. In their conversations with fellow students, they often sounded more like middle schoolers than high schoolers—trash-talking the non-PIE kids for being "uncool" and acting like "sheep." They seemed to think they were more "real" than all the other kids. Yet beneath the banter, they were fragile and afraid of showing vulnerability—of exposing who they really were to one another, much less to an outsider, including me. Over the course of the year, they became more comfortable sharing their interests and writing with me in our conferences, but they were still extremely reluctant to reveal their inner lives to their peers. And they never spoke about having hopes or dreams for their future.

I wasn't sure how best to address this as their teacher. I'd been holding regular PIE "town meetings" with the kids—an idea I'd borrowed from *Summerhill* and from the Brookline school-within-a-school where I'd been a practice teacher. At the meetings we mostly talked about housekeeping stuff, like where to get better furniture and how to divvy up cleaning chores. But near the end of the first semester, I took a risk and proposed that we start a weekly writers' workshop, where kids would share their writing and listen to other students' responses. It would be entirely voluntary, I emphasized. Only a few students, including Jane, came to the first couple of meetings. And strikingly, they flat-out refused to read any of their work aloud. So I led them in a general conversation about writing technique.

After the third or fourth meeting, however, everything began to change. With some encouragement from me, Jane read one of her first revised poems to the group. Her audience was in awe. They had no clue that Jane was interested in poetry, and they praised her work effusively. Others began to bring in journal entries, poems, and stories to read, and soon a dozen students were regularly coming to the workshop.

My next job was to help students understand that just giving one another praise wasn't necessarily going to help them to become better writers. I explained that all writers need to understand the gap between what they are trying to communicate in their work—*what they intend*—and what an audience takes away from the writing—*what they actually achieve*. Our first job as listeners was to understand the author's intention and then to simply respond to the work by saying where and when and how that intention seemed best realized, and where it was less clear, or confusing.

Gradually students began to understand that the opportunity to hear and comment on one another's work really was helping them to become better writers. It was fascinating to see how much my students' writing improved by having an audience other than a lone teacher to write for, and I was intrigued by the fact that the more the students shared their writing, the more diverse their writing became. They would see and hear techniques that worked for another kid, and then experiment with those techniques themselves. Jane never missed a week, and by year two, she routinely brought writing to read aloud to the workshop.

The students' writing also became more intimate over time. They wrote about their loves, their experiences with sex, their bodies. In one early "icebreaker" moment, a girl read a poem about her breasts, ending with the declaration "Why look at my tits? My hands are much nicer." Another student shared a journal entry that began "I have this conflict, whether to let people come close to my serious side or whether to show them the fool side." We often ended up having thoughtful discussions of the writers' chosen topics, not just their writing techniques. I observed that the students who participated in the workshop dropped the bantering and posturing that peppered their conversations outside of class and were more self-assured.

I recalled Elwyn Richardson's description of his teaching and recognized that I was learning to teach writing in a way that he might have—as a kind of collaborative inquiry with my students about what constitutes effective and evocative writing. At the end of the first year, I decided to borrow an idea from his book: I suggested to my students that we publish a PIE literary magazine, with each student picking a favorite piece or two and working to polish it for publication. A couple of art students volunteered to design a cover and illustrations, while others typed up the texts to be mimeographed. Though the first edition was only half a dozen 8.5-by-11-inch sheets folded and stapled in the middle, the students were delighted—especially Jane, who had contributed more writing than anyone else—and our literary magazine became an annual publication.

IT WAS IN MY THIRD YEAR at PIE that the program really took off. Between guidance counselors' referrals and more students requesting the program, enrollment mushroomed. And word of my student-centered approach was getting out. Three senior boys came to me at the start of the year and asked if I would be their AP (advanced placement) English teacher. The head of the English Department was then the only AP English teacher, and his approach to teaching the class was highly structured. These boys wanted some choice of what to read, and they wanted to have discussions about the books, rather than having to listen to lectures. We met once or twice a week for an hour after school, with the students writing essays on each literary work they picked. I had looked at the AP English test and knew that specific texts were not required, but I had never taught AP English before, and I worried about how well they would do on the test in May. I needn't have, though. All three received the top score of 5.

Partway through the third year I made the case to Dr. Reddick that we needed a second PIE teacher, and so a young woman, who was a new teacher, was assigned to us for two periods a day. Knowing that I would have some help, and buoyed by my work with the AP students, I decided to ask the English Department head to assign me one "regular" English class to teach. I was ready to see if the teaching methods I was developing would work in a conventional classroom.

Too late, I realized that I should have been much more

careful with what I'd wished for. The head of the department gave me a class of thirty-nine students, when the average class size for English teachers was closer to twenty-five. I wondered if this was payback for my having "stolen" three of his AP kids. But I made it work. Early in the semester, I told my students that they would take turns in pairs leading discussions of short stories from an anthology, and that I would meet with them when their turn came to help them prepare discussion questions. I also explained to the students that they would have three weeks at the end of the semester to do an extended independent study project.

I met with each student to help them develop their independent study plan and encouraged them to explore genuine interests. As with the PIE kids, I said any topic was okay, so long as it involved some research and writing. At the end of the semester, they presented summaries of their work to their classmates. Their presentations were strikingly diverse—everything from how to fly a model airplane to a biography of baseball player Walter Johnson, the school's namesake.

When I reviewed the written evaluations of the course that I'd asked students to complete, my eyes filled with tears. So many of them remarked on how this was the first opportunity they'd been given since elementary school to pursue a passion in school. I felt a deep sense of satisfaction and accomplishment. I'd come a long way from my first humiliating flop as a student teacher in Brookline.

But I still had much to learn about teaching, and I made some miserable mistakes along the way. My work with Jane, the budding poet, turned out to be among one of these mistakes, I came to see. Through her two years as my student, Jane had developed increasing subtlety and skillfulness as a poet. She earned the English credits that she needed to graduate and announced that she hoped to study poetry at the local community college. Watching her walk across the stage to receive her diploma, I'd felt incredibly proud of her and of the work we had done together. However, a year or so after she'd graduated, I received a letter from her. Riddled with misspellings and incomplete sentences, with no rhyme or reason to her paragraphing, it appeared to have been written by someone only semiliterate. She said nothing about college, only that she was continuing to write poetry. I assumed that if she had tried college, she would likely have floundered. I had failed Jane as a teacher.

Encouraging students to just pursue their interests wasn't enough. I had to help them develop the skills that they would need to succeed in the future and to understand why those skills were important.

BY YEAR FOUR, the PIE program enrollment had grown to two hundred students. The other PIE teacher, who had become a full-time social studies teacher in the program, and I were now able to meet one-on-one with students only every other week, and for a shorter period of time, and so we began offering a variety of seminars to supplement the conferences.

Then, with no warning, we were both told that due to budget cuts we each had to teach two regular classes outside of the PIE program. I wasn't sure how we'd handle the extra workload. In one of the classes, I used methods similar to the ones I'd used successfully with my overflowing regular English class the year before. The other class, though, was a very different story.

We met the last period of the day in a far corner of the school, near the place where the few vocational education kids in the school attended shop classes. And it was a group of these students whom I was assigned to teach. Most were twelfth-grade boys who had already had to stay back a year in school due to failing courses—kids whom the other kids referred to with disdain as "greasers." They all worked part-time jobs after school—pumping gas or bagging groceries—and their only goal seemed to be to get out of school as quickly as possible, with as little work as possible. My question about what kinds of things they might like to read for English was met with sullen silence and stony stares.

I finally persuaded the class to read a short story, but when I tried to lead the discussion of it, the students went mute. No one raised a hand, and several put their heads down on their desks. One boy finally demanded in an exasperated tone, "Why do you want to make us talk? Why don't you just lecture us like all the other teachers?"

I was at a loss. In an effort to engage them, I decided to ask the students about what they did after school and on weekends. It took persistence, but I finally discovered there was, indeed, one topic they were passionate about (and willing to discuss): their problems with cops.

Almost every Friday and Saturday night, students at our school or a neighboring one would hold a keg party. Rumors would spread throughout the corridors at the end of each week about where that weekend's parties would be held, and where hundreds of high school students would turn up. Things seemed to always get out of hand at these events. Students who couldn't get into the house hosting the party would stand outside and drink on sidewalks all over the neighborhood. Bottles were thrown across the streets. There would often be a fight or, worse, a drag race, which would end with one of the drivers seeing how much of a front lawn he could tear up with the wheels of his car. Then the police would come, shout through their bullhorns for everyone to disperse, and throw tear gas into the crowd when their orders were ignored.

The students were furious at the cops. They said they were never given enough warning to leave before the tear gas was used. They also felt that the cops were unnecessarily brutal. A number of the students said they'd been hit over the head with clubs on multiple occasions as they were trying to get back to their cars to leave. So I suggested we hold mock county council hearings to examine the problem.

Students liked the idea and quickly decided who would be on the council, and who would play the roles of parents, teenagers, and the police. When I insisted that students had to do research by interviewing the parents of some of the kids who'd given parties and the lieutenant at the local police station in order to accurately represent their points of view, they agreed. Several students who were role-playing the police perspective even arranged to go on a squad car "ride-along" one evening. When they came back, all they could talk about was the cool stuff in the cars and how nice the cops had been.

On the basis of notes taken during their interviews, students were able to give informed and accurate testimony, learning both how to listen and how to communicate information to others. Those playing the role of the members of the county council asked thoughtful and probing questions, gaining critical-thinking skills. The problem of students' distrust of authorities emerged when some of the students played themselves in the hearings, so afterward we discussed their "testimony," and many of them opened up. They began to see that there was more to their problems with the cops than police brutality. The parties and confrontations were an opportunity to display their strength when they felt weak and helpless. They were perceived to be "losers" by many of the peers and adults in their lives, and they refused to be ignored. Scaring the neighbors and being scared by the cops, they said, was better than staying home and being bored.

But their Saturday night sprees did not offer any real solution for them, and neither could my class. After the mock council hearings were over, we tried doing a play, and although students made somewhat more of an effort because they now realized that mine was a different kind of class, it was nevertheless *school*, and they lost interest.

Walter Johnson had nothing to offer these kids, and there seemed to be little that I could do that might make a difference. They had been largely discarded and forgotten, just as had the black kids in the D.C. tracking system I'd researched for Bill Higgs. These kids needed something different.

After four years of heading up the PIE program, I was beginning to think that I needed something different, too.

I WAS FEELING VERY ALONE and isolated as a teacher. I had gotten to know a history teacher and the school's art teacher, and the three of us would meet in the art studio for a pleasant conversation over our brown-bag lunches. While we shared a dislike of the gossiping and bickering, the cardboard cafeteria food, and the din of the dining area that echoed like a gymnasium, they had zero interest in talking shop.

The other PIE teacher wasn't interested in discussing craft, either. While we sometimes talked about the kids we had in common, she shied away from the kinds of conversations about education philosophies that I'd thrived on in Jay Featherstone's class at Harvard. Nor did she respond to my invitations to visit my seminars with students, and I was never invited to observe hers.

Some of the rest of the faculty were actively hostile. They had heard that I had offered guidance to a group of students seeking to implement teacher evaluations, helping the kids to develop an impartial questionnaire and coaching them on how to enlist the support of Dr. Reddick, who eventually agreed to bring it to a faculty meeting for consideration. The teachers rejected the students' proposal with a near unanimous vote and no discussion. I did not look to see how my two lunch mates had voted. I didn't want to know.

I'd hoped that I might find some support from Dr. Reddick, who had so enthusiastically recruited me to the school. From day one, I had hungered for feedback on my teaching from him. Several times during my first year, he'd popped into my seminars to observe for a few minutes, and I longed to know what he'd thought and if he had suggestions for how I might improve. We finally met near the end of the academic year for my first official evaluation.

I had no idea what to expect. He handed me a two-page form with about forty numbered one-line descriptions and two check boxes in columns to the right of each. One column was labeled "Needs Improvement," the other, "Satisfactory."

"Read this," he said perfunctorily, "and if you agree with the evaluation, then just sign at the bottom of page two."

All the way down both pages, every line was checked "Satisfactory." I signed and fled his office, trying to hide my utter disappointment.

The same scene played out at the end of year two, and then again in year three. The only difference was that at the end of my third evaluation, Dr. Reddick smiled as I handed the signed form back to him and said, "Congratulations. You're tenured now."

I felt disgusted. How could I have been given "a job for life" when I knew that I was still making plenty of mistakes as a teacher? How was I going to get the feedback I needed to become a better teacher?

The following year, my fourth as head of the PIE program, the Montgomery County School District's central office sent the head of its research office down to evaluate what I was doing. At last, I thought, I'll get some feedback. But the process was a bureaucratic fiasco. After months of negotiations, the evaluator reluctantly agreed to my idea of having his staff interview students about their experiences, rather than merely giving students a multiple-choice questionnaire as he'd originally proposed. The interviewer later told me that the students had raved about the program, but that he had no say in how his report might be used. It never saw the light of day. Another sham. My professional development, and ideas for improving the PIE program, were left to me to figure out.

Since the beginning of my first year of teaching, I had kept a journal of my interactions with students in conferences and classes. I kept note cards in my shirt pocket during the week, and whenever I was puzzled by something a student had said or done, or something that had gone well or badly in class or conference, I would jot down a note to myself before I raced off to my next commitment. Then, every Saturday morning, I'd retrieve the cards and review and reflect on them.

I found this discipline of reflection to be invaluable in my development as a teacher. Often, if something had not gone well, writing about it helped me figure out why—and what I might have done differently. And conversely, if something had seemed to go well, I tried to understand why that had happened, too.

Yet my writing was not enough. I longed for external validation and wanted to figure out how I could make better sense of my intuitions and work out my own educational philosophy. The books I'd read in Jay's class offered wonderful descriptions of teachers like me who were discovering new ways of teaching on their own, but they were not research. There was no pedagogical theory backing up their trial-and-error methodologies.

It was a gift, then, when, in my second year of teaching, I stumbled across the work of Jean Piaget, the Swiss psychologist famous for his studies of children's cognitive and moral development. Piaget had written extensively about the implications of his research for education. The first book of his that I picked up was *The Moral Judgment of the Child*. It was incredibly dense—in both number of pages and language—but I persisted, growing more and more excited as I read.

Piaget's clinical observations had led him to conclude that all children were intrinsically motivated to learn. Similar to John Dewey (whose more theoretical work preceded Piaget's), Piaget believed that for kids to make sense of what they saw around them, it wasn't enough merely to fill up their heads with facts; teachers had to challenge and stimulate students to "construct" progressively deeper understandings of how things worked and who they were in the world. He summarized his findings in a short book he wrote in 1948 for UNESCO with the title *To Understand Is to Invent*. This rang true to me. It was just as Stephen Dedalus had said: "By thinking of things you could understand them."

What I found especially fascinating was Piaget's definition of the aim of education. The goal, he said, must be to help children overcome egocentrism in two domains: the intellectual and the emotional. Overcoming intellectual egocentrism meant replacing superstition and uninformed opinions with logic and reasoning. To an extent, that's what I'd accomplished with my mock county council hearing about the keg parties. The kids' views of the problem were broadened by exposure to new kinds of evidence when they went on ridealongs with the police and interviewed parents and others with different perspectives.

Overcoming emotional egocentrism meant, for Piaget, replacing isolated self-centeredness with a sense of oneself in relation to other people. To do this, children need to develop what he called "reciprocity," or what today we would call empathy. He argued that children develop reciprocity naturally when they start playing social games, which requires mutual agreement on the set of rules to abide by. But he observed that when children do their work alone all day in schools and are made to compete against one another for grades, the natural social interactions that would help them learn to take others' perspectives are disrupted.

The writing workshops I had created enabled my students to construct a deeper understanding of good writing. They were absorbing the principles of writing by inventing, then discussing, what worked well, and why. And the more they worked on improving their writing together, the more self-confident they grew. Such self-confidence was the opposite of self-centeredness. As my PIE kids had grown more self-confident in their writing, they were more able to take an interest in the work of others—to learn from them *and* to empathize.

Here was the research and rationale I needed to underpin my teaching methods and better understand what I was seeing with my students.

After reading Piaget's work, I, too, was growing more self-confident—as a teacher. In the summer of 1975, I started to think about writing articles on what I was learning from my conferences and classes. The first was an essay about the patterns I had observed among students, teachers, parents, and administrators in the Montgomery County schools. While things had appeared to bounce back to normal after the chaos of the late 1960s, I'd noticed that students often seemed more driven than curious; parents were obsessed with getting their kids into the "right" colleges and onto the "right" career paths; teachers felt threatened by layoffs; and administrators were caught between unhappy teachers and the school board and central office, which were demanding more accountability through improved test scores. I thought that real student learning was being sacrificed in the daily hubbub, hustle, and stress of school life, and no one was willing to talk about the problem. Just like today. I concluded my article with a call for honest dialogue about what was happening to our students, what we wanted for them, and what our priorities should be for improvement.

I titled my article "All Is Quiet, But Not All Is Well in Suburbia" and sent it off in September to an education publication, the *Phi Delta Kappan*, which I'd found through a cursory search in the school's library. If I had known then that they accepted fewer than 5 percent of all submissions, I wouldn't have dared. But late in the year, I learned that my article had been accepted. When I shared the exciting news with my lunch mates and my fellow teacher in the PIE program, their responses were polite indifference. No one took me up on my offer to read it.

DESPITE MY SUCCESSES in the classroom with students and my discovery of Piaget, I often felt I was swimming against a powerful riptide of education trends, all flowing in the wrong direction. In those days, everybody was enamored with getting "back to the basics"—which meant less student choice and more rote memorization and testing, practices that were antithetical to mine. Two loves buoyed me up: my music and my growing family.

I began to study classical guitar almost by chance. One evening, we had some friends from the neighborhood over for dinner, one of whom was a psychologist. I mentioned in casual conversation that I frequently had dreams about playing the guitar and wondered what that meant. When he suggested that maybe they just meant I wanted to learn to play the guitar, I laughed it off. But then he said, "You know, it's not too late to start." By the end of the following week, I'd purchased an inexpensive instrument and found a teacher.

My teacher was a classical guitar student studying with Aaron Shearer at the Peabody Conservatory in Baltimore, and so we began by diligently plowing through Shearer's *Classic Guitar Technique*. For an hour a day after school, I tried hard to follow his "Recommended Procedure for Practice":

1. First name each note as it is played until all are thoroughly learned.
2. Then say *i, m, i, m* as you play in order to maintain *strict alternation* between the higher and lower string [*i* being an abbreviation for the index finger, *m* for the middle].
3. Finally, count 1, 2, 3, 4 for each beat of each measure. USE A METRONOME.

After a few months, I was able to play the silly simple preludes and études that Shearer had written as practice pieces for students. It wasn't fun. In fact, it was the opposite. The music was boring, and everything was focused on technique and drill.

Toward the end of my first year, I had worked my way to the back of the book and started learning my first real piece of music, "Country Dance," composed by Ferdinando Carulli.

I went on to memorize pieces by Fernando Sor and Mauro Giuliani, whose themes and variations were staples of the classical guitar catalog.

As I learned these pieces, I finally began to enjoy my practice sessions. They were an opportunity to create something beautiful every single day. I splurged on a gorgeous rosewood and cedar guitar, and at the beginning of every session felt a sweet shiver of excitement the moment I cradled it close to my chest. With each sure strum of the strings I could feel my instrument come to life, the throb of the rosewood pulsing next to my own heart. I polished it lovingly every day before laying it to rest in its case.

But my teacher was constantly nagging me to improve my sight reading and my technique with drills, as if I were trying to become a professional guitarist like him, when all I really wanted to do was play some music that I loved. So in my second year of study, I sought another teacher at a different music studio and decided that I would take charge of my lessons.

This teacher had studied with Shearer as well, and he wanted me to start on Shearer's Volume 2. I refused. I told him I wanted him to teach me the techniques I needed in order to play the music I'd chosen to learn. I brought in some tough pieces by J. S. Bach, Heitor Villa-Lobos, and Erik Satie. We worked on them together, one by one, and after three years, I'd memorized an hour of challenging repertoire—music that I looked forward to playing. Yet I'd done this despite my teacher, not because of him. His emphasis was entirely on technique. I was learning nothing about how to play expressively.

Not knowing what to do or where to turn, I decided to ask the owner of the music studio—Mark Ellsworth, who had once played first violin with the Chicago Symphony—to teach me. He told me that he didn't know anything about the guitar and had no extra time, but when I persisted, he agreed to meet with me on Sunday mornings at 10:00 a.m. He taught me the use of vibrato, and the importance of pacing and of varying my tonality. Soon my guitar was beginning to sing in ways I had never imagined. My meetings with him became my Sunday church service, my opportunity to worship the God of beauty and to give thanks that there was music in my life.

I learned valuable lessons for teaching from my experiences in the music studio. First, to maintain students' intrinsic motivation, you have to combine the necessary learning of drills with chances to have fun—*to play*. With writing, students need to learn proper sentence structure and so on, of course, but if these are the teacher's only focus, students will not have a reason to *want* to learn to write well—*to practice*. I also came to understand the importance of combining the head and the heart in learning—*technique* and *feeling*. I realized that if I'd focused only on writing technique in my workshops and ignored the emotional content of my students' work, they would have quickly lost interest.

My other passion in those Bethesda years was my children. My oldest, Daniel, was born in 1972; Sarah followed nineteen months later, in 1974; and our last child, Eliza, was born in

1978. I was often a foolish father. When my one-year-old son began to pull books off the living room shelves, I tried wedging them in tightly. When that didn't work, I strung taut wire across the front of the lower bookcase and attached it to eye hooks I'd screwed into the bookcases at each end. Now, by God, he wasn't going to be able to get those books! But, then, neither could we.

While I made lots of mistakes as a dad, just as I did as a teacher, I tried hard to be a different kind of father from the one I had—more involved and accessible. For starters, I *played* with my kids. With my son, I moved Matchbox trucks across the rug, giving each vehicle a particular purpose and the appropriate noise: "Make way for the ambulance! *Whoop, whoop.*" He'd flash a grin and take the lead with a fire truck. With my daughters, I endlessly rearranged the furniture in miniature dollhouses and fantasized with them about the families who lived in them. We gave their miniature daughters made-up names like "She-sha." With all three, I admired their architectural creations as we assembled intricate Lego forts, houses, garages, and space stations.

But my favorite thing to do with my children was to read to them at bedtime. Every night I would snuggle up in a rocking chair with a child smelling clean and fresh from a bath and feeling warm and fuzzy in soft pajamas. Once they stopped squirming and had settled in against my chest, I would begin. Whether it was *Goodnight Moon*, the Little House series by Laura Ingalls Wilder, or, later, *The Chronicles of Narnia* by C. S. Lewis, it was a joy to feel their little bodies close and warm against mine and to make the books and characters come to life for them. In my Mowglis days, I had thrilled in being read aloud to, but I had forgotten, until I began to read to my kids, that literature is first and foremost an oral tradition, that the sounds of words and the telling of stories can conjure mystery and magic in the dark of night.

IN THE WINTER OF 1976, I learned from a friend that a few teachers from Sidwell Friends School—the well-known independent PK–12 Quaker school in Washington, D.C.—were meeting to discuss moral education, a topic that greatly interested me after having read Piaget's *The Moral Judgment of the Child*. I knew one of the teachers from the Bethesda Friends Meeting, where we had been going, and asked if I could join the discussions.

Sidwell was one of the most sought-after schools among Washington elites—and this was decades before Chelsea Clinton and the Obama girls were students there. A group of teachers and administrators from Sidwell's middle and upper schools had begun to discuss how to strengthen the school's Quaker values and temper what they felt had become a hypercompetitive, grade-obsessed, "me first" culture, where every family seemed bent on admission to an Ivy League college.

We read articles and discussed teaching practices that

might encourage more collaboration and interest in real learning versus just grabbing an A. People were genuinely interested in what I'd learned from Piaget, and I was grateful to be with a group of educators who were also asking important questions. At the end of the third meeting, Ben Shute, the upper school head, encouraged me to apply for an English teacher's position that had opened up.

In early spring, I visited the school for a round of interviews. I was immediately struck by the airy spaciousness of the classrooms, the small class sizes (averaging just sixteen or so students), and the esprit de corps and friendliness of everyone with whom I met.

Ben called a few weeks later to offer me a contract teaching in the upper school for the 1976–77 school year. I was to teach three sections of ninth-grade English and an eleventh- and twelfth-grade English elective of my choosing.

That was the summer I turned thirty. It felt like a milestone. I'd survived the disasters at Avon and Searing and the disillusionments at Randolph-Macon and RPI. I'd been tempered by the tumult of the 1960s and found my own rhythm of learning at Friends World. I'd succeeded at Harvard. And now I had a real profession and a great new job with the promise of colleagueship for the first time. Perhaps, at last, I'd finally be swimming with the current.

SEVEN

A Quaker Education

JUST ONE WEEK INTO THE NEW SCHOOL YEAR, IT BECAME crystal clear how different the Sidwell kids were from my PIE kids in Montgomery County. My new ninth graders all wanted to talk at once, and few felt the need to raise their hands. When I offered them choices of what they might read, the debates would stretch on for half the period. The older students in my elective courses treated discussions of the assigned readings as a kind of game, where winning meant outshining one another with clever arguments to impress me, so that they would get an A in class and punch another hole in their hoped-for ticket to the Ivy League.

Around this time, the famed psychiatrist Robert Coles published his influential essay "Children of Affluence" in the *Atlantic Monthly*. In it, he described his extensive interviews with privileged kids, whom he labeled "entitled": children who "have been brought up . . . to feel important, superior, destined for a satisfying rewarding life." But, he added, being "entitled" did not mean being spoiled. He observed that the children he'd studied were self-disciplined and often highly self-critical. It was as though he'd been sitting in on my classes at Sidwell when he'd done his research.

Teaching entitled kids was a far cry from my work with the assorted rebels and in-school dropouts at Walter Johnson. With many of the PIE kids, my task had been to help them find a reason to stay in school, whereas with Sidwell kids, I decided my goal was to help them develop an interest in learning that was more than getting into a name-brand college. But as I thought more about it, the challenge with both groups was the same: to develop students' intrinsic motivation for learning—in my English classes, an intrinsic motivation for reading and writing.

I took a risk. I met with Ben Shute and outlined an idea for a novel class schedule, and, much to my surprise, he gave me the okay. Rather than meet my classes as a group all five days of the week, I'd tell my students that two days of each week were for independent reading and writing and that I would conference with every student once every two weeks to discuss their work—as I had with my PIE kids.

This unique class format was a hit with students. They immediately had ideas for different kinds of writing they wanted to try and seemed to relish the independence to pursue wide-ranging interests. And, unlike my PIE kids, most came to their conferences ready to talk about what they had been reading and eager to share their writing with me. There were a handful of students who had trouble with the lack of a formal structure, because they didn't really know what they were interested in, in which case I would suggest specific reading and writing assignments to get them going.

Still, in these first few months, I struggled to establish my authority, even with the ninth graders. This was my sixth year as a teacher, and I hadn't mastered how to control a classroom. I felt confused and ashamed. One day I managed to contain my embarrassment enough to seek advice from Hall Katzenbach, the most senior member of the English Department. A wonderfully wise and kindly man, Hall listened sympathetically to my laments and then gave me some simple but effective advice: when class discussions get out of hand, ask for a moment of silence. If the students are still unruly, have them spend some time writing down their thoughts before continuing. When I tried his suggestions, they worked. Mostly.

I had one ninth-grade class dominated by students who all seemed destined to become trial lawyers. They were argumentative, combative, constantly interrupting one another; my begging and pleading for a more orderly discussion went unheeded. Exasperated, halfway through class one day I burst out: "You're wasting my time and yours. Get out!" They silently rose from their chairs and slowly filed out the door—in shock, it seemed. To my great relief, discussions were more civil after that. The shock value would have quickly worn off if I'd had to do it again.

By the late fall of the first semester, I had begun to find the right balance between discipline and freedom, and I grew more consistent in asserting my authority as a teacher in the classroom. But then came Back-to-School Night, when parents followed a miniversion of their child's daily school schedule, visiting each room and listening as each teacher explained their class for ten minutes. Knowing that many of my students' parents were rich or powerful or famous—or all three—I dreaded the event. It was unlikely that these kids had ever had a teacher quite like me, and I was prepared to be cross-examined by their parents. How was I going to explain why I structured my classes in such an unconventional manner?

I spent hours getting ready, in my journal composing a rationale for my approach to teaching like an accused defendant on trial. When the night came, I put on a tie and gave my one pair of leather shoes a good brushing. If I was going to be a different kind of teacher, I had to at least look "normal."

The parents who filed into my classroom were all decked out in professional dresses and suits, and several seemed to eye me suspiciously as they squeezed into the student desk chairs. I'd been right to put on a tie, but that was the easy part. Now I had to put on a real show. My heart was thumping wildly. *Who was I to think that I could or should teach differently from the other teachers at Sidwell? How dare I.* I hid my shaking hands in my pockets, welcomed the parents, and spun out my little spiel. I outlined the four goals of my classes: to teach students to think critically, to communicate effectively, to work collaboratively, and to strengthen students' capacity for independent study. I shamelessly name-dropped when I explained that the skill that had been most important for my success as a student at Harvard was the ability to take initiative and write papers that were based on independent research.

My talk was met with much nodding and positive-sounding murmurs. Most of the parents understood the importance of these skills from the work they did. But then a father demanded, with a scowl, to know how I was teaching grammar. In a slightly shaky voice, I asserted that there were twenty years of research to show that teaching grammar as a separate subject did not improve writing. My method was to discuss students' written work in conference and to go over the common errors I was spotting in students' work when we met as a class.

"What about vocabulary?" he retorted.

Each week, every student was responsible for bringing in five index cards with words they'd encountered in their reading that they did not know, I told him. The cards had to list the dictionary definition of the words, the sentences where they'd encountered them, and a sentence they'd composed using the word. Students then broke up into groups to share and discuss their vocabulary words of the week.

What I did not say to him was that I knew I needed to do a much better job of checking up on students' vocabulary work. I also did not tell him that I picked the vocabulary idea up from Sylvia Ashton-Warner's book *Teacher*, which had been one of my favorite assigned readings in the seminar taught by my favorite Harvard teacher, Jay Featherstone. In the book, Ashton-Warner described how she taught six-year-olds in rural New Zealand to read by regularly asking each student to point out what she called "one-look words" in the stories they read—the words the children didn't know and really wanted to learn and make their own. She'd write each child's words down on a flash card. If they couldn't read the word the following week, she'd throw out that card, believing that it was a waste of time to try to get kids to memorize vocabulary words that had no context or meaning for them. I was trying out a variant of this idea for the first time and had no idea whether or not it would work. I felt a bit like the Wizard of Oz—afraid someone might pull back the curtain and find me out.

As I was wrapping up my defense, a bell rang to announce the change of class periods, and the parents began to file out. The father who had grilled me gave me a grudging nod. The next day, Ben told me that several parents had come up to him at the end of the evening to say how impressed they were with my explanation of my class.

I USED MY TIME over the Christmas break to design a second semester curriculum that wasn't a race to see how many of the classics of the literary canon could be shoehorned into a single semester, as my colleagues seemed bent on doing. Instead, I wanted to focus on fewer books—ones that spoke to themes in my students' lives—and have more time for a wider variety of writing assignments and other kinds of lessons that might stimulate creativity and reflection. Tennessee Williams's *The Glass Menagerie* proved to be a chance for me to teach a work of literature that "spoke" to students—and to teach more imaginatively. And I discovered that when students were more actively engaged with the content of a lesson, class discipline almost took care of itself.

First, I had students read the play's introduction and stage description and then do a drawing of the set. Then we began to read the play aloud, pausing at the end of each scene for discussion. As the class progressed, I noticed that the students seemed very sympathetic to the character of the son, Tom, who had abandoned his mother and disabled sister to join the coast guard, and they were unable to sympathize with his mother, a woman who was always going on about the beaus she'd once had as a young southern belle, and whose husband had abandoned her and her two small children in the depths of the Depression. So I asked the students to write a dramatic monologue from the point of view of Tom, his mother, or his sister five years after the play's events, and encouraged them to tackle a character that might be hard for them to imagine. When they read their monologues aloud, their work showed remarkable sensitivity and insight, and several showed real empathy for Tom's mother and sister.

Deliberating the life challenges that Tom faced also created an opportunity to discuss students' goals for the future and some of the moral dilemmas and tough choices that they might face. I brought up the problem of widespread—and widely acknowledged—cheating in classes. I gave no tests—only essays—and because I knew each student's writing well from conferences, it was impossible to cheat in my classes.

But I'd heard other teachers as well as students gripe about the issue. Students told me cheating on tests was stupid because you might get caught, while cheating on homework was fine. Besides, they argued, cheating didn't actually hurt anyone. "What about the future?" I prodded them. "How do you decide what corners you will cut, what your moral boundaries are?"

Students also greatly enjoyed a unit I designed on advertising. I began by having them analyze a range of TV commercials and categorize them according to the kinds of appeals they used—such as "guaranteeing a happier life," "making you more popular," or "getting the testimony of the doctor in the white coat with a 'cure-all.'" Then I had them work in small groups to write advertisements that illustrated these various seductions. After the groups performed their ads for the class, we discussed the kinds of deceptions they'd used to lure consumers and compared what they'd done with real ads. For their next assignment, I had them write public service ads for products and services they thought might better meet basic human needs—but I insisted that there be no false promises this time. Without any prompting from me, they chose to promote activities like adult education courses (for a sense of belonging) and yoga classes (for a healthier lifestyle). It was exciting to see my students begin to think both more critically and more imaginatively.

Although things were going much better in my classes, I still had the occasional struggle with individual students.

"Diane," a tall ninth-grade girl with a powerful athletic build, a close-cropped Afro, and dark-chocolate skin, was one such student—and one from whom I learned a great deal.

Diane would grumble and complain whenever I announced an assignment, and I sometimes overheard her muttering to the girl who sat next to her that my class was a waste of time. I had several conferences with her after class where I tried to explain what we were doing and why, but she would just slide farther down in her desk chair and glare at me. When I asked her what she thought might be a better use of our class time, she countered in a surly voice: "How am *I* supposed to know? *You're* the teacher, aren't you?"

She clearly had no respect for or interest in what we were doing in class and was a disruptive influence. So I decided that Diane should go to study hall during our class period and work on an independent study project instead. I spelled out why I was not permitting her to come to class and asked what project she'd like to take on. She said she wanted to do a history of race relations at Sidwell, which had been one of the last Quaker schools to integrate.

I met with her several times a week to check on the progress of her research and to offer suggestions. She soon became deeply invested in scrutinizing the official school history. She identified the most prominent people who had sent their children to the school during the time when a powerful minority on the board of trustees still opposed integration and interviewed several of the first black students to enroll. She also questioned the admissions office about minority enrollment trends and the amount of money available for scholarships. It was an extraordinary work of investigation.

When Diane was finished writing up her research, I asked her to come back to class to share her findings. She was hesitant, but I told her that she had something to teach that was of real value. When she finally did present her report, the other students were sobered by her account of how hard it had been to integrate the school and what it had been like for the first black students. This led to a conversation about underlying racial tensions in the school. White students began to understand for the first time that when one of them jokingly remarked in the hall, "Hey, nigger, what's happenin'?," their fellow black students were not amused.

After the discussion, I asked Diane if she wanted to come back to class. She said yes. An uneasy truce settled between us for the rest of the year.

Two years later, I was taken aback when she showed up in one of my eleventh-grade elective classes. As Diane walked into the classroom door on the first day of the fall semester, she gave me a knowing nod, then proudly threw back her shoulders, calling attention to the bold white letters printed across the brown T-shirt that stretched, skintight, across her very considerable chest: I MAY NOT BE PERFECT BUT SOME PARTS OF ME ARE EXCELLENT. I welcomed her into the class while doing my best to stifle an embarrassed smile. She was still a provocateur, but I was no longer the enemy.

. . .

AFTER MY FIRST YEAR at Sidwell, I switched from teaching three ninth-grade English classes to two, and I chose to teach two sections of creative writing for eleventh and twelfth graders—what I called "expressive writing," so that students who didn't think of themselves as especially creative wouldn't be put off. My writing classes were among the most popular electives offered in the department and were always oversubscribed. And it was in them where I really felt myself soar as a teacher.

I still played with my own more creative forms of writing when I had time. One summer I attended the Bread Loaf Writers' Conference at Middlebury College. There I met published authors, had my work critiqued, and talked writing nonstop for an exhilarating ten days. But the expressive writing class wasn't merely about sharing a personal passion with my students. More than anything, I loved helping students develop their individual voices as writers.

I had a talent for drawing students out, I began to see. And the more I trusted my intuitions and insights as a teacher—such as when I gave Diane a free rein for independent study and then asked her to share her work with the class—the more the students' discussions and writing improved. My classes, at their best, became intentional communities, bound by a common aspiration to write more authentically, more insightfully, more artistically. Through their writing, students understood themselves and their world far more deeply. It was just as Piaget had described, to understand the world *really* is to invent it.

Each week, I had students experiment with a different writing genre, just as Mr. Edwards had done with me. One week, it would be a dialogue; the next, an extended physical description. And then a music or restaurant review or an editorial or a letter to the editor that they had to send to a real newspaper—whether it was the *Washington Post* or the school paper, *The Horizon*. More than a few got published.

Once, when I'd assigned students to write an editorial on a topic of their choice, three out of the nineteen had chosen to address the problems of growing old in America. When the third one was read to the class, one girl spoke out impatiently, "It's one thing for us to write about how old people suffer and have a good discussion where we all agree, but we should *do* something!"

"What did you have in mind?"

"I haven't really thought about it, but there must be something we can do."

"Does anybody have any thoughts?"

"We might go give a reading at the nursing home just down the street from school," suggested another student.

The class liked the idea, so two girls who had previously volunteered at the home for the aged near the school agreed to contact the director to see what could be arranged. The students' initial idea of giving a poetry reading was rejected because the home's director said most of the residents were hard of hearing and not particularly interested in poetry. Most of the class was ready to give up after learning this, but I urged them to try again.

When the two girls called back to ask about other options, the director explained that many of the residents were starved for companionship, and that if the students wanted to split up in pairs and just talk with those who wanted company, it would be a real service. However, the visits would need to be after school, because of the home's schedule.

The girls reported back to the class, and a number of students indicated an interest in going, so we set a time and date. I wondered how many students would actually show up now that the visit impinged on their free time and would require much more of them than a poetry reading. Every student but one came.

The minute we walked in the door of the imposing red-brick building, I began to fear I'd done the wrong thing in bringing my students here. The halls were painted dull green, and a heavy antiseptic odor hung in the stale air. Some very elderly people who couldn't control their head or body movements were being wheeled along the corridor; others simply stood and stared with hollow vacant eyes as we passed them. At the main office we were given the names and room numbers of those who had asked for a visit. I made my visit alone, as there was an even number of students, and I wanted all of them to pair off.

I spent my time with a frail ninety-year-old woman who had once been a seamstress for First Ladies and other VIPs. She talked about how some of her clients had been kind to her, while others had taken her for granted. When I left her after an hour and a half, I stopped by the office and was told that many of the students were still at the home, chatting with residents.

The next day in class we talked about our experiences at the home for the aged. The students were surprised at how easy it was to be helpful to another person, and some planned to return. One twelfth grader said that the visit had made her realize how she took her youth and health for granted, and how an awareness of death might help us to live life more meaningfully. Her comment was met with a profound moment of quiet in the room.

Another student broke the silence with a new thought. The residents' physical needs were being met, he observed, but many had complained of being bored and treated disrespectfully by the nursing home's staff. More money might improve the depressing physical appearance of the place. But, he asked, what could change the bureaucratic way in which old people were treated?

None of us had any answers. But it was clear to me that these "entitled" students had had a glimpse of a vastly different reality from their own and had come away with new insights and questions.

AS WORD GOT AROUND among students that I was a good writing teacher, a growing number of twelfth graders sought me out for independent study in writing. I soon discovered that they sometimes wanted to talk about personal aspects of their lives, not just their writing. None was seeking therapy; they were seeking only an adult who was willing to listen attentively. My experiences with three students—a boy, "Bob"; a girl, "Barbara"; and another girl, Elizabeth—provided me with some perspective on the interior lives of my students and on how to make a real difference with some of them.

Bob came to me saying that he wanted to improve his writing. He'd always gotten straight A's in English, as he had in every other subject, but he hated to write and always put his work off until the last minute. The English assignments he brought for me to read were sophisticated and technically flawless, but boring. I asked him what he would most like to write about for his independent study. He had no idea. He'd never been in a situation where he hadn't been told what to write about.

I suggested he go off and think about it for a week. He came back and said he'd like to write an essay on "grading."

"What about grading?" I asked.

Bob replied that he felt students studied only to get an A, that grades got in the way of learning. He had no idea what he was interested in because he'd always just strived to get A's. That, he said, was the problem he wanted to write about.

At our next conference, he told me about several books on education he'd read, but he hadn't done any writing. I asked him why.

"Well, I guess I just want to know what you think about grades first" was his pleading reply.

"I'm not going to tell you until after you've finished your paper," I answered. His eyes became saucers as I went on: "You're a second-semester senior now, so grades don't matter anymore. Why not take a risk?"

At our next conference, Bob turned in a forceful and well-developed essay that described the negative aspects of grading and explored alternative approaches to evaluating students' work, such as portfolios and projects for credit/no credit. It was a fine piece of writing, and he knew it. The fact that I agreed with his opinions was no longer so important to him.

Then he came to me with a new problem. He'd been accepted to two colleges and didn't know which to choose. Everyone had given him contradictory opinions, though most of the people he'd consulted had favored the Ivy League university, and now he wanted to know what I thought. Rather than answer his question, I suggested he keep a journal of his observations when he went to visit both schools in the coming weeks.

After his trips, he showed me his journal and announced that he'd decided to go to the less prestigious college because the students there seemed more sincerely interested in learning, and there were more opportunities for independent study. When I last heard from Bob, he was very happy at the school and was writing for the college newspaper.

I had helped Bob by initially withholding my opinions. But with Barbara, I discovered that the best way I could help her was by offering an honest point of view.

Barbara was a Merit Scholar, and at our first conference,

she said she wanted to keep a journal for independent study. I agreed reluctantly, because I was concerned that journal writing wouldn't be enough of a challenge for her. But in the end, Barbara took on an important challenge of a very different sort.

One of the first entries Barbara showed me described feeling confused and angry because her former best friend now seemed only to want to hurt her. I asked what had happened. Her friend Pam had been going out with a guy for more than a year. Barbara was attracted to him and wrote him a note suggesting they get together. He and Barbara became lovers, and the boy broke up with Pam.

Barbara had told her parents about Pam and her new boyfriend and wondered whether they thought she had done something wrong. They'd replied, "Well, what do you think?" She'd been let off the hook, but she still had a nagging sense that perhaps she'd done something not quite right.

"Is it bad to want something and go after it?" she'd asked me.

"Of course not. But honestly, if I were Pam, I would feel betrayed," I replied quietly.

Shock washed across Barbara's face, almost as if I'd slapped her. I worried that I'd been too candid.

As Barbara was leaving my classroom, though, she lingered at the doorway for a moment and said, "Thank you for being honest with me."

The next piece of writing she brought in began as a letter of apology but ended with Barbara's saying that she felt she deserved the guy more than Pam did because she was able to make him happier. I read the letter back to her in a neutral voice and asked her how she would feel if she were Pam reading this. Barbara could hear the condescending tone of her words and was chagrined.

The last piece of writing she showed me was a sincere letter of apology and an offer of friendship. But Barbara wasn't sure she wanted to risk actually sending the letter. She couldn't stand the thought that the apology might be rejected.

Barbara never did send the letter. Instead, she left a note at Pam's house saying that she was sorry and still wanted to be friends, and inviting Pam to a party she was having. Pam went, but they said very little to each other. It was not until they went off to college together that fall, and Barbara broke up with the boy, that they renewed their friendship.

And finally, there was Elizabeth. Like many Sidwell students, Elizabeth came from a high-powered Washington family. Her father was then serving as the first black person to be appointed as secretary of the army, and her mother came from a distinguished African American family and was a professor of history at George Washington University. I'd observed Elizabeth casually over the course of the year, and she'd struck me as a bit of a social butterfly, but my perception of her changed radically when she showed me her first poem.

The poem, according to the conference notes I wrote at the time, played on a simple theme: it was about feeling angry and being afraid to show it for fear of rejection. After we discussed her poem, she decided to write a short story about the destructiveness of high school cliques. Next was a poem about the joy of dancing—but dance that was solitary and unseen by others, done for the pure pleasure of expressing oneself through movement.

When I asked her about what she'd like to read for her independent study, Elizabeth knew exactly what she wanted to focus on: books by well-known African American authors such as Richard Wright, Ralph Ellison, and Malcolm X. These were works that she'd always been eager to read, but which were not on the syllabus of Sidwell's English courses. Instead, she told me, she'd been assigned several books in middle school that professed to describe "the black experience," but every one of them had been written by a white author.

Elizabeth then set to work on a lengthy editorial for *The Horizon* about how many students at Sidwell were "oblivious to 'Black Reality.'" She began by referring to "the sheltered and pampered atmosphere" of the school and bemoaned how little interaction students had beyond this "small community." She argued that while relationships between black and white students were okay, the school was not doing enough to educate students about the wider black experience in America. She then offered some specific suggestions to improve the dynamic: more outside speakers discussing social issues at school assemblies; more black literature in the curriculum; creation of an urban studies program; and active recruitment of a more diverse student body. It was a powerful and courageous piece of writing.

Elizabeth went on to earn a PhD in English from the University of Pennsylvania, and in 2008 she was appointed chair of the Department of African American Studies at Yale. However, today she is best known as one of America's foremost poets. She was commissioned to write a poem for President Barack Obama's 2009 inauguration and recited her work—"Praise Song for the Day"—at the event.

I didn't teach Elizabeth to write poetry, nor did I teach her about African American literature. I take no credit for her many successes. What I did with her—and with Bob and Barbara, as well as my other independent study students—was to recognize and affirm something essential about who she really was as an individual, separate and distinct from her parents' expectations or her friends' assumptions. I listened with my head and heart to each student, and I took what they said and what they wrote seriously.

If we can find the time and make the choice, teachers have far more important things to impart to our students than just subject matter.

AFTER SCHOOL AND ON WEEKENDS, I set aside time for regular guitar practice and my own writing, outlets that sustained my self-discipline, self-expression, passions, and sense of purpose. I sought time in nature as well. The Shenandoah

Mountain peaks, with their deep hazy-blue shadows, were a few hours' drive away, and they beckoned to me often.

We frequently took day hikes as a family, and several times a year we went camping. When my children were very young, they rode in a kiddie carrier on my back, but soon we could hold hands and toddle along the trails together, discovering the magic and mysteries of the deep woods. I savored these shared moments: a forest of emerald ferns waving in the wind beneath the canopy of tall trees, a rose-colored mushroom unexpectedly emergent from the dark, damp soil—never to be eaten, I carefully explained.

When the kids were older, and my being away for a few days was less of a burden on Connemara, I occasionally headed off to the mountains on my own. I'd backpack, no matter the season, always with my camera hanging around my neck, constantly challenged by the goal of capturing nature's sudden and breathtaking displays of beauty.

The memory of one scene from a winter's hike high in the Shenandoahs is still imprinted on my mind. The ground was snow covered, and the mountains were cloaked close in ghosted fog that clung to the shadowy treetops. I was all alone as I plodded along in this dark, frozen, monochromatic world, the straps of my heavy pack digging deeply into my shoulders. But then, rounding a bend in the trail, I spied a tall bush, with thin red veins for branches, covered with bright round berries, the color of fresh blood. I stopped, stood, and stared spellbound—until at last my gloved fingers began to grow numb and my body started to shiver in an insistent nudge not to tarry in the bitter cold.

Singular beauty is so often there, just waiting to be discovered.

ONE REASON I'D CHOSEN to teach at Sidwell Friends was that it was a Quaker school. I didn't know it at the time, but I think I hoped to bring my spiritual life closer to my professional life. I had attended a Quaker college, and Connemara and I had been married in the San Francisco Friends Meeting. Since moving to Maryland, we'd become members of the Quaker meeting in Bethesda. Over the years, I'd been increasingly drawn to the fundamental conviction of the Society of Friends that there was "that of God in every person," that each person could have a direct, unmediated experience of God without the need of a minister or other higher authority, and that one's life must "bear witness" to one's deepest beliefs.

I also found great satisfaction in the simple practice of Quakerism: the weekly meetings for worship where the congregation met in silence and each person sought to commune with the God within. A few individuals might "be called" to speak during the meeting, but there was no minister, there were no prayers, there were no hymns—there wasn't even a strict definition of what a "belief in God" meant. There were also regular "meetings for business" to decide the affairs of the congregation by consensus, an approach to community decision making that I'd come to appreciate during my days in the civil rights movement. Indeed, Quakers had historically been on the front lines of the struggles for peace, social justice, and women's equality and had, since the founding of the religion by George Fox in seventeenth-century England, believed in "speaking truth to power." Now, as a teacher in a Quaker school, I began to explore what a "Quaker education" really entailed.

While researching the history of Quaker involvement in education, I learned that George Fox had established the first two Quaker schools in 1688, one for girls and one for boys. Around the same time, William Penn was dreaming of a "Holy Experiment" in America where education might be offered to both the rich and the poor. In the colony of Pennsylvania, he set up a public school open to "all children and servants, male and female," who were to be "taught or instructed, the rich at reasonable rates, and the poor to be maintained and schooled for nothing."

Today, more than three hundred years later, there are more than eighty primary and secondary Quaker schools in the United States, as well as a few colleges—notably Swarthmore, Haverford, and, of course, Friends World. They welcome students of all religions, but nevertheless seek to instill in students a few essential Quaker beliefs and practices. Most have weekly meetings for worship, and many offer students opportunities for participation in decision making.

Because of their more liberal education practices, and the good basic education they provide, Quaker schools became increasingly popular in the 1960s. However, the very success of these Quaker schools had led to a problem. It was said by some that "Quakers came to America to do *good* and did *well* instead." Depending on who was speaking, that final "instead" was sometimes replaced with an "also," but the slight was just the same: increasingly, Quaker schools had become havens for the well-heeled, Quaker and non-Quaker alike. By the time I got to Sidwell, there was a growing unease among Quaker educators that the religion's values were being lost as these schools became increasingly proficient in attracting academically talented students and getting them into elite colleges.

The group of Sidwell teachers who had met to consider moral education, which I'd joined before applying for my job at the school, had been formed to address such concerns. During my first semester, the group sponsored a parent night to discuss moral education, which was well attended, and put together a survey to gauge the level of teachers' engagement with the issue. Unfortunately, only about a third of the teachers bothered to respond. Very few were Quakers, and most did not seem to share the disquiet of our small faction. We soon stopped meeting.

In my second year, Earl Harrison became the headmaster. He was a Quaker who had previously been head of another Friends school, and he felt the school's Quaker roots needed more tending. The mandatory weekly meeting for worship didn't go very far in curbing students' sense of entitlement in

Earl's view. And so the upper school instituted a work program where all students were required to do about an hour of chores around the school each week—emptying trash, helping clean up the cafeteria, and so on.

My English classes were running smoothly, and I took great satisfaction in designing imaginative lessons and working with individual students. Yet I kept thinking about what my students had learned when we visited the home for the aged that day. *How might we, as a school, enable every student to have experiences like that?* I wondered. Picking up campus trash didn't expose students to others whose lives were very different. It didn't help them to develop empathy or to discover their own God within.

Early in my third year at the school, I went to Ben Shute with another proposal. I told him that I thought Sidwell should resurrect the long-dormant religion committee, and that I would like to be appointed to be its head and work on some kind of community service graduation requirement. I was one of a small contingent of "card-carrying" Quakers among the faculty, and it was hard to argue against the appointment. I couldn't tell whether Ben liked my idea, but he agreed to let me recruit others to the committee and see what happened.

The committee, which had representatives from the lower, middle, and upper schools, began to gather weekly. At our first meeting, I threw out the idea of a community service program, and people seemed to like the concept. It helped greatly that Hall Katzenbach, who called himself a "Quakapalian"—meaning an Episcopalian with Quaker leanings—lent his support early on.

We wanted the focus of the program to be on learning. So instead of using the term "community service," we chose to call it "service learning." Second, we decided that service learning should take place outside of school, not in a classroom—that such learning should be experiential. Finally, we agreed that it was important to give students meaningful choices in the kinds of service that they could undertake.

By the second semester, we had drafted a proposal for a new Sidwell Friends high school graduation requirement: Students would need to complete sixty hours of service sometime between the ninth and twelfth grades. The service could be fulfilled by working a few hours a week after school during the school year or in a concentrated period of time during a vacation break. We also proposed that the school hire a service learning coordinator, who would approve student proposals for service, review students' writing about their service, and lead seminars where students could discuss what they were learning.

The committee had done thoughtful work, and we had Earl Harrison's and Ben Shute's conditional support—"conditional" because they said that the upper school faculty would have the final say. When it came time for the faculty to discuss the service learning proposal, I felt edgy and vulnerable. This was my first schoolwide leadership effort, and I didn't know what to expect. Hall spoke quietly but forcefully in favor of the new requirement, and the faculty quickly agreed to it with little discussion. Much later I realized it had not been controversial because the program didn't require the existing faculty to do anything additional.

The service learning requirement was phased in, beginning with the 1979–80 school year. And while some students' service learning choices appeared to be more like career internships—such as volunteering at a senator's office—many kids sought opportunities to work for nonprofits serving people in real need.

As far as I know, Sidwell was the first school in the country to make community service a requirement for graduation. Since then, many schools have followed suit. When the Clintons chose Sidwell for their daughter, Chelsea, they said that the service learning requirement was what most attracted them to the school.

The program continues to this day.

I HAD OBSERVED that many Sidwell students aspired to be leaders of some kind, but that they had no idea what real leaders did or what they might actually want to lead *for.* So in my fourth year, I designed an elective seminar on contemporary issues, which met once a week in the evening. The students who signed up were a lively and diverse group—ranging from an academic superstar whose parents were from India to my former ninth-grade nemesis, Diane, who continued to have struggles in school, though not with me.

For the seminar, we read and discussed biographies of many different kinds of leaders—from George Washington to Dorothy Day, who in the 1930s founded the Catholic Worker Movement to aid the poor and sponsored nonviolent, direct-action protests on behalf of the underserved. We then talked about what it meant to be a leader and the things students in the seminar might themselves want to achieve as future leaders.

Over the course of the semester's explorations, the students kept coming back to the topic of the atmosphere and culture of the school. They felt frustrated that Sidwell did very little to encourage students to be genuine leaders. Finally, during a particularly dispirited discussion, one student issued a challenge to the group: "It's time for us to stop all this talk, stand up, and offer some real leadership here in the school—*now*."

The other students seized on the idea, and they began to brainstorm. There was no better forum for getting the school's attention than an editorial in the school paper. Over many late evenings, the group outlined and then drafted their critique of the school's climate. It was near the end of the school year, and they were determined to get the piece done in time for the last issue of *The Horizon*. The Saturday before the paper went to press, they met at my home to go through the final edits of their work, and then one of them rushed their copy over to the editors, who were holding space for them.

The editorial, titled "Leaders Put Down at Sidwell," ran a full page. "One factor affecting [student] leadership at Sidwell is the general lack of respect for others," they began. Students tended toward "verbal aggression"—their description of the way students were constantly finding fault with one another. "Because idealists are ridiculed, ostracized, and constantly challenged," they wrote, "many are afraid to speak out" and say what they really think about any serious topic, whether in class discussions or in social settings. The article called for more guidance from faculty and more leadership opportunities for students. "To become responsible, one must be given responsibilities," they asserted. And students shouldn't be forced into a passive role in the classroom: "Leadership at school could take the form of teaching, mentoring, and directing groups."

Every student in the seminar had contributed to the editorial and signed it. I was proud of them. I had never seen a group of adolescents work so hard and so collaboratively on a project. But because the article appeared in the final days of the school year, it did not spark the changes the students sought. They had not yet discovered that being a leader requires waging a campaign, not merely winning a battle or two—and neither had I.

I learned a great many valuable lessons in my four years at Sidwell. Teaching had begun to feel like second nature. Trusting my professional instincts, my classes and assignments grew increasingly imaginative. I fine-tuned my abilities to listen and to respond authentically to individual students' needs and interests. Above all, I tried hard to give my students the kinds of learning experiences and support that I wished I'd had as a high school student.

I also had some early intimations of how hard it is to lead the kind of "revolution" that Narayan Desai had described as "transforming individual virtues into social values." My work with the religion committee and the student leadership seminar had done nothing to alter the everyday learning environment of the school.

Transforming one's own classroom culture was one thing, and I'd become pretty adept at that. Changing a school culture would be something else entirely.

EIGHT

Lessons from Failure

BACK WHEN I FIRST INTERVIEWED AT SIDWELL, I MET with the head of the English Department, a woman I'll call Yvette. She was plump, with short-cropped, curly coal-dark hair and an even darker disposition. After we'd exchanged pleasantries for a few minutes, she abruptly said, "You know, we like to find people's Achilles' heels here, and when we find them, we gnaw on them." At the time I wondered if she was trying to scare me off, or felt frustrated that her boss, upper school head Ben Shute, was pushing her to hire me, his preferred candidate. Only later did I realize it had been an omen: during the time that I was there, Sidwell wasn't a place where most teachers came together in a spirit of collaboration. The hypercompetitive culture among the students also pervaded the faculty lounge, where sarcastic banter and petty put-downs were as common as they were in the corridors and classrooms.

Any new young teacher would have struggled in such a sink-or-swim environment. But my challenges were made much harder because I was committed to being a different kind of teacher. My philosophy of education and my teaching practices were radically at odds with the mainstream culture. I wasn't going to be swimming with the tide at Sidwell. Actually, the tide was flowing very strongly against me. Yet again.

I didn't know what an innovator was at the time. In retrospect, though, I struggled with the same challenges as some of the young innovators whom I would interview years later. Through research I learned that many innovators protect themselves with an attitude that often comes off as arrogance. If your ideas and insights are fundamentally different from the majority around you, you often feel you have but two choices: you either conclude that there is something flawed in your perceptions (and everyone else must be right), or you arm yourself with an inflated and seemingly infallible belief in your essential rightness. As innovators grow older, the most successful are able to maintain their convictions while listening carefully to the criticisms of others and weighing new evidence. But back then, I had not yet learned this essential lesson.

During my first year at Sidwell, I cloaked myself in the shaky overconfidence of my convictions, with a bit of a cocky veneer to boot. I believed that I had developed much better ways to teach than my colleagues had. I set up conferences with my students, made time for regular independent study, invited students to lead discussions, and challenged them to write on topics of interest to them. I gave my students *voice* and *choice*. No one else in the English Department—or the school, for that matter—was doing anything like that. I had discovered The One Right Way. Or so I thought.

I knew enough not to go around bragging to the other faculty and making myself a target of ridicule, but I definitely gave off a vibe. A "better than you" vibe, even though, in the private land of Oz behind my wizardly curtain, I was constantly questioning myself.

So by the end of my first year of teaching at Sidwell, I felt as alone as I'd been during my first teaching job at Walter Johnson High School. One day in early May, Linda Lucatorto, the dean of students and a member of our defunct moral education discussion group, suggested she and I take our lunch out onto the lawn for a conversation. I'd complained to her a number of times about feeling a lack of connection with my fellow teachers, but Linda had not invited me to the lawn to hear more of my complaints. In a firm yet sympathetic way, she explained to me how I was pushing the other teachers away, that my isolation was my own doing. Though it stung, I sensed the truth in her words. Linda was doing me a huge favor. A friend shouldn't just tell you what you *want* to hear, but what you *need* to hear.

I began my second year resolved to stop thinking of myself as better than my colleagues and, instead, to see what I might learn from them. I asked the other English teachers if I could visit their classes, and they agreed. I sat in on some classes that I thought were well taught, others that weren't; regardless, I enjoyed observing how others taught and how they tried to engage their students. But it was my visit to veteran teacher Hall Katzenbach's class that provided the most powerful gut check to my egotism.

Hall opened his class by lecturing to his fifteen students for a full half hour about a Shakespeare play they were reading. Lecturing from a podium! I considered lecturing to be a form of educational malpractice. Still, it was plain that the way he made Shakespeare accessible captivated his students, and I knew that he was one of the most popular teachers in the upper school. As I watched him conduct a discussion of his lecture from the podium, I realized that the secrets to his success in the classroom were twofold: he had a passion for Shakespeare, which he conveyed luminously, and he was warm and caring with his students. He never cut the kids off or embarrassed them, as I'd too often seen other teachers do, both at Sidwell and elsewhere. He sought to draw out every student and hear what each had to say. Lecturing wasn't in my DNA, but from Hall I learned that there was more than just one way to be an outstanding teacher.

At the end of my second year at Sidwell, the head of the English Department stepped down, and I lobbied Ben Shute to appoint me to the position. I told him that I wanted to lead departmental meetings where teachers talked about *teaching*, instead of having gripe sessions about "the administration." I'd hoped by then that my tour of colleagues' classrooms had created some goodwill, and I knew that many of my fellow teachers now appreciated—perhaps grudgingly—some of my unorthodox teaching practices. In fact, a number of English teachers had begun holding regular one-on-one conferences with their students to discuss their writing. Before I'd arrived, none had done this.

Despite my campaign, Ben turned me down. I was disheartened but took some comfort in the fact that Ben agreed with me that no one could get the English Department to work on anything together. He appointed Hall as interim department chair as a stopgap. Hall didn't want the impossible job of corralling sharks, but he was willing to do it for a year or two.

Seeking some form of collegiality, I approached a couple of teachers in other departments with whom I was friendly and suggested that we meet occasionally to talk about teaching and learning. The five of us—a math teacher, two social studies teachers, a science teacher, and I—began to meet at my house every month or so for pizza, beer, and conversation. Before the first few meetings, I'd circulated some articles about Piaget for discussion. It quickly became clear, however, that the group had come together more to socialize than to talk about education theory. I decided it was better than nothing, and we did end up visiting each other's classes occasionally. But I yearned for a way to make more of an impact on the school.

In my third year, I went to Ben with another idea. How about we spend a faculty meeting discussing an article by

Harvard psychology professor Lawrence Kohlberg on children's stages of moral development, and then watch a video about what educators called "the hidden curriculum"—what teachers implicitly communicate about social norms and values without intending to? I wanted to explore the ways we were ignoring or even enabling students' displays of disrespect for one another. Ben gave me a skeptical look but agreed to try it out.

The meeting was a wasted effort. The whole time the video was playing, I could hear whispering. And when I attempted to lead the discussion of Sidwell's hidden curriculum, I was greeted with a chorus of yawns and paper rustling. A couple of the teachers from my little pizza group responded in earnest when I asked if others were concerned about how kids often put one another down in class discussions; the rest were plainly bored. And Yvette—the woman of the gnawed heels—even defended students' behavior, saying that their barbed comments "were only meant in fun."

I went home feeling utterly deflated. My efforts at professional leadership—beyond my work as chair of the religion committee to help create the service learning requirement for graduation—were going nowhere. And when the religion committee's service learning proposal was approved, there seemed to be no new tasks for the committee—or for me—to take on.

Then, at the end of the year, there was the fiasco of the "faculty follies." The follies were a time for teachers and administrators to let their hair down a bit by putting on skits for the graduating seniors. In one of the skits in which I was performing, another faculty member started carping about the "Bible according to Piaget," then tilted his head toward me with a disingenuous smile. Taken off guard, I tried to toss off a comeback: "Oh, isn't that a watch?" My lame reference to the luxury brand generated loud groans from the audience, and my face was burning as I stepped off the stage. I felt more alone than ever.

So it was that I began the 1979–80 academic year, my fourth and final year teaching at Sidwell. My classes mostly taught themselves, and I craved a new challenge. Since my first essay on education had appeared in the *Phi Delta Kappan*, I'd published half a dozen more articles, which had led to invitations to give workshops at several education conferences. Having seen this glimmer of success, I'd dedicated the past two summers to working on a book based on stories and insights from the teaching journal I'd kept since I had begun teaching. I called the draft book *Educating for Character*. I poured myself into the project, laboring four hours in the morning every day, but when I reread the chapters I'd completed just before returning to school in the fall, I could see how much more I'd need to do to turn my draft into a real book. I was dejected. Writing was hard. And it was lonely work, too. I couldn't face another summer of solitary mornings chained to my Smith Corona.

More than anything, I longed to be part of a professional community, wanted to have a broader impact on education beyond my small classroom. Sidwell offered me neither.

I finally found such an opportunity—or at least I thought I had—in an announcement posted on the faculty bulletin board that September. Cambridge Friends School, a Quaker PK–8 school in Cambridge, Massachusetts, with two hundred students and twenty faculty, was seeking a new head of school, to start in the summer of 1980. I read the notice several times with a growing sense of excitement. Here was a chance to create my own community, maybe even give shape to a model school—and to live in Cambridge again, too. The fact that I had neither administrative nor elementary school experience should have deterred me, but it didn't. I was thirty-three, with nearly a decade in the classroom, counting my time as a student teacher at Harvard. I saw no reason why I couldn't succeed in this new undertaking.

Oh, the hubris of youthful ambition. How little I knew.

THE FIRST INTERVIEW with two members of the search committee via telephone went well, and so I was invited to come to the campus for a day of in-person interviews late in the fall. The little one-story brick and cement school building had been constructed in the early 1960s on a small lot squeezed between triple-decker houses and apartment buildings in the middle of Cambridge. Youths from the low-income public housing project nearby had scarred many of the school's Plexiglas windows with some sort of sharp object and spray-painted graffiti in bold colors on the outside walls. The building and what passed for a soccer field seemed shabby and ill tended. It was a far cry from the manicured lawns and sprawling playing fields at Gilman, Avon, and Sidwell. Though only a mile away, Harvard might as well have been in another country.

But on that visit, I hardly noticed. Nor did I pay much attention to what was going on inside the school. Cambridge Friends prided itself on being progressive—or so everyone kept telling me—and at first glance, the younger students' classrooms reminded me of those I'd seen in Montessori schools, with kids moving from one learning station to another, rather than sitting in rows of desks. With little to lose, I saw only a glorious opportunity to talk about all of my lofty ideas on education to an attentive audience.

I was notified some days later that I was one of three finalists, and Connemara and I were invited back for a two-day visit. I was sent a list of questions that the search committee would be asking, and I prepared by writing down my answers.

In response to the question of why I wanted to be the head of Cambridge Friends, I wrote that what I enjoyed most about teaching was an opportunity "to bring out the best" in my students—encouraging their "reasoning, creativity, empathy, and integrity"—and that I wanted to do the same for an entire school by affirming what I called "two paradoxical principles: a cooperative spirit and support and respect for individual differences."

In answer to a question about my qualifications, I described my successful efforts to create a model school-within-a-school at Walter Johnson and my work with Sidwell's religion committee. And—unbelievably—I said that I'd read a lot of books on education. As if that made me qualified to be head of a school.

The second round of interviews went even more swimmingly than the first. My many mellifluous pronouncements about the importance of Quaker values in schools and all my glib words on the need to educate both the head and the heart seemed to charm the teachers, parents, and trustees alike. I was on my game, high on the experience of so many people hanging on to my every word.

Not so high, though, that I overlooked what was happening with students. On this second visit, there were older kids racing pell-mell up and down the halls, and kids of all ages were constantly interrupting adult conversations. I saw little evidence of intellectually stimulating work being done in the seventh and eighth grades: the faculty wasn't asking hard or interesting questions of their students, and it appeared they didn't believe in assigning homework. I privately wondered whether these kids would be prepared when they enrolled in a new school for ninth grade. From what I'd observed, I knew Cambridge Friends' graduates had no chance of surviving at a school like Sidwell. After my various interviews, several parents confirmed these hunches by coming up to me and privately complaining that the school was too lax and not academically challenging enough.

But when, in public meetings, I asked teachers, trustees,

and parents about the school's strengths and weaknesses, there were always long lists of the former—the Quaker values, the gentle caring nature of the faculty, the dedication of the trustees—and absolutely nothing about the latter. And so when the search committee asked me how I saw the school's strengths and weaknesses, I parroted what I'd heard about all the school's strengths—because they seemed to be true. About weaknesses, I only said that I had some questions and needed to learn more. I had a strong sense that this community wasn't ready to hear anything about my concerns or the complaints of some parents. The way many talked about the school made it sound as though it were a very precious place, perfect as it was—except for the need for some additional classroom space.

It occurred to me that I didn't know what this school wanted its new headmaster to actually *do*. Yet I never asked. I was so ambitious and impatient for new professional challenges that I didn't listen to my own inner doubts about the school and whether I really belonged there.

A week later, in early March 1980, the chair of the board of trustees called to offer me the job. I accepted with a re-sounding yes. As soon as I hung up the phone, I burst into tears of joy.

We returned to Cambridge to house hunt, full of hope and excitement, and soon found a fixer-upper less than a mile from the school. We also enrolled our two older children in Cambridge Friends—something that the search committee had all but insisted upon. The chair of the board, an elderly woman, explained that sending my children to Cambridge Friends would show parents and teachers how much confidence I had in the school.

Then she informed me, almost as an afterthought, that the board had decided to launch a capital campaign in my first year as head to raise money for much-needed facilities improvements. It didn't dawn on me that this would be a huge undertaking—a second job on top of the one I'd defined for myself as the school's "educational leader."

The board also wanted me to attend an eight-day residential summer seminar for new heads of school, sponsored by the National Association of Independent Schools (NAIS). Great, I thought, they're *paying* for me to get a crash course in leadership. I couldn't wait to go.

Ahead of the course, the seminar leader sent us some reading: *Handbook for New Heads* by Dexter Strong. I devoured the book, especially his pearls of wisdom on how to initiate change in a school. "As you begin to exert your leadership," Strong instructed, "you will doubtless want to take the initiative for change . . . your immediate concern, especially at the beginning of your term, should be how soon and how fast you should move." But what was the actual "move" I was supposed to make? The book didn't say. I hoped the seminar would give me the answers I sought.

What I got instead were long days of role-playing, bookended by lectures on the "problems" of power. The psychologist-cum-leadership guru who ran the show told us that as new heads, our priority was to identify our leadership "quadrant" from a map that ranged from dictator to facilitator. Before I could figure out what the middle ground might hold, he implied that the only real option was to be a "benevolent dictator."

We also had to decide when and how we would "give away" some of our power as leaders. It was up to us, he stressed, to decide who could make what decisions. He called it his "window shade" theory. Putting the shade up meant giving more power away; putting it down meant keeping the power to yourself. All you had to do was communicate to everyone how far up or down you'd pulled the shade. The effective head, in other words, was a really smart window shade operator.

The lecturer did get one thing right, though. Over and over he'd pound his fist on the lectern. "If you don't do 'X' or you do 'Y,' you're gonna get killed. I mean really *murdered*." He cited so many different and dire X and Y scenarios that I couldn't keep them all straight in my head and began to panic.

It didn't take very long for this particular prophesy of power to play out for me after I started the job.

I began the school year full of energy and suffering from a swollen ego. I had the power, I'd been told again and again over those eight days. I just had no clue how to use it. Nor did I have any time to figure it out, as I was immediately swept up in the day-to-day business of administering the school. People would rush into my office, urgently beseeching me to deal with one crisis after another: a broken copier, no toilet paper in the girls' bathroom, a floor that didn't get mopped the night before, some boys retrieving a lost ball on the roof.

In between crises, there was a back-to-school-night letter I had to get out to parents, a faculty meeting to plan, conferences with the business manager and the admissions director.

At first I loved the adrenaline surge that came with having to simultaneously juggle so many balls. But I quickly realized that I was drowning in "adminis-trivia," with no time to think about, let alone work on, the school's deeper problems. In my all-too-few classroom visits that fall, I saw kids who seemed unfocused and were disruptive. One boy, "Alex," was sent to my office every day for a talking-to by me. After weeks of this, I started to wonder why Alex's teacher wasn't dealing with him. Had the teacher even called his parents? Or was I supposed to do that? There was no NAIS handbook for how to deal with such situations.

The quiet, nagging doubts that I'd had when interviewing for the job grew into a full-blown fear. I could see that the teachers in the upper three grades weren't asking enough of their students—either academically or behaviorally. The hidden curriculum of the school—its culture—was excessively permissive. How was I going to raise these issues with the faculty? Or with trustees? I had no clue, only a pressing sense of urgency.

And then there was the enormous sinkhole of the school's nascent capital campaign. I had to meet regularly with a committee to understand the school's building and plant needs, studying architectural drawings so that I could make the case for the investment to potential donors. I questioned why the headmaster's new office was to be a tiny, windowless room at the end of a hallway but was told that it was too late to change the plans, as they wanted to start construction the following summer, in less than eight months. In addition, the board had decided to hire a fund-raising consultant, but I was the one who had to interview the candidates. Then I had to work with her on creating a campaign "strategy," budget, and brochure, but the goal—to raise $1 million dollars—had already been ratified by the trustees. The project stunned me. A million bucks was a hugely ambitious undertaking for a school that was only twenty years old. The oldest alumni were barely in their thirties, not yet able to make donations of the scale needed.

This meant the school had to rely heavily on gifts from major donors, most of them elderly, wealthy Quakers. And so I was required to spend far too much time away from school, giving talks at long luncheons and sipping tea with people our fund-raising consultant referred to as "heavy hitters." These gatherings invariably ended with my asking for a specific dollar amount, which I'd been coached to "put on the table." Gushing enthusiasm for a school that I hardly knew and about which I harbored doubts, I felt like a fraud.

I should have been spending my time getting to know the kids, teachers, and parents—getting to know my school. I missed having regular contact with students who weren't being sent to my office to be disciplined.

My first true test of leadership came in December. Alex was spending more time in my office than in classes, where he was constantly acting out. I was totally unprepared for the situation. I still hadn't had time to get to know the faculty involved, or visit their classrooms while they were teaching. Far worse, I'd actually gotten into a shouting match on a phone call with Alex's father, who said his son's behavioral problems were the fault of his teachers. Whether it was true or not, I didn't know, but I'd felt compelled to defend the teachers.

Something had to be done, so I pulled my window shade down a few inches. I announced at a faculty meeting that after consulting with the teachers, I would make the final decision about whether or not the boy should be expelled. I wanted there to be clear consequences for a student's bad behavior. As headmaster, I was ready to take responsibility and make my first "move."

It seemed such a small move. It wasn't even a move, not just yet. But that was when the hostilities first broke out.

At the start of our next meeting, one of the few male teachers told me that for the past twenty years, the faculty had made these sorts of decisions collectively, without the interference of the headmaster. "Why are you trying to change things?" he demanded to know.

How could I say that I'd been told that I was supposed to exert power, show them who was in charge? So I made up something about it being a bad idea to talk about confidential student and family issues as an entire faculty. It was bullshit, and they knew it. I noticed some heads shaking, and I recanted.

A cold war was setting in, however. Later that month, with the Christmas break approaching, I decided to review the school's snow-day procedure and saw another opportunity to try to tug my window shade down again. Cambridge Friends always closed when the radio announced that the city's public schools had canceled classes. A beautifully streamlined system, except for one little wrinkle: as soon as the headmaster heard the announcement on the radio, he was supposed to make a bunch of calls to activate a faculty phone tree that would make sure all the staff knew that school had been called off for the day.

I didn't understand why teachers couldn't get their information from the radio, just as the headmaster and all the parents did. Some teachers seemed to coddle the kids. Was this a way the previous head of the school had indulged the faculty? I saw the issue as an opportunity to send a message, to tighten things up just a bit—to make new policies based on reason rather than on old habit. Idiot novice that I was, I put up a notice on the faculty bulletin board saying that, henceforth, there would be no snow-day phone tree, that the radio announcement should suffice.

I'd made an ally in the admissions director, who had witnessed some of the negative reactions from parents who'd toured chaotic hallways, and thus shared some of my concerns about the school's culture. She pulled me aside and told me that there was a growing chorus of miserable mutterings about the new snow policy. "Why couldn't they just come talk to me if they disagreed?" I asked, frustrated. "Because that's not their way" was her honest reply. So I raised the issue in the next faculty meeting. "Some of us don't have radios," I was told. "Why should we have to listen to the radio early in the morning to find out if there's going to be school?" Another teacher said, "A phone call is so much nicer." Overwhelmingly, the faculty wanted the snow-day procedure to remain as it had been. So I reversed a decision once again.

Now the faculty resistance became a full-blown war of attrition. Teachers started asking increasingly cutting, critical questions about me to one another: *Why is he trying to change the school? What will he spring on us next? Does he want to run the school all by himself? Doesn't he know that it has run just fine without him for years?* But I didn't learn of these interrogations for another three months. It wasn't until March, when one of the trustees, a woman named Mary Johnson, who was a former teacher at the school—and who, I'd later find out, had also been a finalist for my job—told me what was being said behind my back. She said faculty had been calling her since my two disastrous retreats in December.

Like a barely bandaged battlefield wound that had become infected, all sorts of noxious matter soon began to spill out—and the festering couldn't be ignored. Trustees, faculty, and I spent the spring talking about what kind of head I'd been in my first six months and what kind of head the school wanted. This series of meetings was long and painful, but it eventually became clear that the school did not want the type of benevolent paternalist who traditionally ran many independent schools—the kind of leader I'd been coached to be in my leadership course, and which I'd seen in action at Sidwell. They wanted instead an administrator who would take care of problems that shouldn't be of concern to teachers; they wanted a facilitator. Most of all, what they really wanted was the status quo before I'd come along. It was a faculty-run school, and they liked it that way. The parents, meanwhile, were kept in the dark about what was going on.

It was around this time that I learned from a member of the search committee that I hadn't been the faculty's first choice for headmaster. Or their second. Or their third. It was a blow, but it also explained why the teachers had abandoned me before I'd even had a chance to begin.

I've often wondered why the search committee hired me. Was it the Harvard degree? Or my having taught in a prestigious school? Or my Quaker affiliation? I'll never know. I only know that they should never have hired someone with no real experience and that both the committee and I must share the blame for the disaster that unfolded.

MEANWHILE, MY THIRD-GRADE SON, Dan, had decided to take matters into his own hands. Having made his very first best friend in Bethesda the year before, he was furious about the move to Cambridge. And he hated his new school, for reasons that I never fully understood. He was acting out in classes and was constantly being sent to the headmaster's office—my office—for reprimanding. So overwhelmed was I merely by trying to survive in my new job that I had no idea what to tell him and was of little help.

It was one of the worst days of my parenting life when, as

a punishment, I had to forbid Dan from going to the Ringling Bros. and Barnum & Bailey Circus with the rest of the family. He'd thrown a chair in class.

When June came, everyone agreed that we'd make a fresh start of things in the next school year. Dan, too. I spent the summer breathing one long sigh of relief and writing drafts of an article about all that I'd learned about leadership in my first year as a headmaster: about how I'd felt set up for failure by the "crash course" for new heads; about what a misstep it had been to launch a capital campaign the minute I stepped on campus; about the error the school's trustees (and faculty) had made in waiting so long to tell me what was going on; about my many mistakes as an administrator and leader.

Having come from a highly verbal competitive academic school, I was completely tone deaf to the quieter culture of Cambridge Friends. I had missed the many nonverbal cues that were there, for anyone looking. And although I thought it was my responsibility to raise issues that concerned me about the school, I had absolutely no idea how to do so without offending the faculty. I had completely blundered in my first two attempts to assert myself as a decision maker. I wrote the article first to make sense of it all. But I also thought that other new heads might benefit from hearing my cautionary tale.

Over the summer, the trustees had hired Mary Johnson's brother-in-law, Eric Johnson, to consult with them about the school's leadership "crisis." I asked him to review the draft of my article, which he did. He wrote me a note: "Tony, I think it would be a mistake to publish this anywhere now. It's an honest and forthright statement, but there's really not much new in it, and I think it could only damage the school's and your chances of making a go of things in 1981–82. . . . You haven't yet had enough experience to write this." A former English teacher, Eric also made extensive comments in the margins and corrections of my spelling, syntax, and punctuation. If he'd given the paper a grade, it would certainly have been an F.

Fearful, anxious, but resolved to try harder, I began the new school year working to be the kind of "servant leader" the faculty was demanding. I got up much earlier than I had the previous year and was always one of the first to arrive at the school. I stood and greeted the faculty, parents, and students at the doorway every morning. I tried as best I could to deal with all the noise and chaos of the construction project that was now under way in the building. And I proposed that I teach an eighth-grade English class—both to get back to something I loved and was good at and to try to be one of the faculty.

It was all for naught. The teachers had already made up their minds. They sensed my unease about the school, and it made them anxious. They wanted me gone.

Eric Johnson came to see me in early November to urge me to resign. The trustees, he said, had agreed to pay my salary for the rest of the school year, and his sister-in-law, Mary, was to take over as head of school—a position she would hold for the next thirteen years.

The school assembly where I said good-bye to the kids was one of the saddest moments of my life. I had asked if the student chorus would sing one of my favorite songs from their repertoire. After they finished, I faced the concentric circles of young students and, with tears streaming down my cheeks, said that I was leaving, would miss them, and wished them well. I could see looks of bewilderment on the faces of some of the kids, as if to ask, *Why is he leaving so soon?* But I had no answer for them. As soon as the assembly was over, I walked out the door, never to return. My children finished out the school year at Cambridge Friends, but then we transferred them elsewhere.

I spent the next two months at home—moping and brooding, replaying in my head every conversation I'd ever had with the trustees and faculty, every meeting that had taken place. Thinking obsessively about what I should have said, or could have done, differently. I wanted to somehow rewind the clock. I wanted to start over. I was furious with myself. It was the chance of a lifetime, and I had totally screwed it up.

The previous year, I'd had almost no time to write in my journal or practice the guitar. Now, with too much time on my hands, I'd lost all desire to write or make music.

Trying to sleep at night, the looping tape of the Mole's pronouncement ran through my mind: "Wagner, you're a fuckup! You've always been a fuckup, and you're always gonna be a fuckup." The Mole was right. My successes as a teacher had been transitory—flukes. Deep down I knew that I was a total fuckup. That was the reason why I had failed.

. . . .

EARLY IN 1982, I started job hunting. I went first to the headmaster of Sidwell, Earl Harrison, to ask for my old job back. He turned me down, saying only that "you can't go home again"—the title of my favorite Thomas Wolfe novel. And then he revealed that several of my old Sidwell colleagues had predicted that I would "crash and burn" in my new job. He'd sure found my Achilles' heel.

I applied to several schools for the job of assistant head of school and even secured an interview at a progressive K–12 day school in Baltimore. The head and I had similar education philosophies, and we'd gotten along quite well in our daylong discussion when I'd visited the campus. I talked about how much I'd learned from my mistakes and how eager I was to start over and to learn from an experienced headmaster like him. But he finally called to say that he just couldn't take the risk. The risk being me.

I should never have listened to Eric Johnson, I thought. We ought to have found a way to make the job work at least until the end of my second year. Now, I was certain, no one was ever going to hire me again.

In an effort to feel useful while I was job hunting, I began to attend meetings of a group calling itself Educators for Social Responsibility. After President Reagan came into office in 1981, he did an about-face on the established U.S. foreign policy of seeking détente with the communists. He instead chose confrontation, reviving the cold war and seeking to bankrupt the

Soviet Union by ratcheting up defense spending on major new weapons systems, such as the B-1 bomber, the MX "Peace-keeper" missile, and deployment of the Pershing II missile in West Germany.

In 1978, Dr. Helen Caldicott and other physicians in the Boston area had met to revive an organization that had been established in 1961 by a group of doctors concerned about the public health dangers of nuclear weapons testing. The group kept the name of its forebear—Physicians for Social Responsibility—but shifted its focus to the potential medical consequences of nuclear power and nuclear war. The Three Mile Island nuclear power plant disaster in March 1979, and then Reagan's saber rattling, raised interest in the group's mission. Dozens of chapters sprang up around the country, with members numbering in the thousands.

In the fall of 1981, a small group of educators, led by Ro-berta Snow and Sheldon Berman, met to talk about how educators might themselves deal with the growing threat of nuclear war. Having the model of Physicians for Social Responsibility so close by, it was an easy step for them to adopt the name Educators for Social Responsibility, or ESR. I'd seen a flyer for ESR posted in Harvard Square and went to their second organizational meeting.

We began to meet weekly, and our debates about what the new organization should stand for and evolve into were a more-than-welcome distraction from my fruitless job search. Then an article about our little group appeared in the *Boston Globe*, was picked up by one of the wire services, and we began to get inquiries from around the country about how to join and how to form chapters.

By the spring, we had more than 350 dues-paying members, and several groups around the country were calling themselves chapters. It was high time to formally establish a national organization—but we had only a few hundred dollars in the bank. To be a national organization, we needed a full-time director and a real office. We couldn't continue to run ESR out of the basement of the school in Brookline where Shelly taught.

As I scanned the room during one of the meetings where we were wrestling with these issues, I realized that everyone else had a full-time job, and none of them was about to give that up. I, on the other hand, still had three months' severance coming to me from Cambridge Friends and absolutely no job prospects. I could take the risk. When I volunteered to be the full-time executive director of ESR, a couple of people looked at me, wide-eyed and slack-jawed. They were probably thinking that I was a little bit crazy, but someone proposed a vote to accept my offer, and suddenly I had a new job. All I had to do was invent it.

I threw myself into the challenge. First, I went to the folks at Physicians for Social Responsibility, whose national office was in Cambridge, and persuaded them to rent us a tiny bit of space for a nominal fee. Then I found a wonderful full-time volunteer, Susan Alexander, who offered to help me set up the office. Susan was a former English teacher at Wellesley High School and the wife of Dr. Sidney Alexander, one of the founders of Physicians for Social Responsibility. Next, all I needed to do was come up with a mission statement and some money.

The development of the mission statement turned into a struggle between those who wanted ESR to be an activist organization that sponsored demonstrations versus those of us who believed that we should focus on the professional tasks of creating curricula and organizing workshops for teachers. I made the case that ESR could play an essential role in helping teachers learn how to discuss the threat of nuclear war and other controversial issues in their classes. If we sponsored demonstrations, I argued, then people would see us as partisan; they'd be less likely to trust us to be an impartial source of information for their teaching.

But that didn't mean we couldn't demonstrate as individuals. And so I decided to go to the nuclear weapons protest in New York City on June 12, 1982. What a thrill it was to march down Fifth Avenue in the bright sunshine with hundreds of thousands of like-minded people. Different from the Vietnam War protests of the 1960s, which had grown increasingly violent, the demonstration exuded a carnivalesque atmosphere. Smiling mothers pushed baby strollers down the street; high above them, an inflated rubber whale swam in the sky, showing off a sign on its side that read SAVE THE HUMANS. A ten-year-old girl with pigtails held a poster proclaiming ARMS ARE FOR EMBRACING. She held hands with a white-haired man whose placard simply read REAGAN IS A BOMB—BOTH SHOULD BE BANNED.

I couldn't remember the last time I'd felt such joy at a demonstration.

The next day, the *New York Times* reported that, with more than three quarters of a million people attending the rally in Central Park, the demonstration had been the largest in the city's history. And there had not been a single arrest or violent incident. But I had no time to savor the stunning success of the protest. With some helpful guidance from staff at Physicians for Social Responsibility, I'd managed to schedule an appointment with a potential funder in Manhattan—Robert Scrivner, the head of the Rockefeller Family Fund.

Scrivner was an extraordinary man. He'd gone to public school in Kansas and earned a scholarship to Harvard. While a college student, he'd spent his summers building houses in Kansas and roads in Alaska. He'd wanted to go to divinity school after graduation, but his father had pressured him to become a lawyer instead. While studying at Harvard Law School, Scrivner enrolled in a defense policy seminar taught by Henry Kissinger. The seminar was life changing: it opened Scrivner's eyes to the dangers of international conflicts and the specter of nuclear war.

After Scrivner graduated from law school in 1961, he briefly practiced corporate law, which he hated, and so had accepted the offer to join the Rockefeller Brothers Fund. Then in 1967, John D. Rockefeller's grandchildren incorporated another foundation, the Rockefeller Family Fund, as a vehicle for the philanthropy of the fourth generation of offspring.

Robert Scrivner was named the foundation's executive director at the age of thirty-two, a position he held until he died in 1984, at the age of forty-eight, after a long battle with cancer.

According to Richard Chasin, a colleague of Scrivner's who later became director of the Rockefeller Family Fund, Scrivner was from the "troublemaker" school of philanthropy. He urged the foundation's board to take tough stands on a variety of controversial causes. The Family Fund was the first to advocate lawsuits against the big tobacco companies, and it supported the Vietnam vets who had been exposed to the toxin Agent Orange in their successful class-action lawsuit.

However, Scrivner's overriding concern continued to be the threat of nuclear war. The Family Fund was one of the first to give a grant to the International Physicians for the Prevention of Nuclear War, a group that was later awarded the Nobel Peace Prize.

But I didn't know any of this when I met Scrivner at the foundation's midtown Manhattan offices on June 13. The man who greeted me at the door was quite tall and gaunt. With his gray-flecked hair, brown tortoiseshell glasses, and neat charcoal suit, he appeared scholarly, yet he moved with the grace of the basketball player he'd been in high school.

We talked for a bit about the previous day's march and rally before he asked me to tell him about ESR. I quickly related the story of the formation of the group and the growing interest of others around the country, trying not to talk too fast. I also outlined the debate that had gone on within the group about its ultimate purpose and the stand that I had taken on the need for a new professional organization. He nodded his agreement.

Then he said, "Tell me about yourself."

Taken completely by surprise, I wasn't sure what to tell him. I realized, though, that the only thing I could say was the truth. I told him briefly about my teaching experiences and then summarized the Cambridge Friends debacle, saying that it was a job for which I had been totally unprepared. I had the uncanny feeling that he already knew the story.

"What makes you believe that you can succeed with this challenge?" Scrivner asked. He looked long and hard at me, as though he were studying my soul.

"I don't know that I can. But I think it's important to try. Educators need help in figuring out the best way to talk to kids about the threat of nuclear war and other current issues."

"Well, thanks for coming to see me," he said, concluding the interview. He shook my hand warmly but gave no hint as to what he was thinking.

One morning about two weeks later, an envelope was waiting for me at the new ESR office when I arrived. It was from a New York address that I didn't recognize. I tore open the envelope and found a handwritten note and a check:

You have a vital role to play in dealing with the most important issue of our time. If you do it sensitively and well, you will earn the gratitude of future generations. I

hope this will help sustain your efforts until you receive
more significant support.

> *Sincerely,*
> *Robert*

Then I unfolded the check. It was for $10,000. And it was drawn on Scrivner's personal account, not the Family Fund's. Tears of relief and gratitude clouded my eyes—as much for the note as for the money. He believed in me. And I wasn't going to let him down.

IN SEPTEMBER 1983, a year after ESR's official designation as a nonprofit organization, I was invited to join some of the Physicians for Social Responsibility staff at a preview screening of a forthcoming two-hour ABC special movie titled *The Day After*. The film followed a group of characters living in Kansas City before, during, and after a nuclear attack. The consequences of nuclear war were depicted in horrifying detail.

The moment the preview was over, I raced back to the office, called an urgent meeting of my tiny staff of four, and told them that we had to drop everything and spend every available hour and every last dollar to create materials to help teachers and parents talk to their children about what they were going to see on TV that November. We developed guidelines for class discussions for students in different age groups and offered brochures full of advice to parents. We printed a special edition of our newsletter entirely devoted to how to talk to kids about nuclear war and distributed thousands of free copies. Previously the debate had been whether or not to tell kids anything at all about the threat of nuclear war. ABC was making that debate irrelevant. Now the question was *what* to say to them.

The name of our new organization and the guidelines we'd developed began to show up everywhere, including in *TV Guide*. I was quoted on the front page of the *Wall Street Journal* and invited to appear on *The MacNeil/Lehrer NewsHour* (now known as the *PBS NewsHour*) and NBC's *Today*.

The Day After was the highest-rated TV movie in history when it aired. More than one hundred million people in thirty-nine million households viewed the initial broadcast. I'd placed a risky bet, and it had paid off. Educators for Social Responsibility now had a reputation as being both credible and professional.

From that springboard, ESR became a truly national organization, with more than ten thousand members in 125 chapters just four years after our founding. I was in charge of a national headquarters staff of sixteen and published several widely read articles on educating in the nuclear age. There were anxious days when we'd been down to our last few hundred dollars in the bank, followed by days when I'd whooped for joy upon receiving word of a foundation grant for $100,000. Through it all, ESR had sponsored several national Days of Dialogue in schools about controversial issues and had sold thousands of copies of curriculum materials developed by

Sheldon Berman and others in the Boston chapter. The New York City chapter was offering workshops for educators on conflict resolution in classrooms, which proved very popular. We were giving teachers new tools to deal with contentious subjects in their classrooms.

At Cambridge Friends, I had totally failed to create the model school of my dreams and hadn't even managed to survive two years. At ESR, I helped create a model education organization. ESR succeeded in part because I'd taken both personal and organizational risks—but, unlike leaping into the job as head of Cambridge Friends, I had taken informed, intelligent risks.

At the same time, there was much about ESR that wore me down. Fund-raising was a constant source of stress. Additionally, many of the board members were still full-time teachers, and at any given time, a third of them seemed to want my job, though I never understood why. What really wore me down, though, were my distressing doubts about whether or how I'd ever play a useful role in schools again.

Beginning with the 1983 publication of the National Commission on Excellence in Education's report *A Nation at Risk*, a growing number of books about the "crisis in American education" began to appear, and I devoured all of them. *A Nation at Risk* appalled me—first, because the commission included only one teacher and no academics who had actually studied schools, and second, because of its idiotic recommendations for more required courses and a longer school day and year. It was like saying, "The assembly line is broken, so let's lengthen it by 20 percent."

In 1984, three books were published by people who'd studied what was really going on in high schools. Harvard professor Sara Lawrence-Lightfoot profiled six model high schools in her book *The Good High School*. The other two books were devastating indictments of American education: *A Place Called School* by John Goodlad and *Horace's Compromise* by Ted Sizer. Goodlad documented how in most high schools, teachers left virtually no time for discussions in their classes by talking between 70 and 80 percent of the time. But it was Sizer's depiction of the plight of a typical public high school teacher that most spoke to me. The teacher, whom he named Horace, struggled with the unspoken compromise he had made with his students: don't ask too much of them and, in turn, they will behave reasonably.

The book captured the epidemic of boredom and lack of intellectual engagement among American high school students, a problem that Sizer blamed on obsolete education practices, not on teachers. It was the first book I'd read that laid bare the lie of the American high school—a lie that I had seen and lived as both a student and a teacher. The "lie" was simple: everyone pretends there's learning going on when, in fact, there rarely is. In a brilliant yet unassuming way, Sizer had uncovered the truth as no one else had before him.

I had heard that he was starting a new organization to support the transformation of high schools and asked to see him.

We met in his small office just off Harvard Square. Ted's regimental tie and tweed herringbone sports coat, with a gold watch chain snaking down from the lapel buttonhole to the handkerchief pocket of his jacket, were quintessentially Ivy League and trademark Ted. His warmth, humility, and graciousness were anything but Ivy League, however. He listened sympathetically to my Cambridge Friends saga and to my description of ESR's work. But in the end, he said he didn't have a job for me.

I'd have to find another way forward.

EARLY IN 1986, soon after my meeting with Ted, I encountered Robert Kingston, the executive director of the Public Agenda Foundation, at an antinuclear conference in New York. He knew of my success in building ESR from scratch and of my skills as a fund-raiser and seemed interested in sounding me out about a major new effort.

Public Agenda was an operating foundation—meaning that it sponsored projects rather than engaged in philanthropy— that had been cofounded by Daniel Yankelovich, one of the leading public opinion experts in the country, and Cyrus Vance, who had been secretary of state under Jimmy Carter. They were now teaming up with Howard Swearer, the president of Brown University, on a project to improve cold war relations. The goal was to find a way for ordinary citizens to better understand the complexities of the U.S.-Soviet relationship and then make their policy preferences known to lawmakers.

It sounded like a fascinating project, but I didn't think much more about our conversation until Kingston called several weeks later to recruit me to be its director. Although it would be just a two-year commitment, it was a chance to make a larger difference on the national stage, he said. They offered a handsome salary and would pay for my weekly commute between Boston and New York City, where Public Agenda was based; I could even work a day a week from home.

I was flattered to be courted for the position, but I worried about being away from my family for most of the week. I'd miss reading to the kids every night. My bigger fear, though, was about being directionless. I didn't want to be the CEO of a nonprofit for the rest of my life.

In my first months on the project, I focused on coordinating efforts between the public opinion researchers at Public Agenda and the foreign policy experts at Brown University's Center for Foreign Policy Development, and on fund-raising. But very different from ESR, where we struggled for every grant, raising money was comparatively easy because of the reputations of Yankelovich, Vance, and the scholars at Brown. It did not take long to secure commitments for the $4 million required.

I next turned my attention to identifying local media sponsors for a four-city public education campaign, which was to be the culmination of the project, and to helping interpret the focus group research the project was undertaking. Yankelovich had found that opinion surveys measured only what he called "top of the head" viewpoints, which were often fleeting and fickle. Decision makers needed to understand the public's deeper beliefs in order to know what policies would be supported over time. Focus groups enabled researchers to understand the public's "worked-through convictions"—the enduring beliefs and values that were unlikely to be swayed by events of the moment.

Normally, companies rent focus group facilities to test the market for a new product or advertising slogan. We were testing new ways to talk about the complexities of foreign policy in the nuclear age that would be understandable and engaging to ordinary Americans.

Each week, a team of us would travel to midsize cities all over the country, where we'd meet with community, civic, and business leaders during the day to gauge their interest in co-sponsoring a local campaign and to conduct focus groups in the early evening. The focus groups were led by John Doble, Public Agenda's senior researcher, who would facilitate a two-hour discussion with a representative group of local citizens.

I'd sit in the darkened room behind a one-way mirror, munching a deli sandwich and taking notes on the discussion. After explaining the purpose of our research, John would begin with a basic question: "What are your perceptions of the Soviet Union?" Then he'd move on to more challenging subjects, such as "Do you think the policy known as 'mutually assured destruction' is likely to increase or lessen the danger of nuclear war between the United States and the Soviet Union?"

These were questions that few around the table had ever been asked to consider. But John made people feel safe. When participants gave an answer that was unclear, John would ask them to explain further or he would try to summarize what he'd heard a person say and ask if he'd got it right. If someone wasn't yet ready to speak, he'd continue around the room, but then circle back to that person and offer another opportunity. John was a master at drawing out every one of the dozen or so people crowded around the table.

Over the course of a focus group, I watched people arrive at new insights. While some came into the room believing that the arms race was just a fact of life, two hours later many voiced grave doubts about our current nuclear policy and expressed a longing for a U.S.-Soviet relationship that was based on peaceful coexistence—and this happened in even the most conservative towns. I couldn't help but think that Karl Marx had been right: "To make the frozen circumstances dance, you have to sing to them in their own melody." It was John Doble who showed me what this "singing" actually sounded like. It begins with really listening, then probing to make sure you understand what is being said, and finally offering people a chance to hear others and to reflect on a question or issue in a protected environment. Much like what great teachers do.

The focus group discussions helped us identify Four Futures—a framework that spelled out four main alternative visions for the future of U.S.-Soviet relations. We then set up town hall meetings in four American cities, where the Four Futures were debated before attendees voted on their preference for the future. More than seventy-six thousand people participated.

What I learned personally from my meetings with local business leaders and from observing the focus groups was profound. My two grandfathers had been very successful entrepreneurs; my father was one as well. All three were Republican and politically conservative. Like too many on the Left, I believed that the only thing that preoccupied businesspeople was how to make more money. In our meetings and in focus groups, though, I saw decent people who cared about their community wrestling with difficult questions—people like the ones who'd served on my local draft board during the Vietnam War. Much to my surprise, very few responded to the goals of our project with indifference or any sort of ideology.

But it was more than just my bias that was distorting my views of others. For much of my life I'd defined myself by my critical stance to all that I saw around me—by all the ways in which I saw the world differently from how others did. And while I'd learned to listen well to my students without judgment, I rarely offered the same courtesy to adults. What if, instead of arriving at Sidwell full of my own rightness and righteousness, I'd begun by asking what I could learn from others—as I had only belatedly done in my second year there? What if I'd held my worries about Cambridge Friends in abeyance for six months and begun by listening to the teachers, parents, and kids? Might the outcome in both situations have been different?

I couldn't go back and relive the past, I knew that. I had to apply these lessons to my life going forward. But doing what? I still had no idea.

. . .

IT WAS A BRILLIANT afternoon in the fall of 1987. The arc of the autumn sun, swinging lower now in a deep-blue sky, cast long skyscraper shadows throughout midtown Manhattan. I elbowed my way down the sidewalk so that I could hit street crossings in time with every traffic light change, at each corner dodging cars and city buses like a broken-field runner. I was late for my appointment—my first shiatsu massage.

As I disrobed and lay down under the sheet, my whole body felt tense. I'd read that shiatsu was about healing internal imbalances and reducing anxiety and was willing to try anything that might help me to unwind. The constant travel and stress of preparing for the city forums was grinding me down.

The massage therapist began by touching different points in my neck, shoulders, and back with the palms of his hand and his thumbs. They were "acupoints," he explained. Each light touch felt like a jolt, awakening nerve endings that had long gone dormant; each pressure point stirred pent-up pain.

Tears suddenly came. Why was I crying? I didn't know. I knew only that I was finally letting go.

The session over, I dressed slowly and walked reluctantly back out into the cacophonous chaos of rush hour. I could no longer stand the screeching sirens and ceaseless honking. The sunlight was too bright, the sidewalks too claustrophobic. Everything was too much. The massage had stripped me of my armor.

What was I doing, standing here in my Zegna suit, paisley tie, and wing-tip shoes? What was I doing here in New York City? I didn't belong here. I belonged in schools.

A few days later, I awakened having had an incredibly vivid dream: I'd been hired by a college to set up a teacher education program. Standing in front of my student teachers, I told them to keep a teaching journal and write articles. But they shouldn't do it accidentally, as I had. I told them that they needed to think of themselves as social scientists and document good—and bad—education practices, just as Sara Lawrence-Lightfoot had done in *The Good High School*. That way, people would respect teachers more, I had explained.

In some incredible way the dream made it clear to me now. When the Public Agenda project was over, I would go back to Harvard for a doctorate in education. I would become a student again. I would take time to explore what role I might play in the vital work being done to transform America's high schools. And this time, I would *listen*.

NINE

Commencement

WALKING ONTO THE HARVARD CAMPUS IN SEPTEMBER 1988, I found that everything seemed familiar, if not exactly comfortable. I was thrilled to be refocusing my attention on learning, kids, teachers, and schools. But I thought it likely that just as in 1970, when I'd come here for my master's, I would experience struggles and disappointments with the required classes. Fortunately, my degree program in Teaching and Learning was quite flexible and enabled me to choose most of my courses. Even more important, I had the time to explore many learning opportunities outside of class. But it didn't take long to discover that my required courses remained maddeningly irrelevant, as I'd feared.

First, there was the required history of American education where the associate professor lectured twelve of us each week. Or, I should say, *attempted* to lecture us. He was no Hall Katzenbach, however, and so several of us went out of our way to ensure that his mind-numbing soliloquies rarely lasted long. Though we had never discussed it, another independent-minded student, Lois Weiner—a veteran English teacher and union activist from New York City—and I formed a kind of tag-team conspiracy in the class. Each week we let the lecture go on for about fifteen minutes and then one or the other of us would ask a question. The professor would lose track of where he'd left off, and we'd end up having an interesting discussion.

Then there was the required philosophy of education class. It was a large lecture course taught by Israel Scheffler, a much-revered professor who had been teaching at Harvard since 1952. He was so gnarled with ancient wisdom, he was the spitting image of Yoda. But unlike the Jedi grand master, who showered his swampy, hands-on lessons with wit and comedy, Scheffler's lectures were as dry as chalk dust. His course readings were even worse, consisting entirely of out-of-print books written by obscure thinkers that were available to read only in the library on reserve. No Socrates, no Plato, no Aristotle. No Rousseau, no Dewey, no Ted Sizer. The reading list was out of print for a reason: the books were completely disconnected from the realities of classrooms and very poorly written.

Halfway through the semester I made an appointment with Professor Scheffler and asked why we weren't reading any classical or contemporary education philosophers. The wizened instructor gazed out the window of his office for a long moment before replying.

"You see, when I first came to Harvard, someone else taught philosophy of education, and his course readings included all of the greats in education philosophy," he explained. "With all the big names having been claimed by a senior professor, as a young assistant professor, I had to seek out those philosophers who weren't being taught for *my* syllabus."

This stunned me. Scheffler hadn't chosen our readings because they had value to us as educators but because he was stuck in an ossified curriculum, unchanged since the day he came to Harvard. Likely he was using the same lecture notes as well. I was furious at an academic system that permitted such professional negligence.

I wanted to shout, "That was thirty-five years ago! You've been tenured for decades, and yours has been the only philosophy course taught here for years!" I didn't, though. Instead, I decided to take my education into my own hands once again. For the course project, I chose to research and write a paper on John Dewey.

As I read Dewey, I recalled my earlier experience of studying Jean Piaget's work. Both provided powerful validations for my convictions about learning and teaching. And it was no accident that Sizer, Friends World College's Morris Mitchell, and Jay Featherstone, the wonderful teacher from my Harvard master's program, often cited Dewey's work, too. I began to see that there was a long philosophical tradition as well as considerable research supporting the concept of students as active participants, rather than as passive subjects, in their learning—and now I was a part of that living tradition.

Much as I disliked the content of his class, it was in Scheffler's course that I learned the value of study groups. They became a survival strategy. Four of us met over several late nights before the final exam, quizzing one another on the readings and reviewing essay questions that might appear on the test. Scheffler appeared shocked when I stood up, handed him my blue book, and walked out of the two-hour exam after forty minutes. There were two grades on the cover when it was returned to me: a 97, which was scratched out, and beneath it, a 94, with neither an explanation for the downgrade nor any other single mark.

I just smiled; it didn't matter. I had signed up to take all of my courses on a pass-fail basis because I didn't want to have to think about grades. I had returned to Harvard to focus on *learning*. It was what I took away from writing my paper on Dewey, and not the exam results, that mattered most to me.

Having figured out how to crack the nut of my coursework, I had to decide what I was going to do about "The Dissertation." During the first semester, everybody in our cohort was required to attend a weekly seminar where an elderly professor held forth with advice and "support" for us as we began to ascend this holy mountain. Fittingly, she treated our destination as a cloistered shrine. "Your dissertation," she told us one day, "should be a conversation between yourself and only one or two other people in the world." Presumably because there would be only one or two other people who would even understand the arcane topics of most education dissertations, I thought.

"Fuck that," I said to myself. I was not going to spend two years of my life researching and writing something for an audience of two. My dissertation was going to be of value to practitioners—to the people who did the real work in schools.

A few courses did contribute to my learning, and ultimately to my dissertation. They were all taught by people with deep experience in schools, not by tenured academics. Among them was Roland Barth, a former school principal and author of a terrific book called *Improving Schools from Within*, who taught a discussion-based class on school improvement and leadership. Albert Shanker, the legendary president of the American Federation of Teachers, was a guest lecturer for a semester and offered a seminar on the history of education reform efforts in the twentieth century. Both teachers introduced me to the question that would become the focus of my dissertation and the rest of my career: *How do schools change?* But it was an elective course taught by a woman named Catherine Krupnick, who had established a center to improve teaching at Harvard College, that had the greatest influence on me.

Catherine believed that the key to improving teaching was providing teachers with opportunities to review their own lessons and receive peer coaching. Her class consisted of watching videos of teachers and then discussing what we had observed and what feedback we might give to the teacher. Our big project for the semester required us to find a teacher who was interested in receiving this sort of coaching and then reflect on what we'd learned from the interaction. I made contact with a veteran public school teacher in suburban Brookline, whom I'll call Dennis, and established a professional relationship with him, one based on sharing meaningful feedback.

Observing Dennis and talking with him afterward, I came to understand that while no teacher enjoys the process of being "under evaluation," there are also very few teachers who believe they have ever taught a perfect class. When asked if they would like to get feedback on their lessons, teachers welcome the opportunity to learn how to improve. Teachers too often experience formal evaluations as a judgment of their individual worth, rather than as a collegial conversation about how to refine a lesson.

Catherine also had us read *The Teaching Gap* by James W. Stigler and James Hiebert, a study of mathematics teaching in schools in the United States, Germany, and Japan. Stigler and Hiebert had found that Japanese students were many years ahead of their peers. They attributed the success of the Japanese teachers to a process called "lesson study," where teachers of the same course would meet periodically to discuss what learning problems their students were having and then collaboratively design lessons to address these problems. The teachers would take turns teaching the new lessons to their classes while their colleagues observed from the back of the room. At their next meeting, they'd tweak the lessons, based on what was and wasn't helping the students. This iterative process continued until the teachers were satisfied with their lessons.

Most teachers work alone all day, every day, and rarely, if ever, receive useful feedback on their classes. In a decade of teaching, I never had. Not in my student teaching during my Harvard master's program, not at Walter Johnson, and not at Sidwell. Left to their own devices, the vast majority of teachers teach in the ways that they were taught as students, because that is all they know. I didn't, only because the teaching I'd experienced in high school, college, and graduate school hadn't worked for me as a student.

Lesson study was a revelation. It changed how I viewed the challenge of improving learning for all students, as well as how I approached my conversations with Dennis. I began to see that teaching was not changed by administrative fiat, or a different curriculum, or having faculty attend a random workshop, like the one I'd put together at Sidwell—or even by reading great books like Ted Sizer's. At the heart of the process of lesson study was a commitment and a process for *continually* improving teaching. Catherine's class and the Japanese teachers' experience showed me that teaching *could* be improved— but only through regular, collaborative conversation and shared reflection about the problems of the classroom.

But this revelation raised new questions for me: How do we make time in the school day for teacher collaboration? How do we persuade teachers to work together to improve their lessons? And how do we transform how teachers are prepared for their profession? I didn't just want to know what I might have done differently to have avoided the Cambridge Friends fiasco. I wanted to understand what all schools could do to improve students' learning.

But first I had to find out what a reimagined high school actually looked like.

TED SIZER'S ORGANIZATION, the Coalition of Essential Schools, had taken off after its founding in 1985. He was actively recruiting public and independent high schools to join the program and adopt the coalition's common principles. Among these were:

- the purpose of school is to teach all students to think, and "less is more"—depth is more important than breadth;
- students learn best when they are assigned work they consider worth doing;
- you have to know your students well in order to teach them;
- exhibitions of mastery are the best form of assessment, because they motivate students more than tests and help teachers to see what kids really know.

I was dying to see these schools in action, so in the winter of 1988–89, I visited several of them.

The first was Central Park East, a public school in Harlem that had been established in 1984 by Deborah Meier. The school had six hundred students, in grades seven through twelve, most of whom were minority kids growing up in poverty.

Several things about the school immediately struck me. All of the courses were interdisciplinary and team taught by pairs of teachers whom students called by their first names. Rather than being organized around a checklist of facts or dictated by textbooks, the courses focused on a yearlong "essential question." As students dug more deeply into this question, they sought to master academic skills such as research, writing, and weighing evidence. The question in a humanities class I visited was "What is an American?"

Students spent half a day each week outside of school doing internships or community service. The teachers used this time to meet for collaborative lesson planning.

Another striking feature of the school was the "advisory"— a hybrid of the homeroom concept and the traditional role of a guidance counselor. In an advisory, a teacher met with about fifteen students for four hours a week, exploring non-academic topics such as sex education, bullying, substance abuse, and how to apply to colleges. The students remained in the same group for several years, developing into an extended support network, becoming almost a family.

What most intrigued me, though, was that in order to

graduate, students had to complete a portfolio of their work, then present and defend it to a committee of teachers, community members, and students. The portfolio had a dozen required elements, including writing a research paper, conducting a science experiment, and demonstrating proficiency in a second language.

The focus on learning academic skills, rather than course content, along with the school's caring culture, was wildly successful. Central Park East graduated nearly all of its students, and most went on to college—a dramatically better record than that of other large urban high schools serving comparable kids, where the graduation rate averaged 50 percent and few attended college.

This was the first time I'd seen the "merit badge" approach to completion of a high school diploma, and it transformed my thinking about what a high school could be. We shouldn't give a high school diploma—or a college diploma, for that matter—based on serving the prescribed amount of "seat time"; a diploma should be a certificate of mastery based on completion of required and elective merit badges. I'd earned my orange axemanship ribbon from Colonel Elwell by demonstrating mastery of a specific set of skills, rather than by merely putting in "forest time." Why shouldn't school be the same?

But the visit was also personal for me. Sadistic teachers like the Mole at Avon would never have been tolerated in a learning environment like the one being nurtured at Central

Park East. What if I'd attended a high school like this one instead? How might my life have been different? Could every school and every classroom offer the attention to students that I was observing here? And what role might I play in helping to bring about this reimagining of high school?

The second school I visited was Brimmer and May, a PK–12 independent school with two hundred students in the suburbs of Boston. Brimmer had been an all-girls prep school for most of its history, but in 1987, under the leadership of Anne Reenstierna, the school had joined the Coalition of Essential Schools and was in the process of adopting a classroom model like the one I'd seen in Harlem. I visited a ninth-grade class, taught by upper school head Judy Guild, and was riveted by what I saw. It was the epitome of Sizer's most well-known aphorism: "Student-as-Worker, Teacher-as-Coach." Two students co-led a discussion on Chaucer's *Canterbury Tales* for the entire period. Judy interceded only a few times, asking for clarification of something a student had said or evidence from the text for an interpretation. Impressive, I thought, but I wondered if Judy might be an exceptional teacher, or that the kids chosen to lead the day's discussion might be exceptional students.

On the drive back to Cambridge, the seed of an idea for my dissertation sprouted to life: I could study Sizer-influenced high schools that were in the process of change over an extended period. Sara Lawrence-Lightfoot taught a course at Harvard on the ethnographic methodology she'd used in writing *The Good High School*, which she called "portraiture."

She described it as "a method of social science inquiry distinctive in its blending of art and science, capturing the complexity, dynamics, and subtlety of human experience and organizational life." I would take her class and learn how to study and write about high schools as they worked to create new models of teaching and learning. And Brimmer and May would be the first school I would study.

A year later, I'd lined up two additional high schools to study. Cambridge Rindge and Latin High School, the large urban public high school in Cambridge, had decided to divide into six smaller schools-within-a-school to give students greater choice of approaches to learning, and I had secured the necessary permissions to study one of them—The Academy, led by Ruben Cabral, who had also been influenced by Sizer's ideas. The third school was the Hull Junior/Senior High School, the only public high school in the working-class community of Hull, located on Boston's South Shore. The new school superintendent, Claire Sheff, was equally committed to refashioning the town's high school according to coalition principles.

From mid-1989 until the end of the 1990–91 school year, I spent an average of half a day a week in each of these three schools. I filled notebooks full of my observations and reflections as I sat in on countless classes and conducted in-depth interviews with students, teachers, administrators, parents, board members, and community leaders. And I was a fly on the wall at many teacher meetings as well as parent nights.

There were things I saw that made me laugh and conversations that brought me near to tears. Several still come to mind, years later. I remember how Superintendent Sheff decided to empower her teachers to make more decisions at the Hull High School as part of a hot new education trend called "site-based management." I sat there as the Hull site management team struggled during two meetings to try to decide whether or not to allow chocolate milk to be sold in the cafeteria—only to conclude that they lacked sufficient information. They should have been discussing instead what to do about the high school's 30 percent dropout rate. But they'd never been asked to consider that depressing data point. In fact, it was likely that no one had ever shared the real numbers with them.

It was a conversation at The Academy with a ninth-grade African American boy, whom I'll call Dwayne, that most moved me, though. He was failing three classes out of five and often sat in the back of the room, making scornful side comments. When his English teacher summarized the tone of the play *Even Colored Girls Get the Blues* as having "a lot of anger," Dwayne replied with an acidic, "No, *really?*" Even the teacher's attempts to connect more personally with students were scoffed at. When she acknowledged that some kids had said they wished they had read the play much earlier in the semester, Dwayne muttered, under his breath but loud enough for most to hear, "Yeah, if we'd read it sooner, then maybe we would have liked the course."

Yet I saw a very different side of Dwayne when I interviewed him after class one day. He told me that the one thing he'd done all year in school where he'd actually learned something was an independent study project on the filmmaker Spike Lee, who was his hero. Dwayne spoke at length about the problems in his "real" life—violence, gangs, guns, drugs, war—and how he looked up to Lee for speaking out about them. "Spike Lee is the only activist we have right now," Dwayne said. "If I was president, there'd be no such thing as a MAC-10"—a type of machine gun. "War'd be something you play on Nintendo. War in other countries, war in the streets—it's crazy!"

Dwayne was engaged, passionate, political, and at times eloquent. School was a silly game, irrelevant to his life. It didn't challenge him. "There's nothing for me to really think about in class," he said. "They don't give me anything I can use my mind on."

That was exactly how I had felt throughout high school and most of the time at Randolph-Macon and RPI. And even in too many of my Harvard graduate school courses.

I could take care of myself now, but the Dwaynes of the world were powerless. After that conversation, I made a commitment to ensuring that adults heard what students really thought and felt.

LATE IN THE SUMMER OF 1989, a year after I'd gone back to Harvard, I received an urgent call from Anne Reenstierna at Brimmer and May. There had been a last-minute resignation. "Would you consider teaching a senior English class?" she implored. I accepted without hesitation.

Being back in the classroom was a total joy. The students

readily took on the responsibility I gave them for leading discussions, pursuing independent study projects, and presenting their work to one another. They also embraced the conferencing structure I had developed at Sidwell. But this experience was so much better than Sidwell because I was now in a coalition school, where many of the teachers were exploring similar approaches. I wasn't an outlier here.

Soon after I began teaching at Brimmer, Anne offered me another opportunity. When we had first met late in 1988, I had handed her my new business card, on which I'd given myself the title of "Consultant for School Improvement"—an entrepreneurial aspiration that I hadn't yet tested. Anne was the first educator who actually wanted to hire me as a consultant. At the faculty meetings at the end of the previous school year, concerns about student behavior had surfaced, she explained. Some teachers felt that students did not treat either one another or the faculty with respect. I proposed to Anne that I spend some time observing things at the school and then facilitate a half-day workshop where I would share my data with the faculty for discussion.

The problems were much the same as I had seen at Cambridge Friends. Kids routinely interrupted one another as well as adults, they ran and bumped into one another and teachers in the halls, and they shouted to faculty members on duty in the dining room to bring them more food at their lunch tables. The faculty was at best inconsistent and at worst indulgent in confronting these behaviors. A few who spotted kids running in the halls told them to go back and walk; others appeared to have stopped noticing.

I facilitated a faculty workshop where I described my time observing the school and explained that I was now merely reporting on what I had seen and heard. The evidence spoke loudly for itself. I then broke the faculty into small groups to address three questions: Which student and adult behaviors were of greatest concern? Which behaviors would they like to see more of at the school? And finally, which explicit values might the school adopt to support better behaviors?

The conversations were animated. Waves of pent-up frustration and relief seemed to break throughout the rooms. The teachers were delighted to discover how much they agreed and had no difficulty coming to consensus on four core values they believed should be promoted in the school: respect, honesty, responsibility, and citizenship. I thought to myself that Narayan Desai would have been proud. The faculty was attempting changes that might, indeed, turn "individual virtues into social values."

But they couldn't do it alone. The next step was to involve students. I proposed to conduct a focus group with twelfth graders around the same questions and then to teach the seniors how to lead similar dialogues among students in grades seven through eleven. Some faculty members were skeptical that students could facilitate discussions about their own behavior and thought that adults should be present. I resisted. If there were adults in the room, the students might not feel free to say what they were really thinking.

Much to the faculty's surprise, in the focus group I conducted, the students immediately went to work answering
the questions, and also put lack of respect—for one another
and for teachers—at the top of their list of problems. But the
students had a concern of their own: teachers sometimes gos-
siped about students, they said. When I reported this back to
the faculty, many nodded their heads, and it was agreed that
teachers' conversations about students needed to be more
professional.

The final step was to bring parents into the process. Late in
the fall, the largest group of parents in the school's history—
more than 150 people, representing three quarters of student
families—gathered for an evening discussion of moral education. Many parents left the evening saying that it was the most
informative school-sponsored event they had ever attended.

I drove home that night exhausted and exhilarated. I had
failed in my attempts to get either Sidwell or Cambridge Friends
to focus on problems of student behavior. But I had learned
new skills and acquired a little humility over the years. Jay
Featherstone had shown me that asking good questions was the
essence of good teaching. And watching John Doble, I'd seen
how focus groups enabled adults to reflect and to see things in
a new light. Now I understood that facilitating deliberations of
the right questions, rather than offering preconceived answers,
was the essence of good school leadership as well.

During the rest of my time at Harvard and for many years
afterward, I consulted widely to schools, school districts,
foundations, corporations, and state agencies. I used the same

basic approach of gathering evidence—often including focus groups—and presented it along with other kinds of relevant data in ways that provoked inclusive and focused deliberation of the right questions. It was the lesson study process, only on a larger scale. I was bringing together "communities of practice" to improve the lives and learning of young people.

I could now see that many problems of teaching practice might be best addressed with improvements to the training we gave our student teachers. So on top of observing the schools for my planned dissertation, teaching at Brimmer, and accepting the occasional consulting job, I signed up to be a so-called university supervisor of students in Harvard's master's degree teacher preparation program. The Graduate School of Education had discontinued the intense six-week summer program that had been my first introduction to teaching. Instead, the school now employed doctoral students like me to "supervise" the student teachers who were placed for the academic year with a full-time master teacher in a public school, much as I had been.

At first I stuck to the standard protocol: a preliminary conference with each student teacher during which she outlined her proposed lesson; then an observation of the lesson when it was taught; and finally, an assessment to review how the lesson had gone. I was supposed to do this four times through the semester with each of my student teachers. I quickly discovered, however, that the process did nothing to improve the quality of their teaching. The first meeting was informational; the student teachers told me what they were going to cover, and I was supposed to simply listen. The observation was a staged show, of course. And in order to accommodate everyone's teaching and class schedules, the review meetings often didn't occur until many weeks later. I had to rely on memory and my scribbled notes from the day to generate a couple of pointed questions and suggestions—and usually these came too late to affect the student teacher's next lesson plan.

The entire supervision model was too little, too late. Imagine that a sports team had a coach who showed up only four times a season and could talk only about a game the team had played weeks earlier. New and even experienced teachers need regular coaching every bit as much as sports teams do. And the best coaches, it occurred to me, used video replays of games as their key coaching strategy—something I resolved to try if ever I had a say in how supervision was done.

The so-called master teachers weren't of much help, either. Out of curiosity, I'd watched most of them teach, and their lessons hardly qualified as "masterful." And like Allen, my master teacher years ago in Brookline, these old pros enjoyed their free periods and did not feel the least bit compelled to stay in the class when the student teachers took the helm. Nothing had changed. Harvard was still graduating students into full-time teaching jobs who were as unprepared as I had been.

I saw an opportunity to try something different at Brimmer and went to Anne with a proposal. For a modest stipend, I proposed to be a peer coach to the new teachers whom she was hiring, suggesting that it could be an important element in the strategy of getting more of the school's classes to adopt coalition principles. She loved the idea, and so I took on this responsibility in my second year at Brimmer, in addition to continuing to teach my twelfth-grade English class.

Though I couldn't videotape their lessons because of logistics, I did a number of other experiments to create opportunities for learning among Brimmer's new teachers. I invited them to observe my lessons at any time without notice, and most took me up on my offer. I established a seminar group that met weekly after school where teachers took turns sharing their lessons and critiquing one another's work. To help build camaraderie and trust, I invited the group to my house for a series of potluck suppers. After a year, we had built a real community of practice. The new teachers were becoming better, more confident professionals, unafraid to share problems of teaching and solve them together.

In making a real difference in these teachers' lives, we were making a real difference in their students' lives. It was the most satisfying work I'd ever done. To be a teacher of teachers— that was the job I wanted most. That fleeting fragment of a dream from my final days in New York was becoming a reality.

BY JANUARY 1991, I had completed most of the course requirements for my doctorate. My qualifying paper—a mini-version of my dissertation-to-be documenting Brimmer and May's work implementing coalition principles—had been accepted. I had done well in Sara Lawrence-Lightfoot's class and recruited her to serve on my dissertation committee—which had been a vital political move.

Most education dissertations were based on quantitative data, not the qualitative approach of portraiture. My own faculty adviser, who wasn't tenured, had turned on me in the middle of my dissertation proposal defense, asserting that my research design wasn't rigorous enough. I was stunned. I think he was trying to prove to his two tenured peers that he was as academically demanding as they were. But I recovered quickly and responded by citing what Dr. Lawrence-Lightfoot, who was sitting at the table, had written about her methodology, and I saw her nod and smile. My proposal was approved by the committee, and so I was allowed to paint my portraits of the process of change I'd observed for the past year and a half.

Now all that remained was the actual writing—and a hunt for a teaching position. I needed to pay the rent while having adequate time to finish my dissertation. I decided I was willing to take a job only where teacher education came first. At Harvard, research came first, and teacher preparation was an afterthought.

It was a lucky day when I saw the posting for a position for the 1991–92 academic year in the University of New Hampshire's Teacher Education Program, one of the first five-year master's degree teacher preparation programs in the United States. I applied immediately. Within weeks, Mike Andrew, who had created the program, invited me to join the faculty as a tenure-track assistant professor of education. He was looking for practitioners like Roland Barth, Albert Shanker, and

Catherine Krupnick—people who had spent considerable time working in schools, not just studying them—and liked my years of experience as an innovative classroom teacher. But he warned me not to dally in completing my dissertation. He was taking a chance in hiring me before I'd received my doctorate.

I was given responsibility for supervising eight student teachers and teaching three sections of a course on education structure and change required of all education majors. Other professors were teaching the course, too, but there was no textbook, and I had complete freedom in choosing what students read. So I chose contemporary books on education that offered a range of perspectives—from Xerox CEO David T. Kearns's *Winning the Brain Race*, which made the case for a better-educated workforce, to Tracy Kidder's *Among Schoolchildren*, a wonderful account of the year he spent shadowing a fifth-grade teacher.

I also had complete freedom in how I organized the class and had great fun creating an innovative course structure. I divided the forty students into study groups of four that took turns leading the first third of the two-and-a-half-hour class, meeting with each group ahead of class to give them a little help in finding ways to engage their peers in a discussion of the week's readings. Some weeks there were simulations of classroom situations; in others there were games. I even required that they supply snacks for our class break—and jokingly told them that the snacks would be graded.

In the middle third of the class period, I had the students

meet in their study groups to share and discuss the papers they had written in reaction to the week's reading. Finally, after our snack break, the full class would come together to discuss the week's readings, again with the students leading the conversation. I sat back and listened, resisting the temptation to step in when students were obviously struggling with ideas and adding my voice only at the end of class. Having listened closely, I could surgically focus my comments on clarifying concepts they hadn't understood or introducing new ideas for their consideration.

My grading policy gave every student in the class a B if they met my performance standard. I'd observe their level of participation in class and study groups and assess their written work, which consisted of their weekly reaction papers and a final paper, a profile of a school. All of their written work was put into a portfolio, which I collected periodically for review. If any of their papers did not meet my standard for quality, I told the student to revise it. If a student continued to struggle on the paper, I asked a stronger student to help out. For those students who wanted an A in the class, I gave the option of writing a description of what they thought "excellence" as a performance standard looked like and then making a case for how their work met their own standard.

I broke new ground in how I supervised my student teachers as well. In addition to observing the student teachers onsite in their schools, I required that they bring a short videotape of a portion of a lesson they had taught to our weekly group seminar. I encouraged them to bring in tapes of lessons that illustrated a teaching problem they were working on, such as how to begin a class, rather than tapes of lessons they were proud of. I'd ask the student teacher sharing the video to open the discussion with thoughts on the problem captured, so that he'd have the first opportunity to critique his own work.

What a difference it made in discussions of lessons. Instead of having to rely on notes or memory to reflect on something a teacher said or did, we could just replay the tape and pause the action.

A weak link remained in my work, however: the quality of the veteran teachers to whom my student teachers were assigned was extremely uneven. Many students complained that they were not learning anything about how to teach well in their school placements. Midway through my first year at UNH, I found an innovative way to solve this problem, too. I learned that the town of Amherst, New Hampshire, was building a brand-new high school that was to be a member of the Coalition of Essential Schools, organized according to Sizer's principles. I met with the school's newly hired principal, Bob Mackin, in the spring of 1992, a few months before the school opened its doors to students. He told me that he was recruiting teachers from throughout the country to help him put into place several of the teaching approaches used at Harlem's Central Park East—an interdisciplinary curriculum, regular teacher team meetings, advisories, and student portfolios. In other words, everything that I wanted my student teachers to experience. I pitched the idea of placing all eight of my UNH interns in his school and conducting my weekly supervision seminars there in the school, and he agreed.

I was ecstatic. I had found a way to solve the last problem that remained in devising a better way to prepare my new teachers. My student teachers would work with *real* master teachers who were collaborating to create new approaches to learning and teaching.

In my decade as a classroom teacher, I had worked to redefine what was important to learn in the English curriculum and how best to engage students. Now, with both my graduate student classes and my student-teacher seminars, my goal was to give future teachers a new model of teaching and ways of improving our craft. It was gratifyingly creative work. I was reimagining how teachers should be prepared and what would help them continue to improve.

THROUGHOUT THE 1991–92 school year, I commuted three or four days a week to the UNH campus and spent the rest of my time writing my dissertation. At first I was drowning in the hundreds of pages of notes I'd taken over a year and a half. But as I read them again and again, a pattern began to emerge. All three high schools in my study were dealing with the same three basic tasks: how to establish clear academic standards for student work that focused on real competencies, not merely content coverage; how to create a culture centered around core values that provided standards for student behavior; and how to inspire teachers to collaborate.

I discovered something else, too, something more important. Most of the teachers in my three schools didn't understand why they were supposed to change their approach to teaching, whether that involved adopting team teaching, cooperative learning, Ted Sizer's "Student-as-Worker" model, or some other approach. The schools' leaders had never explained *why* they wanted teachers to transform their practice of teaching.

What was the problem that joining the Coalition of Essential Schools—or any other education fad—was intended to solve? Teachers had no idea. Most thought that students' lack of motivation for schoolwork was laziness or bad parenting and had nothing to do with the content of their classes and how they were taught. And they had no way of knowing how many high school graduates left school ill prepared for work, citizenship, and lifelong learning. They felt they had little say in a curriculum that was largely dictated by the expectations of higher education and standardized tests. Given these circumstances, what reason was there to risk change?

I realized that teachers were being treated by their administrators and school boards just the same as students were being treated by the teachers. The message in both cases was "Do it because I told you to." But mere compliance to edicts does not create a continuing commitment to improvement, any more than it motivates real learning. In a compliance-driven culture, the goal is to do the minimum that's expected—whether you're a teacher or a student.

Yet neither was the mere passion to be a great teacher enough to improve the actual practice of teaching. To be a truly great teacher, you have to develop a discipline for continuing to hone your skills. Having a coach or multiple coaches—a team— who trains alongside you in a culture of mutual standards and shared accountability is the springboard to continual improvement. And genuine teamwork was altogether missing in most schools. I resolved that in my future work I would help educators better understand *why* to change, as well as *how* to create a team-based learning ethos for adults as much as for students.

Now I couldn't wait to start writing my dissertation every morning. I loved the work of trying to make the classes, meetings, and interviews come alive on the page using language that was accessible to everyone, not just academics. It was as though everything that I had done to become a good writer since my tutorials with Mr. Edwards at Searing, and later with Robert Leverant in San Francisco, was coming to fruition. I finished my dissertation on time, and less than two years later it was published as my first book, titled *How Schools Change*, with a gracious foreword by Ted Sizer.

Graduation day at Harvard in May 1992 began with a colorful, boisterous parade. We marched boldly through the empty early-morning streets of Harvard Square in our black-and-crimson robes beneath the schools' bright banners snapping in the breeze. It was an exhilarating moment, but then we trooped back to our respective graduate schools for the rest of the day's formalities.

My parents, who had divorced soon after I turned twenty-one, came to see me graduate. My younger brother came, too, and we all went out with my three teenage children for a festive dinner. When the subject of my spotty school history and "underachievement" came up, Mom told my kids that I'd just been "a late bloomer." Dad offered a quiet toast and said how pleased he was that I'd finally learned to "straighten up and fly right."

Faint praise was the best he could do. Earlier in the day, at the awards ceremony, he'd turned to me and asked why I hadn't earned any special award or recognition. I'd let his comment slide. He couldn't understand that there were no honors for me because I'd earned a doctorate *my* way.

I'd accomplished a great deal in four years, and I was proud of my work. I had learned how to become an effective teacher of teachers. Perhaps most important, I'd become deeply engaged with a set of challenges that I'd observed in the schools I'd studied—and have confronted in countless schools since.

Education fads and reforms come and go and most are not grounded in research about how children learn best or in the importance of intrinsic motivation. Nor are they informed by a larger conversation about the purposes of education—particularly, *what* is important to know and which skills are essential to master in a time of radical disruption and profound change.

In addition, teachers are almost never given opportunities to understand and discuss the modifications being proposed in schools. And they rarely receive any meaningful feedback on their lessons or time to plan collaboratively. Education administrators are ill prepared to be instructional leaders, while school board members typically expend more energy on political and monetary considerations than on substantive education issues. This frayed spiderweb of circumstances and conventions is the primary reason why teaching and learning in most classrooms are not fundamentally different from what one would have found fifty or seventy-five years ago, despite the introduction of new technologies and the well-meaning efforts of many professionals.

Doing Harvard "my way" had meant finding every opportunity to learn more about these issues. I sought out the best teachers and classes and numerous educational opportunities beyond Harvard, and I wrote papers in order to gain a deeper understanding rather than for a grade. And I relentlessly pursued a dissertation that would be useful to other educators.

In a quiet, personal acknowledgment of having completed Harvard on my terms, I'd given myself a graduation present: a beautiful Mad River Canoe, with ash wood gunnels, oak thwarts, cane seats, and a Kevlar hull the color of Harvard crimson. I left town a few days later for a maiden solo voyage.

The Green River Reservoir was near the Vermont-Canada border, a four-hour drive from Cambridge. According to my paddling guidebook, the reservoir had nineteen miles of wooded, mountainous shoreline and was one of the last wilderness canoe areas in New England. I parked my car in the empty dirt lot at one end of the long, thin lake, loaded up my canoe with enough camping gear and food for a few days, and pushed off from shore.

It was a cool, cloudless early June afternoon, with a steady breeze out of the north that made the paddling rough going. Still, I loved that familiar feeling of wind and sun in my face, the work of leaning into the paddle and pulling hard, the boat responding to my every stroke as the bow sliced and sloshed through the blue-gray water, leaving glinted specks of sunlight in its wake. I loved the vast silence, broken only by the occasional call of a loon, seeking its mate. The way the lush green mountains came tumbling down out of the deep blue sky to meet the rocky shore reminded me of the lake at Mowglis, where I'd first learned to love learning.

Only this lake was even more pristine. No shouting campers, no motorboats. No other boats of any kind. I was alone here. I was "unheeded, happy, and near to the wild heart of life"—just like Stephen Dedalus in James Joyce's *Portrait of the Artist as a Young Man*. I had first read the book that summer before I'd started at Friends World, so full of hope. It had become like a bible to me. It had traveled with me to Mexico and then to San Francisco, Vermont, Cambridge, D.C., and back to Cambridge. I reread it every few years and knew many lines by heart. And so I had them with me now in this wilderness.

On one of the tiny little islands that dotted the lake, I found a good campsite, with a cozy clearing for my tent surrounded by tall whispering pines. Close by, there was a smooth ledge that sloped gently to the shoreline. The blood-red sun sank slowly behind the inky ridge of mountains as I finished my supper and cleaned up. The wind had died, but now the crisp air was turning cool. I threw another couple of logs onto my campfire and sat down on the flat rock nearby to watch as the fingers of flame reached higher and shot showers of orange sparks into the enveloping darkness.

There, in the absolute stillness of the moment, my favorite lines from the novel's closing rose to consciousness once more. In a clear strong voice, I proclaimed them to the phosphorescent shimmer of stars swimming in the black sea-sky: "Welcome, O life! I go to encounter for the millionth time the reality of experience and to forge in the smithy of my soul the uncreated conscience of my race. . . ."

I knew now that I wasn't going to be the novelist that I'd once aspired to be. And yet I could also see that I *am* an artist, of a different kind. My art is teaching, my canvas the classroom, my brushstrokes my imaginative lessons. My teaching is creative play—disciplined, adult play with a purpose.

Yes, I *had* welcomed life. In response to so many setbacks, I had found nurturance in nature and the burning passion to persist. And I had sought the unique spark of life in each of my students and kindled it as best I could.

And yes, God knows, along the way I *had* grappled with the reality of my experiences. Whether good or bad, most had taught me something—far more than what I had learned in the majority of my classes—but only when I had taken the time to make my own meaning from them, through writing and reflecting.

I met great teachers along the way, too, but most had not

stood in front of me in a school. I saw their faces in the faint shadows of memory now just beyond the flickering firelight: the patient Cheyenne who showed an awkward, lonely camper how to dance; Mr. Edwards, who volunteered to teach creative writing to a "fuckup" and invented an end-of-year award to praise his progress; the radical lawyer who welcomed a three-time dropout into his family's home and, reciting poetry, gave him a glimmer of hope; the Catholic priest who asked a confused adolescent if he'd yet met God and sent him to an Aztec temple where he discovered his wings; and the Gandhian khadi spinner who taught an earnest young man the real meaning of revolution.

All of this and so much more I'd forged in the solitary smithy of *my* soul. There was the hot anger from which I'd forged the Mole's curse into a vow that no student should ever experience such abuse from a teacher. There was the naked fear as I stood vigil against the Klan in Victoria, Virginia, which I transformed over time into a deep commitment to social change. There was the solitary struggle and stress of a decade's work to become a good teacher that I'd hammered into a hunger for a professional community and a conviction that schools must be reimagined. And finally, there was the fiery forge of shame from my time at Cambridge Friends, from which I had fashioned the life lesson that you can—you must—learn from failures.

The ultimate failure of my traditional schooling, I now knew, was in my teachers' inability to help me make sense of myself and the world around me. But it wasn't their fault. No one had told them that these are the most important lessons they had to impart. No one had prepared them for such difficult and demanding work.

Teachers cannot do this work alone. We must all play our part. We are all teachers—stewards of future generations—if we choose to be.

From the reality of his experience, Stephen Dedalus had forged "the uncreated conscience of my race." That was not my calling. But to contribute to creating the conscience of my profession, of teaching? *Yes!*

ACKNOWLEDGMENTS

Thanks, first, to my agent, Esmond Harmsworth, who has done a superb job of representing me yet again. But Esmond did much more than merely represent me for this book. When we realized that I needed help in learning how to write a memoir, Esmond went on a six-month search and finally found Robin Dennis. Robin has been my coach and teacher throughout the writing of this book and has been an absolute joy to worth with. I am grateful for all that I have learned from her.

Several people helped greatly in my research for different parts of the book. Carol Rodgers has written extensively about the life and work of Morris Mitchell and generously shared her knowledge. Keith Helmuth, who was once my faculty adviser at Friends World, has chronicled the history of the college. It was wonderful to reconnect with him as he assisted me in filling some of the gaps of my memory. Finally, I wish to thank Nick

Robbins, director of Camp Mowglis, and James Hart, director of Development & Alumni Relations, for spending a morning with me at the camp and for introducing me to Colonel Alcott Farrar Elwell's dissertation.

The people at Penguin have also been most helpful. Thanks to Kathryn Court and Victoria Savanh for their editorial guidance and to Susan Johnson for her excellent copyediting of the manuscript.

Finally, I wish once more to express my deep appreciation to PJ Blankenhorn, my wife. For all seven of my books she has been my thought partner, first reader, and wise critic.

SELECTED BIBLIOGRAPHY

Ashton-Warner, Sylvia. *Teacher* (New York: Simon & Schuster, 1986).

Barth, Roland S. *Improving Schools from Within: Teachers, Parents, and Principals Can Make the Difference* (San Francisco: Jossey-Bass, 1990).

Coles, Robert. "Children of Affluence," *Atlantic Monthly*, September 1977.

Dewey, John. *Experience and Education* (New York: Free Press, 1997).

Duckworth, Angela. *Grit: The Power of Passion and Perseverance* (New York: Scribner, 2016).

Dweck, Carol S. *Mindset: The New Psychology of Success* (New York: Random House, 2006).

Freire, Paulo. *Pedagogy of the Oppressed* (New York: Herder and Herder, 1970).

Fromm, Erich. *The Art of Loving* (New York: Harper & Row, 1956).

———. "The Revolutionary Character" in *The Dogma of Christ and Other Essays on Religion, Psychology and Culture* (Greenwich, CT: Fawcett, 1973), 137–54.

———. *The Sane Society* (New York: Holt, Rinehart and Winston, 1955).

Goodlad, John. *A Place Called School* (New York: McGraw-Hill, 1984).

Gopnik, Alison. *The Gardener and the Carpenter: What the New Science of Child Development Tells Us About the Relationship Between Parents and Children* (New York: Farrar, Straus and Giroux, 2016).

Illich, Ivan. *Deschooling Society* (New York: Harper & Row, 1971).

Kidder, Tracy. *Among Schoolchildren* (Boston: Houghton Mifflin, 1989).

Kroeber, Theodora. *Ishi in Two Worlds: A Biography of the Last Wild Indian in North America* (Berkeley: University of California Press, 1961).

Lawrence-Lightfoot, Sara. *The Good High School: Portraits of Character and Culture* (New York: Basic Books, 1983).

Meier, Deborah. *The Power of Their Ideas: Lessons for America from a Small School in Harlem* (Boston: Beacon Press, 1995).

Mitchell, Morris. *World Education, Revolutionary Concept* (New York: Pageant Press, 1967).

Mitchell, Morris (writing as Benjamin Harrison Chaffee). "Mine Own People," *Atlantic Monthly*, October 1925, 496–501.

Nearing, Helen, and Scott Nearing. *Living the Good Life: How to Live Sanely and Simply in a Troubled World* (New York: Schocken Books, 1970).

Neill, A. S. *Summerhill* (London: Penguin, 1968).

Piaget, Jean. *The Moral Judgment of the Child* (London: K. Paul, Trench, Trubner, 1932).

———. *To Understand Is to Invent: The Future of Education* (New York: Grossman, 1973).

Richardson, Elwyn. *In the Early World* (New York: Pantheon Books, 1969).

Sizer, Theodore R. *Horace's Compromise: The Dilemma of the American High School* (Boston: Houghton Mifflin, 1984).

Stigler, James W., and James Hiebert. *The Teaching Gap: The Best Ideas from the World's Teachers for Improving Education in the Classroom* (New York: Free Press, 1999).

Wagner, Tony. *Creating Innovators: The Making of Young People Who Will Change the World* (New York: Scribner, 2012).

———. *How Schools Change: Lessons from Three Communities* (Boston: Beacon Press, 1994).